THE ROMAN EMPIRE

BOOKS ON HISTORY BY

ISAAC ASIMOV

THE KITE THAT WON THE REVOLUTION

A SHORT HISTORY OF BIOLOGY

A SHORT HISTORY OF CHEMISTRY

ASIMOV'S BIOGRAPHICAL ENCYCLOPEDIA OF SCIENCE AND TECHNOLOGY

THE GREEKS

THE ROMAN REPUBLIC

THE ROMAN EMPIRE

THE ROMAN EMPIRE

BY ISAAC ASIMOV

HOUGHTON MIFFLIN COMPANY BOSTON

To all the nice people
at Houghton Mifflin

937
ASI

w 10 9 8 7 6 5

COPYRIGHT © 1967 BY ISAAC ASIMOV
ALL RIGHTS RESERVED INCLUDING THE RIGHT
TO REPRODUCE THIS BOOK OR PARTS THEREOF IN ANY FORM
LIBRARY OF CONGRESS CATALOG CARD NUMBER: 67–14700
ISBN: 0–395–06577–1
PRINTED IN THE U.S.A.

CONTENTS

THE ROMAN EMPIRE

1

AUGUSTUS

INTRODUCTION

In my book *The Roman Republic*, I recounted the rise of Rome, which began as a small village on the Tiber River in Italy.

It had been founded, according to legend, in 753 B.C.; that is, 753 years "before Christ," or before the traditional date of the birth of Jesus.*

For centuries, Romans struggled to develop an efficient government. They got rid of their early kings and established a republic. They worked out a system of laws and strengthened their hold on surrounding areas.

They suffered some defeats and at one point the city was

---

* The Romans counted their years from this date, which they referred to as 1 A.U.C. or "Ab Urbe Condita" ("from the founding of the city." Throughout this book, I will give important dates according to the Roman system as well as our own.

nearly destroyed by invading barbarians. The Romans held on, though, and by the time their city was five centuries old they had gained control of all of Italy. Rome then began to undertake wars against the other great nations of the Mediterranean world. Once again she came near to defeat, but once again she held out till final victory. By the time the city was six centuries old, it was the strongest power in all the Mediterranean.

Prosperity and power brought problems and Rome began to suffer from insurrections of slaves, revolts of allies and, most of all, from wars brought on by competing generals.

For a while it seemed that peace had come when the greatest of the Roman generals, Julius Caesar, gathered all control into his own hands. In 44 B.C. (709 A.U.C.), however, Caesar was assassinated, and the civil wars began again.

This time, they lasted only briefly. Julius Caesar's grand-nephew, Octavian, seized power in his turn, defeating all his rivals. In 29 B.C. (724 A.U.C.) peace had truly come at last. The wars of seven centuries were over, both the major wars of conquest and the terrible tearing civil wars.

The fighting might continue in border areas and distant places, but the civilized lands about the Mediterranean settled down, gladly, to the joys of peace. It was at that point that my book *The Roman Republic* came to a close, and it is at that point that this present book takes up the tale.

THE PRINCIPATE

With peace won, Octavian set about reorganizing the government. Up to his time, Rome had been ruled by the Senate, a group of men drawn from the rich and noble families of the city. This form of government had worked well when Rome was a small land, but, despite all efforts to adjust it to the government of a great realm stretching across thousands of miles it was now badly outmoded. The Senators, who were all too often corrupt, looted the provinces they were supposed to govern and resisted necessary social changes at home which would have weakened their own power.

For a century there had been constant opposition within Rome to the Senatorial party on the part of politicians who were not Senators and who wanted a part of the power and the loot for themselves. (To be sure, there were also idealists on both sides who would have liked to see honest and efficient government.) Both the Senate and the Opposition made use of force and it was this which brought on half a century of civil war.

Julius Caesar was planning to end this by suppressing the Senate as a purely Roman institution consisting only of men born and brought up in Italy. He was beginning to make an effort to bring into the Senate men from the various provinces. In this way, a government would be established in which the general interests of the whole realm would be represented. No doubt he also felt that in a government that included many men from outside Italy, he could make himself king. The Romans of Italy had a great prejudice against kings but the people of the provinces were quite used to kings and would have accepted a "King Julius." Then, with one-man rule established, Rome could be made more orderly and efficient, provided the one man who ruled was a capable person who knew how to govern — and this Julius Caesar certainly was.

In the long run, this might have been of inestimable value to western civilization, but the difficulty was to make this ideal of racial and national equality work. Too many of the Romans of Italy considered themselves masters of the realm and would not give up their prerogatives. No doubt this national prejudice played a part in the motives of the men who assassinated Caesar.

Once Octavian was in charge, he realized that one-man rule was indeed needed if the government was to be reformed. He had learned, however, by his great-uncle's fate, to go about matters cautiously. He decided not to risk either monarchy or the spreading of power away from Italy. Both lines of action would make him too unpopular and the risk of the assassin's knife too great. He declared it his intention, therefore, to restore the Republic and to rule under the good old institutions to which the Romans were accustomed.

And this he did, in a way. He removed those foreign Senators whom Julius Caesar had introduced and left only those of acceptable Italian descent. Octavian then went out of his way to treat the Senators and the Senate with all respect and to reserve all Senatorial power in the hands of Italians. He arranged to have the Senate debate government business to their heart's content, go through all the old forms, make recommendations, have a voice in the government of certain provinces and in the appointment of certain lower officials.

But it rested with Octavian himself (who controlled all the important offices of the government) to say who was to be a Senator and who was not to be a Senator, and every man in the Senate knew it. Consequently, though they talked freely, they always ended by deciding to do exactly what Octavian intended them to do.

Octavian also drew the "equites" to his side. These made up the middle class of the realm, the businessmen. They were called "equites" from a Latin word for "horse." This was because, when called up to serve in the army, they could afford a horse and the military equipment that went with it. They could then serve as horsemen in the cavalry, while foot soldiers were drawn from the poorer classes. They might be called "cavaliers" which is from another Latin word for "horse." Sometimes they are referred to as "knights" because that is the name applied to the horsemen in medieval armies, but medieval knights are quite different from the Roman equites and I will not use that word in this book.

The equites were rich enough to be Senators, usually, but did not belong to the old Senatorial families. Octavian made some of them Senators, but others he placed in important administrative positions. They became the "civil servants" of the realm, so to speak. The middle classes, so well treated, became ardently loyal to Octavian and his successors.

An important part of Octavian's power was his absolute control over the army. It obeyed only him, since only he had the money to pay it.

Octavian carefully scattered about ten thousand soldiers over the length and breadth of Italy. These made up the "praetorian guard" (a name derived from the days when a general or *praetor* made use of a group of soldiers as his personal bodyguard.) The praetorian guard was Octavian's private force and it supplied the iron fist under the velvet glove of his deliberately moderate policy. There was also a special force of about 1500 men who served to police the city of Rome itself. This prevented the street riots and disturbances that were so marked a feature of the period of social unrest and civil war in the century before Octavian.

The major portion of the army was not, however, kept in Italy, where rebellious generals might intrigue with the Senate and rise in sudden revolt. Instead, the Roman legions (twenty-eight of them, of six thousand men each, plus enough auxiliary forces to bring the total to about 400,000 men) were stationed at the outer boundaries of the realm in just those places where there might be trouble with the barbaric tribes beyond the border. In this way the troops were kept occupied and busy about their own affairs and yet remained under the control of Octavian who could send them here or there as suited him. Octavian saw to it, moreover, that the army officers and the elite troops remained Italian. This, too, fixed the supremacy of Italy over the provinces and made certain that the army would be run by people with some feeling for the Roman tradition.

What's more, although the Senate was awarded its traditional right to rule over the provinces, this rule was restricted to those in the interior where no armies were stationed. The border provinces that contained armies were under the personal control of Octavian. And even the Senatorial areas were under Octavian's command when he really wanted to exert his influence.

The Senate, in other words, controlled no part of the army, and they knew that any stirring on their part would leave them, helpless and defenseless, facing armed men who would kill them on order without any compunction. The Senators were well-behaved, therefore, and made no trouble.

To be sure, in 27 B.C. Octavian announced that the emergency was over; that peace had been restored; that all was tranquil; and he therefore resigned all his special powers, including his control of the army. This, however, was not meant seriously and the Senate knew it. What Octavian wanted was to be given the powers back again by the Senate. He would then have them quite legally and no one could raise the cry of "illegal usurper" against him.

The Senate played its part tamely. Octavian was humbly asked to accept numerous powers, including the crucial one — command of the armed forces. He was also asked to accept the title "Princeps" meaning "first citizen." (It is this word from which our term "prince" has developed.) For this reason, the three-century period of Roman history beginning in 27 B.C. (726 A.U.C.) is sometimes called "The Principate."

Octavian was also given the title "Augustus" that year, a title which previously had been applied only to certain gods. The implication of the title was that the person of the god so named was responsible for increasing ("augmenting") the good of the world. Octavian accepted the title and it is as Augustus that he is best known in history. In this book I will refer to him, henceforth, only as Augustus.

The army meanwhile considered him the "Imperator," which means "commander" or "leader." It was a title he had borne since an early victory of his in 43 B.C., during the disorders that followed the assassination of Caesar. This has become "Emperor" in modern English, and Augustus is therefore considered the first of the Roman Emperors and the realm he governed is called the "Roman Empire."

Nevertheless, if Julius Caesar's grand-nephew had become a prince and an emperor and even, as Augustus, almost divine, he did *not* make himself a king. That, he felt, the Romans would not have endured. Although he had all the powers of a king and more, he never made use of the name; it was quite enough for him to have the reality. Rather than be king, he had himself elected consul (the traditional office of the Roman executive, held by election for one year) each year. Since the Romans always elected two consuls, Augustus would have someone else elected with him. The other consul, in theory, had as much power as Augustus had, but in actuality he didn't, and he knew better than to dream he had.

Later on, Augustus resigned the consulship, leaving it as a means of rewarding different Senators from year to year. He made himself tribune for life instead, a position which he arranged to have greater legislative powers than that of the consul. He also made himself pontifex maximus, or high priest, and, one after another, took over additional offices as well.

As a result of his various offices, he controlled the direction of government by means of the old Republican customs. Few of the Romans of the time felt any practical difference in the manner in which they were governed, except for the fact that there was no longer civil war — which was, of course, a great change for the better.

Only the Senators, dreaming of the time when they were true masters, and a few idealistic intellectuals, really noted the difference. They sometimes hankered after the old Republic which in their memories or historical reading grew to seem much better than it really was. And the further off in time it receded, the more dreamily noble it seemed.

Nor was it just Augustus' military command and his official authority that kept Rome quiet under his rule. There was also the matter of finances. The Roman Republic had always had a most inefficient method of raising necessary money for governmental use. What taxes were collected often lined the pockets of the collectors and the government had to be kept going by outright loot from conquered lands. Roman citizens were freed of taxation as a reward for having conquered the ancient world; indeed many of the poorer Roman citizens were supported by the state outright with money taken from the provinces.

In the century before Augustus, the provincials were ground to bits, first by legitimate taxation, then by graft and robbery whereby the provincial governors enriched themselves personally, and finally by the illegal demands of generals who might be fighting their civil wars in a particular province.

So grinding were the financial demands and so little of the money found its way into the central treasury that when the period of conquest came to an end and the sources of fresh loot dried up, the Roman government faced bankruptcy.

Nor could Augustus plan new conquests to stave off financial ruin. All the rich areas of the civilized world within reach of Roman armies had already been gobbled up. What was left were barbarian cultures which, even after being conquered, would yield very little in revenue no matter how mercilessly they were squeezed.

If the old extortion were continued, Rome would necessarily sink into anarchy. For one thing, the soldiers would not be paid and that meant they would revolt and Rome would fall apart into quarreling sections as the empire of Alexander the Great had done three centuries earlier.

Augustus therefore did his best to initiate an honest system. The provincial governors were put on a generous salary and it was clearly understood that any attempt to add to that salary by graft would be dealt with quickly and severely. In the old days, grafters knew the Senate would go easy on them because each Senator had done the same in his time or planned to do the same at the first opportunity. The Emperor, however, had no need of graft for himself because he was already the richest man in the Empire. Indeed, every penny stolen by a corrupt official was a penny out of the Emperor's treasury and Augustus could therefore be relied on to show no leniency.

Furthermore, Augustus tried to introduce reforms in the system of taxation itself so that a larger percentage of the money collected went to the treasury and a smaller percentage into the pockets of the collectors.

Such innovations as these kept the provinces quiet and reasonably happy. They might resent the loss of the political power that had seemed at hand under Julius Caesar, but really the Roman aristocracy had no political power, either. And at least the provinces could now look forward to reasonably honest and efficient government and that was more than they had had previously — even, very often, under their own kings.

But despite tax reform and the control of corruption, the income of the Empire still did not meet all its needs and expenses, especially since Augustus was engaged in a huge program of beautifying the city of Rome (he found it brick and left it marble, he is supposed to have said), of attempting to establish a fire-fighting brigade, of extending roads throughout the Empire, and so on.

Augustus made use of the Empire's financial necessity as another way of consolidating his rule. When he defeated Antony and Cleopatra, he took over Egypt not merely as a Roman province but as his own private property. No Senator was even allowed to enter Egypt without special permission.

Egypt was the richest portion of the Mediterranean world at this time. Thanks to the annual floods of the Nile, its agriculture was unfailing and its crops huge, so that it served as the granary, or food supply, of Italy. All the taxes collected from the long-suffering Egyptian peasants went into Augustus' personal treasury. So did a great deal of other money obtained by various legal devices. (Many rich men left Augustus some of their estates, either in gratitude for the peace he brought them, or perhaps as a bribe in order that he might see to it that their heirs got the rest without trouble.)

Augustus could therefore advance money from his own purse to fill many of the needs of the Empire. You might suppose that it would be less trouble to let the money go directly to the state but Augustus' reasoning was that if the money went to the state by way of the Emperor, the Emperor could withhold it as a form of punishment, or earn gratitude if he gave. Then, too, he alone could guarantee payment for the soldiers so it was to him alone that the soldiers would be surely loyal.

Augustus tried to strengthen the position of Italy by social as well as political legislation. He tried to restore the religious customs to what they had been before the more colorful and dramatic cults of the East had invaded Rome. These cults were brought in by the slaves from the conquered East. Since Roman custom allowed such slaves to be freed under certain conditions, non-Roman "freedmen," with the rights of free men but often without the Roman traditions, were increasing in number in Italy. Augustus didn't want the old Italian population drowned out and his least admirable reforms were those which tried to restrict the liberation of slaves.

And so, in this manner, for forty-five years after he had won power, Augustus ruled over Rome in prosperity and, at home at least, in peace.

There is no question but that Augustus' reforms marked an

important turning point in history. If he had not been as wise as he was, or lived as long, Rome would have continued its civil wars and, perhaps within a few generations, fallen into decaying fragments. As it was, the Roman realm remained strong and intact for four centuries. This was long enough to fix Roman culture over much of Europe so firmly that even the disasters that followed could not wipe it out. We ourselves live in the midst of the heritage of that culture.

It should be remembered, too, that Christianity, the chief religion of the western world, evolved under the Empire, and might not have spread and developed as it did if a broad, united realm had not made it possible for its early missionaries to travel freely over many populous provinces. Even today, the Catholic Church retains much of the atmosphere, as well as the language, of the Roman Empire.

THE BORDERS

Let us now take a quick survey of the extent of the Empire at the time that Augustus became Emperor in 27 B.C.

All the shores of the Mediterranean either belonged to Rome outright or were ruled by kings who were nominally independent but who knew that they were in the absolute power of Rome. These kings could not take their thrones without Roman permission and they could be deposed at any time. For that reason they were completely subservient to the Emperor and often kept their satellite-kingdoms more safely in the Roman pocket than Rome might have managed if she ruled them directly.

Suppose, then, we begin with Egypt (Augustus' private es-

tate) at the eastern end of the southern shore of the Mediterranean and move westward.

West of Egypt were the provinces of Cyrenaica, Africa, and
Numidia in that order. The province of Africa included what
had once been the realm of Carthage, a city that had nearly defeated Rome two centuries before. The old city of Carthage
had been completely destroyed by Rome in 146 B.C. (607 A.U.C.)
but shortly before his assassination, Julius Caesar had established a Roman colony on the site. A new Carthage, a Roman
Carthage arose, which was to remain large and prosperous for
six centuries.

West of Numidia, in the spot occupied now by the modern
nations of Algeria and Morocco, lay the still-independent
kingdom of Mauretania. This was so named because it was
inhabited by a tribe which called themselves "Mauri." (It is
from this name that the Spaniards in later history derived their
own word "Moros" to describe the inhabitants of north Africa,
and from this we get, in English, the equivalent expression
"Moors" and the name of the modern kingdom of Morocco.)

The king of Mauretania was married to Cleopatra Selene, a
daughter of Mark Antony and Cleopatra. By her he had a son
named Ptolemy (the name borne by fourteen kings of Egypt
who had preceded Cleopatra). Ptolemy succeeded to the kingdom in 18. *

North of the Mediterranean Sea there were, to the west of
Italy, the two rich regions of Spain and Gaul. Spain (which
included modern Portugal as well as Spain itself) was first entered by the Romans two centuries before Augustus. In all that
time, however, the natives of Spain had resisted Roman arms
manfully, and had retreated only step by step. Even in Au-

* Dates that are later than the traditional year in which Jesus
was born can be written with the initials A.D., standing for "Anno
Domini" or "in the year of the Lord." In this book, however, such
years will be written without initials. We will speak of 18 B.C.,
but instead of A.D. 18, we will say simply 18.

gustus' time, northern Spain was still not pacified. The Cantabri, a tribe bordering on the Bay of Biscay, north of Spain, fought against Augustus' armies for several years and were not subdued until 19 B.C. Only then, did Spain, in its entirety become a peaceful and quiet part of the Empire.

Augustus directed peaceful operations in Spain as well as warlike offensives, and founded cities, two of which can be mentioned particularly. Both were named for himself: "Caesaraugusta" and "Augusta Emerita" ("Augustus, the Retired Soldier"). They survive today under distortions of those names — Saragossa and Merida respectively.

Gaul (which included modern France, Belgium, and those parts of Germany, the Netherlands, and Switzerland west of the Rhine River) had been entered much later than Spain, but its conqueror had been Julius Caesar, who had done the job thoroughly. The Alpine border between Gaul and Italy remained, however, in the hands of the native tribesmen at the time Augustus became Emperor.

East of Italy lies the Adriatic Sea. The opposite shore of the Adriatic Sea was part of what the Romans eventually called "Illyricum" but in English would more commonly be called Illyria. It is roughly equivalent to the modern nation of Yugoslavia. When Augustus became Emperor, Rome held only the Illyrian coastline, a section sometimes called Dalmatia.

Southeast of Illyria were Macedonia and Greece, both of which were firmly in Roman hands.

East of Greece is the Aegean Sea and across it is Asia Minor (included in the modern nation of Turkey). In the period when the Roman Republic began to expand eastward, Asia Minor was a patchwork of Greek-speaking kingdoms. By the time Augustus came to power, the kingdoms in northern and western Asia Minor were Roman provinces. The rest were firmly under indirect Roman control.

South of Asia Minor lay Syria, which was a Roman province,

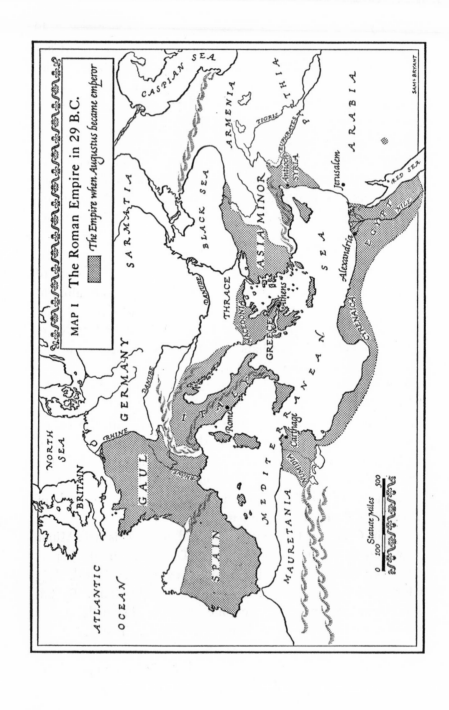

MAP I   The Roman Empire in 29 B.C.

The Empire when Augustus became emperor

and Judea, which had a king of its own who ruled with Roman permission. Southwest of Judea we come to Egypt again.

Augustus, in surveying the Empire could see it well-knit together by roads stretching out of Italy into the provinces in an ever-lengthening and thickening network. And most of its borders were tight. In the south and west, it was completely secure from foreign invasion, for in both directions the Empire had reached an absolute limit. To the west was the boundless Atlantic Ocean and south of most of Roman Africa lay the equally boundless (for all any Roman could tell) Sahara Desert.

South of Egypt, the Nile River continued to some misty source that was unknown to the ancients. The tribes of Ethiopia which lay along the river to the immediate south of Egypt had, a thousand years before Augustus' time, fought great wars with Egypt. Those days were long gone, however, and Ethiopia now lay quiet, for the most part. The Ptolemies of Egypt had placed colonies in Ethiopia but had never seriously tried to conquer the land.

After the Roman occupation of Egypt, the governor, Gaius Petronius, responded to an Ethiopian raid by launching a retaliatory expedition in 25 B.C. He marched southward and occupied part of Ethiopia, but to Augustus this seemed useless work. Ethiopia was too far off to do Rome any good and was not worth the expediture of men and money. He recalled the army and thereafter there was unbroken peace on the southern border of Egypt. (A half-hearted attempt to cross the Red Sea from Egypt and take over southwestern Arabia was also called off by Augustus.)

Southeast of Syria and Judea was the Arabian desert which, like the Sahara, represented a limit to Roman arms and a protection against enemy attack from that direction. In later years, the Roman realm did expand somewhat into the desert, but not far.

To the east, the situation was far more dangerous. There lay the only organized power that bordered on the Roman realm and was truly independent, and even hostile, to it. This was Parthia, which spread over the region occupied chiefly by modern Iran.

Parthia was actually a restoration of the old Persian monarchy that had been disrupted and destroyed three centuries earlier by Alexander the Great. ("Parthia" is a form of "Persia.") Greek culture had pushed into the Parthian realm under Alexander's successors, but it never took strong root.

Most of the Asiatic section of Alexander's Empire was taken over by his general, Seleucus, after Alexander's death, and came to be called the Seleucid Empire in consequence. As the Seleucid Empire weakened, the Parthian tribes established their independence about 250 B.C. and extended their power westward at the expense of their old masters.

In 64 B.C. Rome annexed the remnant of the Seleucid Empire (by then confined to Syria) and made it into a province. Now she faced Parthia directly to the east. In 53 B.C. (700 A.U.C.), a Roman army attacked Parthia without provocation and was catastrophically defeated. Parthia captured the flags of the defeated legions, something that was considered a great disgrace for Rome.

Fifteen years later, Roman armies again invaded Parthia and won some victories. This was vengeance of a sort but Parthia still had those captured flags. After that, there began a long, long tug-of-war between Rome and Parthia, with the kingdom of Armenia as the rope that was being pulled from either side.

Armenia is located at the eastern edge of Asia Minor just south of the Caucasus Mountains. Roman armies first penetrated as far as Armenia about 70 B.C. and established their influence over the kingdom. However, as often as the Romans placed one of their own satellites on the Armenian throne, the Parthians would manage to replace him with one of their own.

Augustus did not feel himself to be in a position to resolve this problem in a grand, conquering way. It was slow work reforming the Empire's financial policy and money was tight. To go to the vast expense of a Parthian war would surely wreck his reforms and possibly face him with a defeat that would ruin his prestige. He decided therefore to place a careful, minimal pressure on Parthia.

As usual, two candidates — a Roman puppet and a Parthian puppet — were quarreling over the Armenian throne. Using the plea for help on the part of the Roman puppet as an excuse, Augustus sent a Roman army into Armenia under his stepson. The Roman puppet was placed on the throne and the Parthian puppet was defeated and killed.

Parthia was in no mood to fight either, since she was having her own internal troubles, and when Augustus indicated his readiness to sign a peace treaty, the chance was gladly seized. In 20 B.C. peace was restored and Parthia agreed to hand back the battle flags captured thirty-three years before. Roman honor was satisfied and Augustus' caution had paid off magnificently.

(However, Armenia did not remain securely in Roman hands. For a thousand years it was to remain a buffer state that slipped in and out of Roman influence with the shifting tides of war.)

THE GERMANS

To the north of the European section of the Empire, the situation was again different. Here there were no deserts nearly empty of men; nor was there a settled, more or less civilized realm, with whom a more or less firm peace could be made.

There were instead wild and trackless mountains and forests inhabited by warlike barbarians. The Romans called them "Germani" and the word has come to us as "Germans."

The first Roman experience with the Germans had been in 113 B.C. when the Cimbri and Teutones left their tribal homelands somewhere on the north German shore and moved southward. They were finally defeated in southern Gaul and in northern Italy but Rome had had a good scare. She realized that to the north there lurked a serious danger.

The danger was partly removed by 51 B.C. when Julius Caesar had conquered Gaul and had established Roman power on the Rhine River. If Roman legions camped themselves strategically along the western shore of the Rhine, those armies and the Rhine itself would represent a formidable barrier against the Germans; one that, in fact, remained standing (though with occasional leaks) for over four centuries.

Caesar had gone even further. On two different occasions, in 55 B.C. and 53 B.C., he had sent small forces raiding across the Rhine into Germany. This was not with any intention of conquering Germany, but was meant to make the Germans aware of Roman power and keep them quiet.

East of Gaul, the Roman border was less satisfactory. It lay along a ragged line of mountainous territory that was not very well defined and not easy to hold. About 150 miles north of the boundary, however, lay the large Danube River, coursing across Europe from west to east. It seemed necessary to reach the Danube and interpose another clearly marked, easily defended barrier between the Roman realm and the northern barbarians.

Augustus sent his armies northward therefore in the major aggressive warfare of his reign. Even this advance, though, was not a true imperialism: it was a hungry reaching for a line that could be defended; an attempt to conquer in order that conquest might be safely stopped.

Slowly and doggedly, the Roman armies advanced, first taking over the Alpine mountain areas that curved in a semicircle about the north of Italy. There, in 24 B.C. Augustus founded the city of "Augusta Praetoria" ("Augustus the General") a city which survives today as Aosta.

The territories north and east of the Alps were also taken. Illyria became Roman and to the east of that was established the province of Moesia (taking up what is now southern Yugoslavia and northern Bulgaria). North of Italy and Illyria, the land to the Danube was eventually divided into three provinces which were, from west to east, Raetia, Noricum, and Pannonia. Roughly, these correspond to the modern Bavaria, Austria, and western Hungary respectively.

By 9 B.C., the Roman legions stood along the Danube from its mouth to its source. There were some rebellions that had to be crushed later but that was just a detail. The only territory in the entire region that was left to self-rule was Thrace (in what is now southern Bulgaria). Since Thrace was not actually on the Danube, and since its local chieftains were safely in the Roman pocket, it was left unannexed for another half-century.

It would have been well for Augustus if he could have left matters at that, and, in all probability, he would have liked to. Unfortunately, it is often easier to make war than to make peace. The Germans did not want the establishment of the strong Roman power in Gaul. From a consideration of Rome's past history, it seemed almost certain that Rome would next attempt to conquer Germany.

Various German tribes attempted to form a federation, therefore, in order to present a united front against the Romans. In addition, they did what they could to foment revolt in Gaul. In both respects, they succeeded somewhat, but only somewhat. It was difficult to unite all the self-willed German tribes and some insisted on holding aloof from any attempt at united action. Furthermore, as soon as Gallic rebellions broke out, they were crushed.

It seemed to Roman generals on the spot that an invasion of

Germany was the sensible next step. It was the one way to make sure Gaul would remain pacified and it might serve to prevent the formation of a dangerous German union in case the quarrelsome tribes ever found some dynamic leader who could enforce unity upon them against their will.

The generals involved were Augustus' two stepsons.

Augustus never had sons of his own, but in 38 B.C., before he came to power, he fell in love with and married Livia Drusilla, a shrewd and capable girl — she was only nineteen — fit in every way to be the wife of Augustus. When Augustus (still Octavian at the time) fell in love with her she was already married, but this was no obstacle in the Rome of that day. Augustus forced her husband to divorce her and that was it. (He had had two previous wives himself, both of whom he had divorced — divorce was very easy in the Rome of the time, and very common among the upper classes.)

At the time of Livia's marriage she already had a four-year-old son and was pregnant with what turned out to be a second son. Both grew up to be capable generals.

The older was Tiberius (Tiberius Claudius Nero Caesar) who, when he was only twenty, was already fighting in the campaigns against the Cantabri in northern Spain. Two years later, in 20 B.C., it was he who led the Roman armies into Armenia and made it possible to recover the battle flags from the Parthians. He was then sent to help his younger brother Drusus (Claudius Nero Drusus) in the battles north of Italy that led to the establishment of the boundary on the Danube.

In 13 B.C., Tiberius and Drusus were sent to Gaul to guard the Rhine, but there were revolts along the Danube and Tiberius had to be called away to that theater of war. Drusus carried on alone at the Rhine and did well. When a German tribe incautiously raided Gaul in 12 B.C., Drusus turned it back, then pursued it across the Rhine. In the next three years he marched and countermarched, always victorious (though once he was

ambushed and would have been defeated if the Germans —
too sure of victory — had not let down their guard and fallen
into disorder in their effort to begin looting.)

By 9 B.C. (744 A.U.C.) Drusus reached the Elbe River, 250
miles east of the Rhine; a line that is now the boundary between
West Germany and East Germany.

It is conceivable that under the further leadership of Drusus,
Rome might have conquered Germany and the history of the
world might then have been different. It is even possible that
Rome might have advanced to the line of the Vistula and
Dniester Rivers running from the Baltic Sea to the Black Sea.
That would have been a much shorter boundary than the Rhine
and Danube and much easier to defend. The Germans within
the Empire might have been civilized and Romanized and —
well, imagination boggles and anyway it didn't happen, so why
talk about it?

On his way back from the Elbe to the Rhine, Drusus' horse
stumbled and threw him. The injuries he suffered were fatal.
He was only thirty-one when he died and his death was a great
loss to Rome.

Augustus at once replaced Drusus by Tiberius, and things
might still have been well. Tiberius proceeded to make sure
the Germans didn't grow overconfident because of Drusus'
death. He repeated his brother's feat of marching his army
back and forth between the Rhine and the Elbe.

Unfortunately, Tiberius was suffering a personal tragedy.

It seems that Augustus had a daughter, Julia, by his first marriage, and since she was his only child, any sons she might have
could well succeed Augustus as Emperor. She had five children, including three sons, but in 12 B.C. her husband died and
left her a widow at the age of twenty-seven. Livia, her step-
mother, now saw her chance. If she could arrange a marriage
between the young widow and her own son, Tiberius, that
would increase Tiberius' chance of becoming the next Em-

eror, if Julia's own sons were too young to reign when Augustus died. After all, Tiberius would then be not only Augustus' stepson but also his son-in-law.

Augustus was won over by Livia (who had great influence over him). There was only one catch to Livia's scheme. Tiberius, it seemed, was already married to a wife whom he dearly loved. Augustus, however, forced him to agree to a divorce and to marry Julia, who was a frivolous, immoral woman whom the somber and moral Tiberius couldn't abide. The forced marriage broke Tiberius' heart, and left a mark on him from which he never recovered.

After his campaign in Germany, Tiberius felt he could bear it no longer and he got permission to retire to the Greek island of Rhodes where he could be away from his hated second wife and where he could drown his sorrows in study.

Augustus was angry indeed at this behavior of his new son-in-law for he felt him to be deserting his soldierly duties and to be behaving insultingly to Julia. Eventually, therefore, when Tiberius asked for permission to return to Rome from his self-imposed exile, that permission was first refused and then only grudgingly allowed. Indeed, he did not really become engaged in affairs of state again until 5 when it was necessary to call on his military services to crush a rebellion in Pannonia. Tiberius handled that task skillfully and by 9 the region was quiet.

During the fifteen-year period when Tiberius was away from Germany, that region fell into inferior hands with dire results for Rome and the world. Tiberius' forced marriage was indeed an expensive matter for everyone, then and now.

In 7, Augustus had decided that some twenty years of Roman occupation had made the region between the Rhine and Elbe good, solid Roman property. He decided to organize it as a Roman province and for the purpose sent Publius Quintilius Varus to Germany. Varus had served as consul in 13 B.C. and had later governed Syria with rather more graft than one would expect of an employee of Augustus.

Varus went about the business of Romanizing the Germans with great arrogance and no tact. He at once roused the Germans to thoughts of revolt. They found their leader in the twenty-five-year-old Arminius (the Latin form of the German name, Hermann.) Arminius had served with the Roman armies in his younger years. He had learned Latin, become Romanized, and even gained Roman citizenship. All this, however, didn't mean he was ready to submit to the kind of Roman arrogance represented by Varus.

Arminius began a campaign of clever deceit. He won Varus' trust and persuaded him, in the year 9, to leave the safety of the Rhine fortification and to establish his camp deep in Germany. Arminius then arranged for a small revolt to call Varus still farther into the German forests, with Arminius and his German contingent marching along as the rear-guard. Once Varus was sufficiently entangled in the section of the forest known as the Teutoburger Wald, about eighty miles east of the Rhine, Arminius broke away. He roused the countryside by a prearranged signal, and then launched a sudden wild attack from all sides that thundered down upon the unsuspecting, but neatly surrounded, Varus.

Varus and the Romans fought back bravely but the cause was hopeless. In three days, three Roman legions were totally destroyed.

The news struck Rome like the tolling of doom. No such defeat had battered down a Roman army in more than two centuries. Augustus was prostrated with grief. He simply could not replace the three legions without placing an unacceptable tax burden on the Empire, and the Roman army was therefore reduced from twenty-eight to twenty-five legions for a long time. The story is that Augustus beat his head against his palace walls crying, "Varus, Varus, give me back my legions!"

But Varus did not give them back. He was dead with his men.

Tiberius was rushed to the front and quickly led expeditions

across the Rhine to demonstrate to the Germans that Rome was
still mighty and to discourage the Germans from any attempt
to follow up their victory by invading Gaul.

But the German marches of Tiberius had no further significance. There was no attempt at a conquest of Germany, not
then and not ever again. The Roman frontier, so briefly on the
Elbe, was withdrawn to the Rhine (although Roman forces
continued to occupy the coastline of what is now Holland and
Frisia east of the Rhine) and remained there.

The battle of the Teutoburger Wald was truly one of the crucial battles of world history. The Germans retained their independence and never felt the warming touch of Romanization except from afar. And four centuries later, the German
tribes, still free but still barbaric, were to turn on Rome and
tear it to bits.

THE AUGUSTAN AGE

In the reign of Augustus, peaceful in Italy and in the settled
provinces, there was a flowering of culture. The "Augustan
Age" of Latin literature forms, together with the preceding
period in which the orator Cicero was prominent, Rome's cul-
tural Golden Age.

Augustus himself was greatly interested in literature and
encouraged and supported writers. Even more notable in this
respect was a close friend and minister of Augustus, Gaius
Cilnius Maecenas. Maecenas had been close to Augustus ever
since the latter was a schoolboy. During the last years of the

civil wars he remained in Rome, taking care of affairs at home while Augustus was fighting the final battles. After the coming of peace it was Maecenas who urged Augustus not to reestablish the republic on the ground that all the old disorders would spring up again.

About 16 B.C., Maecenas, who was by now immensely wealthy, retired from public life and used his riches in order to continue and enlarge his favorite hobby of supporting and encouraging Rome's artists, writers, and scholars. So famous did he become in this respect that ever since the expression "a Maecenas" has been applied to any rich man who devotes himself to the patronage of the arts.

The most prominent writer who benefited from Maecenas' patronage was Publius Vergilius Maro, commonly known in English as Vergil (or Virgil).

Vergil was born in 70 B.C. on a farm near Mantua. After the battle of Philippi, in which Augustus won his final triumph over the assassins of Julius Caesar, the victorious soldiers were rewarded with grants of land in Italy. (This was common practice during the civil wars.) Vergil's father was evicted from his farm in 42 B.C. in order to make room for one of these soldiers.

Vergil, however, had already gained some reputation as a poet and he was known to one of Augustus' generals, Gaius Asinius Pollio (himself a poet and orator) who was in power in that region of Italy. Asinius Pollio saw to it that Vergil's land was restored, then introduced him to Maecenas.

Vergil's works consist first of a number of short pieces called the *Eclogues.* Of these, the Fourth Eclogue, written in 40 B.C., speaks of the imminent birth of a child who is to bring a new reign of peace to the world. No one knows exactly whom he had in mind. He may simply have been meaning to flatter one of his patrons whose wife was expecting. The later Christians, however, thought it possible that he was predicting (pos-

sibly unconsciously) the birth of Jesus, and for that reason he
became of great importance in Christian legend. In Dante's
Divine Comedy written thirteen centuries later, it was Vergil
who was pictured as guiding Dante through Hell.

At the suggestion of Maecenas, Vergil composed the *Georgics*
in praise of agriculture and country life. (The name is from
a Greek word for "farmer.") The purpose may have been to
encourage a revival of agriculture in Italy for Augustus had
this as one of his aims.

(Augustus, indeed, tried to restore the Romans to all the
imagined virtues of a simpler day, when their honored ancestors were pictured as truthful, honest, dutiful, brave, hard-
working farmers who were loyal husbands, noble fathers, and
devoted patriots. Unfortunately Augustus did not succeed in
this, for in many respects the Italy of his day was a sophisticated example of an "affluent society" like ours today. Luxuries
poured in from all the Empire and the upper classes found
little to do but enjoy themselves. They married often, got divorced easily, ate and drank well, enjoyed leisure. As for the
poorer classes, there was free food, and plenty of pageantry
and games to amuse them. Moralists disapproved of this and
compared Rome unfavorably with other nations and with their
own ancestors, but despite the hard words conditions did not
change. And although Vergil's *Georgics* are considered Latin
perfection, they were read chiefly by the leisure classes and
did not cause a rush of aristocrats back to the soil.)

Vergil's later years were devoted to a grand epic in twelve
books called the *Aeneid*, begun, supposedly, at the request of
Augustus himself. The *Aeneid*, in terms of plot, is actually a
feeble imitation of Homer. The Trojan warrior, Aeneas, is the
hero (a rather anemic one) and the epic tells of his escape
from burning Troy, his long voyage filled with adventure that
brings him finally to Italy and lays the groundwork for the even-
tual founding of Rome by his descendants. Indeed, Aeneas is
described as having a son named Julus, from whom the Julian

family (including Julius Caesar and Augustus) were descended.

The poet worked on the epic many years and was still polishing it when he died in 19 B.C. Unsatisfied with anything short of perfection, he left directions to have the manuscript burned. This was overruled by Augustus, however, and the *Aeneid*, after some final bits of polishing by others, was published. Vergil is generally accepted as the greatest of the Roman poets.

Second to him is Horace (Quintus Horatius Flaccus), the son of a freedman, who was born in 65 B.C. in southern Italy, and educated in Rome and in Athens. He was clearly meant for the literary life for his attempt at soldiering was disastrous. While he was in Athens, Julius Caesar was assassinated and Horace joined the army raised in Greece by the assassins. At the battle of Philippi, where Horace served as an officer, he took to flight and reached an inglorious safety.

Horace did not lose his life for the crime of being on the losing side, but he did lose his family property in Italy. He went to Rome to try to make a living and attracted the attention of Vergil who introduced him to Maecenas who, in turn, saw to it that he was granted a farm that would allow him the necessary financial independence. His work rapidly won him the regard of Augustus and his short poems, odes and satires, retain their popularity even today. He died in 8 B.C., shortly after the death of Maecenas.

The last of the great poets of the Augustan age was Ovid (Publius Ovidius Naso) who was born in 43 B.C. about seventy miles east of Rome. He was of independent means and enjoyed life, especially since his poems were popular enough in his own lifetime to impress rich patrons and thus keep his means independent.

His poems dealt so unabashedly with love, however, that they proved shocking to the straitlaced Augustus and to those men in the government who were anxious to reform the Roman way of life. Ovid's most famous book is the *Metamorphoses*

which is a retelling of Greek myths in Latin verse. The myths
were usually pretty ribald, too, and Ovid obviously enjoyed
that.

In later life, he was involved in a scandal that concerned
Augustus' frivolous daughter, Julia. The Emperor, broken-
hearted, exiled his daughter and never forgave her and he certainly wasn't going to forgive any of her accomplices. Ovid, of
whom Augustus disapproved anyhow, was ordered into exile in
8. He spent the last eight years of his life in a barbarian town
at the mouth of the Danube, and although he wrote reams of
melancholy poetry intended to persuade Augustus to relent
and allow him to return to Rome, all failed. He died in exile
in 17.

The greatest prose writer of the Augustan Age was Livy (Titus Livius) who was born in Padua in 59 B.C. Although he
openly expressed republican sympathies all his life, Augustus
tolerated that good-humoredly since Livy did not indulge in
politics but devoted himself entirely to the literary life.

At Augustus' request he wrote a tremendous history of Rome
from the time of its founding to the death of Drusus. The whole
was in 142 books, and he may have intended several more to
carry matters to the death of Augustus, but his own death in
17 prevented him from doing so.

Livy was the most popular of all the Roman historians, both
in his own time and since, though, unfortunately, only some 35
of the 142 books survive. The rest are known to us through sum-
maries but that is not the same thing. Livy wrote to be popular and that is his weak point. In his anxiety to tell interesting
stories and capture the imagination of the reader, he repeated
all sorts of mythical and legendary material without in the least
worrying as to whether it could possibly be accurate or not.

Most of our knowledge of Roman history comes from the
surviving writings of the Roman historians themselves. In most
cases, as in that of Livy, only parts of those writings have survived. It is the accidents of survival that allow us to know some

portions of Roman history in great detail while others are known only sketchily.

THE JEWS

Yet the outstanding event of Augustus' reign and, very likely, the most important single happening in civilized history, did not involve a conquest or a defeat, a reorganization or a reform, a work of art or of literature. It was simply the birth of an obscure individual in an obscure corner of the Empire — a fact that went unnoticed at the time.

South of Syria lay Judea. Its inhabitants (Judeans, or Jews) had a fiercely monotheistic religion which they traced back nearly two thousand years to the patriarch Abraham. For four centuries, between 1000 B.C. and 600 B.C., they had gloried in an independent kingdom, which had been moderately powerful at first under the conquering king David, but had then gradually weakened.

In 586 B.C. (166 A.U.C.), the kingdom had been wiped out by the Babylonians. Less than a century later, the Babylonians were in turn conquered by the Persians and the Jews were permitted to rebuild their Temple at their old capital, Jerusalem.

The Jews remained in Judea, under Persian domination, without a king and without either political or military power, but clinging to their religion and their memories of past independence. The Persians were succeeded by the empire of Alexander the Great and then by the Seleucid Empire. In 168

B.C., the Seleucid monarch, Antiochus IV, had declared Judaism illegal and had attempted to convert the Jews, one and all, to the Greek culture and way of life, with extinction as the alternative.

The Jews rebelled and, under the leadership of Judas Maccabeus and his brothers, actually won their independence from the Seleucids. For about a century, this independence was maintained under the house of the Maccabees and Judea was able to go its own way briefly, although under kings who were not of the revered "house of David."

In 63 B.C., the Romans were cleaning up the East. By that time, members of the Maccabee family were fighting among themselves over who had the right to rule Judea, and the losing side called in the Romans. The Roman general felt the safest thing was to wipe out the Maccabean kingdom altogether and to place over Judea someone who could be counted on as being safely pro-Roman. He did this by making a certain Antipater the ruler of Judea.

The cleverness of the move lay in the fact that Antipater was not really a Jew, but an Idumaean (or Edomite, in the language of the Bible.) Idumaea, or Edom, lay just south of Judea, and although the region had been conquered by the Maccabees and forcibly converted to Judaism, there was a traditional enmity between the two neighboring peoples that dated back for over a thousand years. The Jews felt Antipater the Idumaean to be an alien no matter how closely he adhered to Judaism and they resented his rule no matter how efficient and just he tried to make it. The Romans knew therefore that he could never count on his own subjects and that he would have to rely heavily on Rome for protection.

The second son of Antipater was Herodes (better known in English as Herod). In 37 B.C., he gained control of Judea. The land was restive, however, and Herod found it difficult to remain in power.

He tried to win over his Judean people by practicing Judaism and by improving the Temple at Jerusalem to the point where it far surpassed the original Temple of Solomon. However, he was a cruel and suspicious man who married some ten times and who had no compunction about ordering the executions of wives and sons when he felt them to be dangerous. (Augustus is reported to have said, upon hearing of one such execution, "I had rather be Herod's pig than Herod's son.")

The Jews detested Herod and among them a hope had been growing for some time. As centuries passed with one people after another — Babylonians, Persians, Greeks and Romans — tyrannizing over them, they began to dream that some day a descendant of David would return to be their king and give them their independence and their rightful place in the world.

Since the Jews consecrated their kings by anointing them with holy oil, they referred to the king as "the anointed one," much as moderns who consecrate their kings by crowning them refer to them as "crowned heads." In Hebrew, the phrase "the anointed one" is "messiah." The Jews, therefore, were waiting for the coming of the messiah.

The example of Judas Maccabeus, who had beaten the Seleucid kings when that had seemed impossible, was always before them. Another such man, a still greater one, could defeat Rome.

Other Jews, who were aware of the fact that Rome was far stronger in Augustus' time than the Seleucid Empire had been in the time of Antiochus IV, were less confident of a purely military solution. Instead they began to think in terms of a mystical and supernatural messiah; one who would do more than merely liberate Judea, one whose coming would begin a new reign of justice and holiness on Earth, with all the world turning toward the one true God.

Many individuals in Judea in those years claimed to be the messiah and there were always some who were ready to believe in the messianic character of anyone who claimed it.

There were revolts under the leadership of such men, all of which were put down. Herod and the Romans remained warily on the watch for all such supposed messiahs, recognizing them as an almost invariable source of all sorts of problems and troubles.

According to the story in Chapter 2 of the Gospel of St. Matthew in the New Testament, the birth of a baby called Jesus (the Greek form of Joshua) in Bethlehem toward the end of Herod's reign fulfilled the various prophecies concerning the messiah that appeared here and there in the books of the Old Testament. Herod, hearing of the rumored birth of such a baby, ordered all the children in Bethlehem who were under two years of age to be killed, but the infant Jesus was spirited away to Egypt in time.

There is no record of this event anywhere but in the New Testament and I mention it only because it is important in setting the time of birth of Jesus.

About five centuries after the time of Herod, a Syrian monk named Dionysius Exiguus, after making a careful study of the Bible and of Roman historical records, decided that the birth of Jesus had taken place in 753 A.U.C. This came to be accepted by the people of Europe generally, so that 753 A.U.C. became the year 1 of the Christian Era, and the founding of Rome was placed in 753 B.C.

However, Dionysius must have made a mistake because it is quite certain that Herod died in 749 A.U.C. which is, by Dionysius' reckoning, 4 B.C. If Herod had been disturbed at the reports of the birth of Jesus, then Jesus must have been born no later than 4 B.C. and possibly even some years earlier. (It is odd to think of Jesus being born four years "before Christ" but Dionysius' reckoning is so firmly embedded in history books and in documents that it is quite impossible and undesirable to change it.)

When Herod died, there still remained three sons of his

whom he had not got round to executing. Each of them inherited part of the realm. Herod Archelaus ruled over Judea
itself, together with Samaria, the region north of Judea. Herod
Antipas was set over Galilee, to the north of Samaria, and over
Perea, east of the Jordan River. Finally, Herod Philip ruled
over Iturea, northeast of Galilee.

The two latter, Antipas and Philip, remained in power for a
generation, but not so Archelaus. His rule was over the center
of the Judean dominion with its capital at Jerusalem itself, and
the Jews complained constantly to Rome over his misgovern-
ment. In 6 he was deposed by Augustus and exiled to Gaul.
For a period of time after that, Judea and Samaria were ruled
by Roman procurators appointed by the Emperor.

Although Jesus is recorded as having been born in Bethlehem, a small town south of Jerusalem which, according to tradition, was to be the place of birth of the messiah (since a thousand years before it had been the place of birth of David),
his family lived in Nazareth, a town in Galilee. It was in Galilee then, in the territory of Antipas, that Jesus grew up. As a
grown man, he gathered a group of devoted disciples about
him for his teachings proved popular and his personality mag-
netic.

Some of his disciples began to believe him to be the Messiah,
(and now the word is capitalized and so will pronouns refer-
ring to Jesus be, for hundreds of millions of men have since
that time believed in the Messiahship and divine nature of
Jesus). The Greek word for "the anointed one" is "Chris-
tos" and so what in Hebrew might have been "Joshua the Messiah" became in the English version of the Greek, "Jesus Christ."

The authorities, both Herodian and Roman, must have
watched Jesus narrowly for signs of Messianic tendencies that
might give rise to rebellions and troubles. The Jewish religious leaders were also wary of such things for they realized
how easily revolts could get out of hand and spark off a Roman

reaction that would destroy the nation completely. (This was actually to happen a half-century later so that their fears were anything but foolish.)

When Jesus' popularity was at its height, He traveled to Jerusalem to celebrate the Passover there and, in doing so, He tacitly accepted the role of Messiah, for He entered riding on a donkey. That was how one Old Testament prophet had predicted the Messiah would arrive in Jerusalem and the crowd caught the symbolism.

That was enough for the authorities. As soon as an opportunity offered itself to arrest Jesus quietly (so that no rioting would start among his disciples or among Jewish nationalists generally with possibly disastrous consequences) he was taken. One of Jesus' disciples, Judas Iscariot, revealed the place he was staying and made the quiet arrest possible, so that the name Judas has become a byword for treachery as a result.

To the Jewish leaders, Jesus' crime was that of blasphemy — claiming to be the Messiah when, in their opinion, He was not. To the Romans, His crime was purely political. The Messiah was someone whom the Jews recognized as king. If Jesus claimed to be the King of the Jews, He was rebelling against the Roman Emperor who alone had the right to appoint kings.

It was perhaps in 29 (782 A.U.C.) that Jesus was brought up for trial before Pontius Pilate, the sixth procurator to govern Judea since the deposition of Archelaus. He had been appointed to the post three years earlier. According to the Biblical account, he was reluctant to convict Jesus and did so only under pressure from the Jewish religious authorities who felt that to release Jesus would make a nationalist rebellion, followed by Roman repression, inevitable. The high priest, Caiaphas, is recorded in the Bible as saying, "It is expedient for us, that one man should die for the people, and that the whole nation perish not."

If Pilate convicted Jesus, however, he had to convict him of a Roman crime over which alone he had jurisdiction. Jesus was

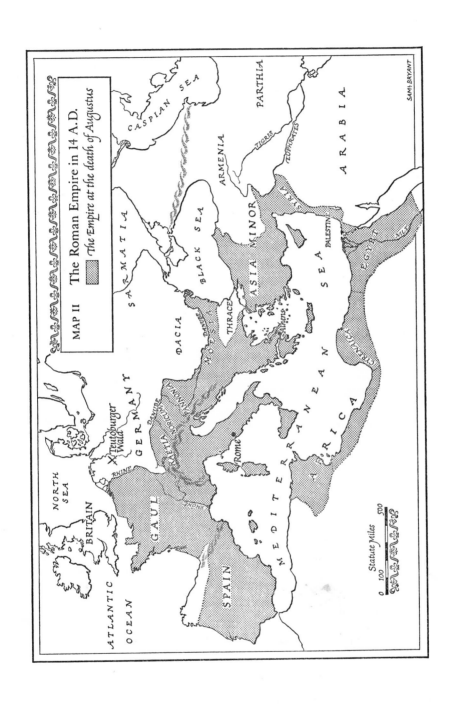

MAP II   The Roman Empire in 14 A.D.

The Empire at the death of Augustus

ATLANTIC OCEAN

NORTH SEA

BRITAIN

GAUL

SPAIN

GERMANY

X Teutoburger Wald

RHINE

RAETIA NORICUM

PANNONIA

DANUBE

DACIA

SARMATIA

MOESIA

DANUBE

THRACE

Athens

BLACK SEA

CASPIAN SEA

ARMENIA

TIGRIS

EUPHRATES

PARTHIA

ASIA MINOR

MEDITERRANEAN SEA

AFRICA

CYRENAICA

PALESTINE

SYRIA

EGYPT

NILE

ARABIA

Rome

Statute Miles

0   100   500

SAM: BRYANT

therefore convicted of treason against Rome and one common punishment for such treason was crucifixion, a type of torture common in the East and in Rome, although never used by either the Jews or the Greeks. As an example of the Roman use of crucifixion in quantity there is the case of that gladiatorial revolt in Italy which had been suppressed in 71 B.C. At that time, no less than six thousand of the captured rebels were crucified on miles of crosses all along the Appian Way, Italy's main highway.

So Jesus was crucified, as simply one more rebel getting the usual punishment, and that would seem to end that. No Roman at the time could have imagined at that moment that this particular crucifixion marked only a beginning.

2

THE LINE OF AUGUSTUS

THE SUCCESSION

Augustus was in his seventies and the shadow of death was closing in. He had to worry about the succession — the question of who was to succeed him as Princeps. If he were a king, the closest of kin might succeed automatically, but he wasn't king. He was the first Princeps and no tradition existed for the manner of choosing the next.

It seemed clear to Augustus that if he died without making provision for the succession, various generals might try to become Emperor, using their armies for the purpose and the civil wars might start again. Augustus would therefore have to choose a successor before he died and make the Senate and the people accept him in advance. Naturally, he would have liked to choose someone from his own family for the purpose.

The obvious choice in all such circumstances would have

been one's own son, but Augustus had no son of his own. He had only a daughter, Julia, who had upset and disgusted Augustus with her easy-going, pleasure-loving way of life. She had made a mockery of his program of reforming the Romans and she was sent into exile.

Her first husband, however, had been Marcus Vipsanius Agrippa who had been a close friend and advisor of Augustus from their schooldays, when they had studied together. When Augustus, who had little military ability of his own, was struggling for mastery over the Roman realm, it was Agrippa who fought and won his battles for him. In the peace that followed, it was Agrippa who supervised the rebuilding of Rome and built its most beautiful temple, the Pantheon ("all gods"), plus a number of aqueducts to insure the city's water supply. This Agrippa and Augustus' daughter, Julia, had five children before Agrippa's death in 12 B.C. There was that, therefore — Augustus had five grandchildren who were also the children of the Emperor's dear and loyal friend, Agrippa. And three of them were boys.

The two oldest sons, Gaius Caesar and Lucius Caesar, were full of promise. Lucius, however, sickened and died in Massilia (Marseille) in 2. As a young teen-ager, Gaius was sent off on a minor military expedition to Asia Minor, where he was wounded in action and died on the way home in 4. The youngest son of Agrippa and Julia, born after his father's death, proved of unsound mind, and was consequently kept in isolation under guard.

Of Augustus's two granddaughters, one was Julia, who seemed to be as pleasure-loving as her mother and namesake had been. She, too, was punished by the rigid Augustus. He sent her into exile as he had sent her mother, and she lived out twenty years of her life without ever being allowed to return to Rome. That left only the second granddaughter, Agrippina, who will be mentioned later.

With these tragedies dogging his personal life, Augustus was forced to turn to his stepson Tiberius again. Tiberius was not a blood relation but he was a son by adoption (which counted for a great deal in Roman times) and was the natural son, moreover, of Augustus' beloved wife. Tiberius was a member of the aristocratic Claudian family on his natural father's side and, through his adopted father Augustus, a member of the equally aristocratic Julian family. The line of related Emperors that begins with Augustus is therefore often spoken of as the "Julio-Claudian line."

Another advantage of Tiberius was that he was a grown man, in his fifties during Augustus' last years, and a general of proven worth. He was also honest, conscientious, and rigidly moral. There was no question but that he would govern well. Unfortunately, he was a dour, withdrawn individual (especially since the forced divorce of his beloved wife) and did not inspire liking in anyone.

Later on, there were historians who related that Tiberius had stage-managed the whole business in an evil and deceitful way with the help of his mother, Livia. Tales are told that he poisoned Augustus' grandsons, that he maneuvered Augustus' own death, and so on. His character was blackened and he was made to seem a monster of cruelty and lust.

Actually, it is doubtful that any of this can be believed. The writers from whom we hear these things were members of the Senatorial party of a couple of generations later, who longed for what seemed to them to have been the good old days. They resented the Emperors who had ended the Republic and they delighted in writing scandalous stories about them. Listening to these historians is something like listening to keyhole columnists in the tabloid newspapers and believing everything they say about celebrities.

Finally, in 14 (767 A.U.C.) Augustus lay dying. He was seventy-seven and had reigned forty-three years. Almost his last words to those around him were "Do you think I have acted my part in life well? If so, applaud."

Certainly he had acted his part in life well. The Empire was well established and its five million citizens and nearly hundred million non-citizens were at peace. All the centuries of struggle of ancient history seemed to have reached its climax in this final peaceful and enlightened "world government."

It remained only to keep it so for as long as possible.

TIBERIUS

With Augustus dying, Livia (who lived on for fifteen more years, dying in 29 at the remarkable age, for those days, of eighty-six) sent out messengers to Tiberius. He was on his way to Illyria on a campaign but, upon receiving the message, took command of the army at once and returned to Rome to assume the office of Emperor.

He offered, as Augustus had once done, to lay down all those powers and restore the Republic but again this was a device to force the Senate to hand him those powers personally. He would then be Emperor by the will of the Senate as well as by that of Augustus and his position would be completely legal and doubly secure. The Senate understood this, and understood also the dangers of anarchy if, by some odd chance, Tiberius were serious.

They hastened to vote him all Imperial power.

On his accession, Tiberius had to face the rebellion of legions on the Danube and on the Rhine. To take care of the Danubian legions, he sent his son Drusus Caesar (sometimes called Drusus the Younger, to distinguish him from Drusus the Elder, who had been Tiberius' brother). Drusus the Younger managed to bring those mutineers back into line.

The situation on the Rhine was more dangerous. Since the

defeat of Varus, the Rhine frontier had been particularly sensitive, and special efforts had to be made to keep morale high there. The Roman soldiers on the Rhine had idolized Drusus the Elder and Drusus had had a son in 15 B.C. who had been named Germanicus Caesar in honor of his father's German victories. The boy had been only six years old when his father died, but when Arminius had won his great victory over Varus' legions, Germanicus was twenty-four, a gallant young man and the model of a young Roman nobleman. What's more, he married Agrippina, the virtuous granddaughter of Augustus.

Augustus was so impressed by his grandson-in-law that he sent him to the Rhine frontier along with Tiberius in the critical time after Varus' defeat. They did well there and when Augustus was arranging to have Tiberius succeed to the Imperial throne, the old emperor insisted that Tiberius adopt Germanicus as his son and heir to the exclusion of Tiberius' own son. This Tiberius did.

In 14, Germanicus was sent to the Rhine a second time, and alone, while Tiberius was sent to Illyria. When Augustus died and Tiberius returned to accept Imperial honors from the Senate, it was Germanicus who was on the spot and who had to deal with the suddenly rebellious legions.

The soldiers were demanding more pay and, in essence, shorter hours, for they complained that the campaigning was too arduous. Germanicus, with a mixture of tact, affability, and firmness, and with the offer of more money, won the legions over.

To keep them occupied and give them the excitement of victory, he then led them into Germany once more. He defeated the Germans in several battles and showed them that the victory over Varus was very much a one-shot affair and not likely to be repeated easily. He even led his army through the Teutoburger Wald where they came across the bleaching bones of Varus' three legions and where they buried the remains they found. Germanicus had occasion to fight Arminius and his Germans again, and defeated them with much slaughter, recovering the standards lost by Varus' legions.

In Tiberius' judgment, a great deal had been accomplished. The Germans had been taught their lesson and they would no longer presume on their one victory. Nevertheless, to him, as to Augustus, there seemed no point in trying to reestablish the Elbe line. It was too expensive both in money and in men for any worth it seemed to have to Tiberius. In 16, therefore, he ordered the Roman legions back to the Rhine and recalled Germanicus.

The Senatorial gossip-mongers of later times were sure that this was done out of jealousy and hatred for his nephew, whom he was supposed to resent as his heir and to dread because of his popularity with the army. And yet this is by no means certain. Tiberius' strategic judgment was right. The Germans *had* been taught a lesson and the Rhine frontier remained quiet for two centuries thereafter. On the other hand, Germanicus had lost a considerable number of soldiers and his victories had not been easy ones. Had he continued his campaign it is quite possible that the Germans might eventually have won a second victory and that after such a second victory, a German invasion of Gaul would have followed with results of unpredictable consequence.

That Tiberius was not seriously jealous of Germanicus seems to be demonstrated by the fact that he placed the young man in a position of power over the eastern portion of the Empire. His mission in the east was to settle matters concerning Armenia. Parthia was once again stirring up trouble there, as it was to do many times in the future.

Germanicus, unfortunately, had no chance to solve this problem. In 19, he died at the age of thirty-four. There is nothing intrinsically surprising at this. It is only in modern times that infectious diseases have been conquered and in ancient times there were many diseases and infections that were fatal that today would scarcely even be serious. The general length of life in Roman times was much shorter than it is today. Although occasional individuals might, like Augustus and Livia, survive well into old age, the average Roman was probably dead by forty.

Nevertheless, this never seemed to be allowed for when a popular figure died young of no clear cause, particularly if he were in line for a position of power. The gossip-mongers then and later always assumed the scandalous worst. Rumors arose at once, for instance, that Tiberius had had Germanicus poisoned and Germanicus' wife, Agrippina, seems to have believed that.

But Tiberius had no more luck with his heirs than Augustus had had. If Tiberius had poisoned Germanicus in order to make his own son the Emperor, this hope was dashed. In 23, Drusus the Younger died at the age of thirty-eight.

Tiberius continued Augustus' prudent policy in peace as well as in war. No more than Augustus did he seek the expense and risk of foreign conquest merely for the sake of conquest. No more than Augustus did he neglect to see to it that the provinces were governed honestly and efficiently. He seized the opportunity whenever he could to unify the Empire by annexing a satellite kingdom as a province, but not by force. He rather chose to seize a strategic moment as when an old king died. Thus, when the king of Cappadocia, in eastern Asia Minor, died in 17, Tiberius made it into a Roman province.

Tiberius was already elderly when he became Emperor. By the time he was sixty-five, he was weary indeed and only too willing to shift the burden of government to younger shoulders; to select the equivalent of a prime minister, in other words.

He chose Lucius Aelius Sejanus for the purpose. Sejanus was the chief of the praetorian guard which, under Augustus, had been scattered in small detachments over Italy. Sejanus persuaded Tiberius to order these men concentrated in a camp near Rome. This made them handier in case of emergencies and increased Sejanus' power. (It also made them more dangerous to the Empire as later years were to show.)

The stories whispered in later years make out Sejanus to be an incredible monster. It was he who supposedly engineered the poisoning of Drusus so that he himself might possibly succeed to the Emperorship. It seems likely that Sejanus' real offense was to take stern measures to make Tiberius' power supreme over the Senate.

Tiberius did not have Augustus' gift for winning over people. Where Augustus could walk the streets unprotected, Tiberius had to guard himself. As the Republic receded farther off in the mists of history, more and more Senators began to praise an idealized past. Sejanus persuaded Tiberius to act strongly against such Senators as spoke openly against the Principate and the later Senatorial historians execrated him and Tiberius in consequence.

It was not only the Senate that represented a possible danger. Agrippina, the widow of Germanicus, seems to have intrigued against Tiberius whom she suspected of poisoning her husband, and to have dreamed of placing one of her own children on the throne. Sejanus persuaded Tiberius to exile her in 30 and she died three years later, still in exile.

By 26, Tiberius was well enough assured of Sejanus' ability to run the government to feel that he could afford to retire completely from the cares of state and from his sorrow at the death of his son. He therefore took up residence in restful retirement on the island of Capri in the Bay of Naples.

Popular rumor, afterward, had Tiberius indulging in all sorts of cruelties and lustful orgies on the island, but it is difficult to imagine anything more ridiculous than such stories. In the first place, Tiberius had led a most unluxurious and abstemious life and it is not likely that the habits of a lifetime would suddenly be cast way. Secondly, he was sixty-eight when he retired to Capri and it is not likely he could have indulged in much in the way of orgies even if he had wanted to.

In his absence, though, Sejanus appears to have gone to extremes. The laws against treason were sharpened to the point where any unguarded statement that might be interpreted as displeasure concerning Tiberius or the Principate could constitute cause for a death sentence. People were encouraged to report such statements and were rewarded for it so it is not surprising if reports of such statements were sometimes false. Professional informers became one of the horrors of the period.

Sejanus may have deliberately encouraged the reign of terror with the intention of breaking the spirit of the Senate, if it required further breaking.

Eventually, though, the suspicious Tiberius became suspicious even of Sejanus. The prime minister was arranging to marry Tiberius' granddaughter and thoughts of the succession may well have been in his mind at that. Perhaps Tiberius resented this. In any case, the Emperor sent a letter from Capri in 31 denouncing Sejanus and his till-then all-powerful prime minister was executed at once.

CALIGULA

Tiberius died in 37 (790 A.U.C.) after a reign of twenty-three years, and there was again a problem of succession.

Tiberius had no living children and Germanicus, his nephew, who had originally been his heir was long since dead. Germanicus, however, had had children. Some were already dead, but one son remained alive. This was Gaius Caesar, the grandnephew of Tiberius, the great-grandson of Livia (Augustus' wife) through his father, and the great-grandson of Augustus himself, and of Mark Antony, too, through his mother.

Gaius Caesar had been born in 12, while Germanicus and Agrippina, his father and mother, were in camp in Germany. He spent his first few years among the legions, and the rough legionaries apparently adored the novelty of having the baby of their commander in their midst. Germanicus, making use of the child in his campaign to keep soldier morale high, dressed him in a soldier's outfit, including a small version of army boots. The soldiers went wild at the sight and called the youngster nothing but Caligula ("little boots.") The nickname stuck and he is known to history by that silly name only.

Caligula, unlike Augustus and Tiberius, had no grounding at all in the old tradition of Rome. He had been brought up in the Imperial court where on the one hand he was deferred to as a possible heir and experienced all possible luxury and where, on the other hand, his life was in constant danger through court intrigue so that he had to learn to be fearful and suspicious. Then, too, he had as his friends several of the princes of the Eastern satellite kingdoms who were in Rome for one purpose or another. One in particular was Herod Agrippa, a grandson of the first Herod of Judea. From these friends, Caligula absorbed a liking for the Eastern type of monarchy.

Caligula's rule began quietly enough and was, in fact, greeted with rejoicing, for the court was gayer than in the days of gloomy old Tiberius and the young Emperor seemed liberal and pleasant. He was so liberal, in fact, that he gaily spent in one year all the surplus that Augustus and Tiberius had prudently stored up in the treasury over nearly seventy years of careful government.

In 38, however, Caligula fell seriously ill and when he recovered all was changed. There is no doubt that the illness had affected his mind and that he was quite unbalanced during the last few years of his life. The later Senatorial historians traced his mental illness back into early life and made him a monster from the beginning and while they undoubtedly exaggerated, there may be a streak of truth in this.

After 38, Caligula's spending mania increased and he was forced to take unusual measures to obtain the money he needed. The need for money is a strong temptation to tyranny for if a rich man is convicted of treason and executed his property can be confiscated by the state and flows into the Emperor's pockets. If the conviction is unjust that doesn't matter. As a particularly flagrant example, Caligula had Ptolemy, the harmless king of Mauretania, and a fellow descendant of Mark Antony (see page 12) brought to Rome and executed. He was then able to confiscate the Mauretanian treasury.

Caligula attempted to alter the Augustan Principate into an Eastern monarchy and to have himself worshipped as divine.

Actually, divine worship was accorded to dead human beings and sometimes to living ones in most ancient cultures (the Jews being a conspicuous exception to this). The Roman Emperors were often deified after death and routine ritual honors were paid them. It didn't mean much in a polytheistic society and it pleased the Senate since it was up to them to vote the divine honors or not. It often happened that the only way the Senate could get back at an Emperor that tyrannized over them in life was to refuse him divine honors after death. It did no harm to the dead Emperor, of course, but it made the living Senators feel good.

Caligula went beyond this in his megalomania, however, and wanted to be granted divine honors while still alive. This was against Roman custom but it was not without precedent in other cultures. The Egyptian Pharaohs were considered to be living gods, for instance. This was not as ridiculous to the Egyptians as it seems to us, today, for a great deal depends on one's definition of "god." The security and ceremony with which a modern head of state is surrounded doesn't make him seem godlike to us, who are well aware of the transcendent power of the God we worship, but it might have made him seem quite godlike to an ancient culture to whom gods were many and often quite humanly weak in their characteristics.

To the Romans, though, the sight of a young Emperor dressing like Jupiter and demanding that his own statue be put in place of Jupiter's in the temples was very disturbing.

Augustus and Tiberius had merely been "first citizens." Their title was Princeps. Whatever their powers they were merely Roman citizens in theory and other Roman citizens were their equal — in theory. If Caligula became a god-king, however, he would be a good deal more than a citizen. All the peoples of the Empire, including Roman citizens, would be his subjects and slaves alike. A Roman citizen would then have no more rights than any noncitizen provincial.

Conspiracies rose against Caligula. One of these finally succeeded and in 41 (794 A.U.C.) he, along with his wife and daughter, were murdered by a contingent of the Praetorian guard. He was not yet thirty at the time.

CLAUDIUS

In a way, this first assassination of an Emperor (not the last by far) was a golden opportunity for the Senate. Now that a mad Emperor had shown what he could do, the gloss was off the Principate. Its "image" had risen high after seventy years of firm, reasonable rule but now it was permanently tarnished for it clearly gave mad boys the life-and-death rule over all the realm. Here, then, was a good time to restore the Republic.

Unfortunately for the Senate, the decision was not theirs to make. It had been the soldiers who killed the Emperor and it was the soldiers who would pick a new one.

As it happened, Caligula's uncle was with the emperor at the time of the assassination. This uncle, Claudius (Tiberius Claudius Drusus Nero Germanicus), was the younger brother of Germanicus and the son of Drusus the Elder, the two military heroes of the early days of the Empire.

Claudius, unlike his brother and father, was sickly and unattractive in appearance, so he tended to be shoved aside and neglected. He found it safest to cultivate obscurity and was widely felt to be feeble-minded, which probably further helped keep him safe against intrigue since he seemed a threat to no one.

In actual fact, Claudius was not feeble-minded at all, but was a scholar who did historical research and wrote competently of the Etruscans and Carthaginians. This probably further convinced the gayer members of the Roman aristocracy that he was an eccentric, however.

Caligula may have felt some affection for his harmless uncle, or he may have thought him an amusing court jester. At the beginning of Caligula's reign, he served as consul along with the Emperor and, as mentioned earlier, he was with Caligula when the assassins burst in.

Claudius, in panic, hid behind some furniture, while the soldiers raged about, killing blindly at first in the fear that they might themselves be set upon. When their fury was spent, they spied Claudius in his hiding place and dragged him out. Quakingly, he pleaded for his life but there was no intention of killing him. The soldiers recognized the need for an Emperor and Claudius was a member of the Imperial family. The pleading was on the other foot; they begged him to be their Emperor.

Claudius probably did not like the idea but there was no way in which he could argue with armed soldiers. He not only agreed, but promised to reward the soldiers with a general bonus on his accession. This set a bad precedent, for the soldiers learned they could charge for the throne and they gradually charged a higher and higher price.

The Senate, their hopes of a restored Republic dashed, had to agree to whatever the soldiers wanted and Claudius was Emperor.

Claudius was fifty years old at the time. He had spent his life in scholarly pursuits and was not a man of action or decision. In fact, he was rather timid and weak-willed. Nevertheless, he did his best to be a good Emperor. He carried on building programs in Rome, extended the Imperial road network, and drained lakes to reclaim valuable farmland. He respected the Senate and, under him, the court was freed from the danger of divine kings for Claudius was merely First Citizen in the tradition of Augustus.

Under Claudius, timid though he was, the Roman Empire again began to expand somewhat. For one thing, Claudius continued Tiberius' policy of sweeping up the satellite-kingdoms when conditions were right. Mauretania was without a king since Caligula had had Ptolemy executed and the Mauretanians had rebelled at Caligula's clumsy attempt to make it a province. Claudius had the rebellion crushed and Mauretania became a province in 42.

Lycia, in southwestern Asia Minor, was made a province in 43, as was Thrace, north of the Aegean Sea, in 46. Only one or two odd corners of the Empire remained self-ruling. One example was Commagene, a small region in eastern Asia Minor that Caligula, out of a whim, had made a monarchy again after it had already been part of a Roman province. It retained its kings for a generation.

Still more to the point, the Roman Empire jumped across the sea from Gaul into Britain.

The island of Britain (now called Great Britain and including England, Wales and Scotland), lying north of Gaul across the narrow arm of the sea now called the English Channel, was known only vaguely to the ancient world before the time of Julius Caesar. The Phoenicians and Carthaginians are supposed to have sent ships to Britain in search of tin, a metal needed for the manufacture of bronze, carefully keeping their tin sources a commercial secret.

When Caesar conquered Gaul, he became aware of Britain since the Celtic inhabitants of that island were akin in language and culture to the Gauls. What's more, feeling secure on their island, they did not hesitate to send help to the Gauls in their fight against the Romans.

To put a stop to this, Caesar mounted two raids into Britain in 55 and 54 B.C. In the second, he achieved considerable success, advancing beyond the Thames River. He was of no mind at the time, however, to be entangled in the distant island and, having accomplished his purpose of cowing the Britons, he left and went about his greater business.

The Britons had a respite of nearly a century. Still, as they watched the Roman power growing ever more settled in Gaul, and the Gauls themselves growing ever more Romanized, they must have become increasingly nervous. They felt it the part of self-defense to continue to encourage trouble in Gaul.

Under Claudius, conditions in Gaul had grown more favorable to Rome, however, and less favorable to Britain. The narrow policy of Augustus and Tiberius with respect to citizenship was being reversed and Gauls of distinction were being admitted to citizenship. This farsighted action helped make the land a secure base for a further outhrusting of power. (By 48, a generation after Augustus' death, the number of Roman citizens had increased to about six million.)

The internal politics of Britain also made an invasion seem advisable. A pro-Roman ruler in Britain, Cunobelin (the "Cymbeline" of Shakespeare's play) had died and had been succeeded by a pair of anti-Roman sons. A pro-Roman British leader called for help from Rome against the new rulers and Rome responded. A Roman army landed in southeastern England (the modern Kent) in 43 (796 A.U.C.). Southern England, which had already been peacefully penetrated through commerce and trade and was half-Romanized in consequence, was conquered and made a province of the Empire. Claudius himself joined the army and his young son, born the year before, was given the surname Britannicus.

The Britons fought back hard, particularly in the wild hilly regions of the north and west. The British leader, Caractacus, was not captured till 51. Then, in 61, a fierce revolt on the part of Boudicca (usually spelled, incorrectly, Boadicea), queen of a region in eastern England north of the Thames, nearly undid all the Roman work by virtually erasing a Roman legion. It took some thirty years before what is now England and Wales were reasonably pacified.

At home, Claudius had his troubles for he was governed and hen-pecked by his womenfolk. His third wife, to whom he was married at the time he became Emperor, was Valeria Messalina. She was the mother of Britannicus. The later Senatorial historians have filled her life with such an amazing list of vices that the word "Messalina" has now come to be used for any abandoned and depraved woman. Apparently, Claudius himself was finally convinced that Messalina was perhaps planning to kill him and replace him on the throne with one of her lovers, for he ordered her executed in 48.

He then married Agrippina, Caligula's sister and his own niece. She had been married before and had a son, Domitius, who adopted the Imperial names, Nero Claudius Caesar Drusus Germanicus, when his mother became Empress. He is known to history as Nero. Nero was the grandson of Germanicus and the great-great-grandson of Augustus.

Agrippina's driving ambition was to see her son Nero become Emperor. She persuaded Claudius to adopt Nero as his son and to make him his heir in preference to his own son Britannicus, who was younger than Nero. In 53, Nero's position was made more secure by his marriage to Octavia, the daughter of Claudius. At the time, Nero was fifteen and Octavia was eleven.

When all this was done, Agrippina needed Claudius no more. According to the story of the later Senatorial historians, she had Claudius poisoned in 54 (807 A.U.C.) and arranged to have the praetorian guard recognize Nero as his successor at the cost of the promise of a generous bonus. If the soldiers said yes the Senate was in no position to say no. Nero became the fifth Emperor of Rome.

NERO

Nero, sixteen years old at the time of his accession, began his reign, as Caligula did, in such a way as to give rise to optimistic hope. Yet when one is young and finds one can have any wish gratified, whatever it may be, it is hard to learn restraint.

Very soon, Nero was learning to kick out of his way anything that might act as a barrier to the continued gratification of his wishes. He had Britannicus poisoned; he divorced his young wife, had her banished, and eventually done away with. By 59, he had grown so willful he did not hesitate to have his mother executed because she tried to dominate him as she had dominated Claudius.

Oddly enough, Nero never really liked the business of government. What he really wanted was to be a performer on the stage. He was what we would today describe as "stage-struck." He wrote poetry, painted pictures, played on the lyre, sang, recited tragedies. It was his eager desire to perform in public and receive applause. It is impossible, of course, to tell how proficient he was in his performance because there is no impartial record of what he did. He got wild applause on all occasions and was constantly being awarded the prize over professional performers, but was that because he was good, or because he was the Emperor? Almost certainly the latter. On the other hand, the later Senatorial historians derided his abilities and perhaps he was not quite as incompetent as they liked to say.

Perhaps if Nero had been a performer rather than an Emperor, he might have led a reasonable life and even attained some minor measure of renown. He might have been a respectable citizen and even a good man. As it was, however, his position as Emperor allowed him plenty of opportunity to go down in history as one of the most blackened villains who ever lived.

But regardless of how luxurious and wasteful Nero's personal rule was, the business of the Empire went on.

Trouble arose in the East once again, and the problem, as almost always, rested with the tug-of-war between Rome and Parthia for the buffer state of Armenia that lay between them. Shortly after the death of Claudius, the Roman puppet-ruler of Armenia was killed by border tribesmen and the Parthian king, taking advantage of what he felt might be a period of unsettlement in Rome, invaded Armenia and made his brother, Tiridates, king of the land.

Nero sent Gnaeus Domitius Corbulo east to take care of matters. Corbulo had served effectively in Germany under Claudius and was a thoroughly competent general. He spent three years reorganizing the legions in the east and revitalizing their morale. In 58 (811 A.U.C.) he invaded Armenia and in the course of the next year occupied the country, driving out the Parthians, and setting up a new Roman puppet.

If Corbulo had been given a free hand, Parthia might have been resoundingly defeated. Nero, however, was concerned lest any one general become too successful and he replaced Corbulo with a general far less competent who, in 62, was badly defeated. Corbulo was then placed in charge once more and he managed to restore the situation so that matters ended in a stalemate. Tiridates, the Parthian, remained king of Armenia in the end, but in 63 he agreed to come to Rome and receive his crown from Nero, thus establishing Armenia, in theory at least, as a Roman satellite.

Meanwhile, however, a crisis was arising in Judea. The Jews were growing increasingly restive under the rule of the Herods

and the procurators. Their messianic longings were growing
more acute and they were in no mood to compromise their religion in any way. Their memories of the Maccabees and their
gloriously successful rebellion on behalf of religion and against
Antiochus IV, two and a half centuries before, remained fresh
in their minds.

Thus, they continually objected to any form of honor that
might be construed as worship for the Emperor or for any of
the symbols of Empire. When Pontius Pilate entered Jerusalem
with standards on which the figure of the Emperor Tiberius was
painted, violent disorders broke out among the population, for
the painting was counted as an idol. Pontius Pilate was astonished, for there seemed no harm in a battle flag. Nevertheless,
Tiberius desired no unnecessary and expensive rebellion over
so trifling a cause and he ordered the troublesome symbols removed.

Such intransigent behavior, however; such certainty that
their God was the one, true God and that all other objects of
worship were evil and disgusting; made the Jews increasingly
unpopular with the other peoples of the Empire, who welcomed
a multiplicity of gods and were each largely indifferent to the
beliefs of their neighbor. The Jews were particularly unpopular with the Greeks who considered their own culture the one,
true Culture and thought as little of other cultures as the Jews
thought of other gods.

In Alexandria, the capital of Egypt, the largest Greek-speaking city in the world at that time and second only to Rome itself
in the Empire, there was a large colony of Jews who remained
Jews — almost a city within a city. They had been given
special privileges by Augustus (who was grateful for their support of him in the final civil war) such as exemption from the
necessity of participating in the rituals growing up about the
person of the Emperor and freedom from military service. This
too, annoyed the Greeks.

The Greeks in Alexandria broke out in anti-Semitic riots and the Jews sent a deputation to appeal for justice to Caligula. The Greeks, uncertain as to what whim might inspire the mad Emperor, hastily sent a counter-deputation to argue that the Jews refused to participate in the Emperor-cult and were therefore traitors.

Caligula, who was desirous of having himself worshipped outright, had ordered his statue set up in the various temples of the Empire. In many places, the order was obeyed at once. What was another piece of stone in a temple, more or less? Now, however, Caligula specifically ordered that his statue be placed in the Temple at Jerusalem and this was refused. The notion that a human figure be adored in the House of the one, true God was completely unacceptable to the Jews and they were quite prepared to die rather than accede. The governor of Syria wrote to Caligula, telling him just that, and desperately delayed implementing the order. Caligula, in his wrath, might well have ordered the destruction of Judea. He was killed, however, just in time to prevent an insurrection and that destruction was delayed another generation in consequence.

Claudius, on becoming emperor, had placed Herod Agrippa, Caligula's old friend, on the throne of Judea, giving it a measure of self-government again. Herod Agrippa labored to win over the Jews, and actually grew to be quite popular despite the fact that he was an Idumaean. (The story is told that at one Passover he wept because he was not a Jew and that the spectators, weeping also, called out, "You *are* a Jew and our brother.")

Unfortunately, his reign was short and ended, after three years, in 44 with his death. His son, Herod Agrippa II, ruled for a time over parts of Judea but the main portion of the land was once again made a province and handed over to procurators.

These procurators were often rapacious and one in particular, who had been appointed by Nero, rifled the Temple treasury. The anti-Roman extremists among the Jews (called the

"Zealots"), whose influence had been growing, provoked riots. Herod Agrippa II, who happened to be in Jerusalem at the time, urged calmness and caution, but he wasn't listened to. By 66 (819 A.U.C.), Judea was in full furious revolt against Rome.

The intensity of the rebellion caught the Romans by surprise. The army on the spot could not handle it and Nero had to send three legions eastward under Vespasian (Titus Flavius Sabinus Vespasianus). Under Claudius he had served in Germany and had then participated in the conquest of southern Britain, leading the forces that conquered the Isle of Wight. He served as consul in 51 and then as governor of the province of Africa. The new task now set him he performed efficiently, if slowly, for the Jews were fighting to the death.

In 69, Vespasian left Judea to return to Rome but his son Titus (Titus Flavius Sabinus Vespasianus, like his father) continued the job. On September 7, 70 (823 A.U.C.) he took Jerusalem and the Temple was destroyed for the second time. (The first time it had been destroyed by the Babylonians five centuries before.) Titus celebrated a triumph in Rome the next year, and the Arch of Titus, which still stands in Rome, was erected in honor of the victory.

Those Jews who survived and remained in Judea found themselves living amid devastations, their Temple destroyed, their priesthood abolished, and the force of a Roman legion permanently established in Jerusalem in their midst.

PHILOSOPHY AND CULTS

And yet the battle between Roman tradition and Jewish religion was being carried on, in a way, beyond the borders of

Judea. The fight there was to be longer and the verdict different.

The Roman religion, largely borrowed from the Etruscans, was, to begin with, predominantly agricultural in nature. The numerous gods and spirits represented forces of nature and much of the ritual was designed to ensure fertile soil, adequate rain and, in general, good harvests. In a society in which the alternative to a good harvest was starvation, this is certainly understandable. There were also numerous gods and spirits who presided over different facets of the home and of individual life from birth to death. Religious rites were comparatively simple — the kind of thing busy farmers could spare the time for.

The chief refinement brought to the old religion by the Empire was the "Imperial Cult" in which a kind of routine lip service was paid to the reigning Emperor and Empress, and in which dead Emperors and Empresses were granted divine honors.

When upper-class Romans discovered Greek culture, the official Greek religion was, to a certain extent, fused with that of the Romans. The Roman Jupiter was identified with the Greek Zeus; the Roman Minerva with the Greek Athena, and so on.

However, the official religions of both Greece and Rome alike were virtually dead by the time of the Empire. The upper classes practiced the official Roman and Greek religious rites in a mechanical, absentminded fashion.

The primitive beliefs, after all, were no longer suitable for a society that was not made up of uncultured farmers only, but which included aristocratic, well-read, city-dwellers who had come to work out sophisticated views of the Universe. Their interests extended beyond the mere hope of a good harvest. There was the question of the good life, the fruitful spending of leisure time, the cultivation of intellectual interests, the desire to understand the workings of the universe. The Greeks developed elaborate philosophies to satisfy their gropings in this direction, and the Romans adopted some of these philosophies.

One popular variety of philosophy was founded by Epicurus, who had been born on the Greek island of Samos in 341 B.C. He had established a school in Athens in 306 B.C. and it remained extremely successful until his death in 270 B.C. Epicurus adopted the beliefs of certain earlier Greek philosophers and viewed the universe as made up of tiny particles called atoms. All change consisted of the random breakup and rearrangement of groups of these atoms and there was little room in the Epicurean thought for any purposeful direction of man and the universe by gods. The philosophy was essentially atheistic although the Epicureans were not fanatic about that; they would cheerfully go through rituals they considered meaningless in order to avoid giving unnecessary offense or create useless trouble for themselves.

In a universe consisting of atoms in random movement, man could be conscious of two things: pleasure and pain. It stood to reason that man should behave in such a way as to enjoy a maximum of pleasure and a minimum of pain. It remained only to decide what was actually a maximum of pleasure. To Epicurus, it seemed that if a little of something gave pleasure, a lot of it did not necessarily give more pleasure. Starvation through undereating was painful, but indigestion through overeating was also painful. The maximum of pleasure came from eating in moderation, and so with other joys of life. Then, too, one must not forget the pleasures of the mind; of learning, of improving discourse, of the emotions of friendship and affection; pleasures which, in the view of Epicurus, were more intensely pleasant and desirable than the ordinary pleasures of the body.

Not all the Epicureans of later centuries were as wise and moderate as Epicurus himself. It was easy to place the pleasures of the body first and it was hard to set any limit to them. After all, why not enjoy all the luxury you can get right now.

Tomorrow might be too late. So the word "epicurean" has entered our language and come to mean "given to luxury."

So popular did the Epicurean philosophy become that to the Jews in the centuries after Alexander, all Greeks seemed Epicureans. Any Jew who abandoned his religion for Greek ways became an "Epicurean" and to this very day, the Jewish term for a converted Jew is "Apikoros."

The Romans picked up Epicurean beliefs. Rome was far more wealthy and powerful than any Greek city had ever been and Roman luxury could reach higher levels than Greek luxury could. Consequently, Roman Epicureanism tended to become grosser than the Greek version. Under the Empire, Epicureanism often became an excuse for the worst kind of self-indulgence.

An example of a Roman Epicurean is Gaius Petronius. He was a man of ability who served as consul at one time, and at another as a governor of Bithynia in Asia Minor. He preferred, however, to pass his life in pleasure and luxury (rather like members of today's "jet set.") Perhaps he did not altogether admire this way of life, for he is best known today for a book called *Satyricon* which it is believed he wrote. In it he makes excruciating fun of the gross and tasteless luxury of people who have more wealth than cultivation and whose only use for money is to waste it.

Nevertheless, so famous did he grow for his judgment in matters of pleasure that he became a boon companion of Nero, who relied on him to dream up new kinds of fun and games to make the time pass pleasantly. He was the "arbiter elegantiarum" ("the judge of taste and style") and is, in consequence, often called "Petronius Arbiter." Like many of Nero's friends and associates, however, Petronius came to a bad end. Nero's suspicions, always easily aroused, were turned on Petronius, who chose to commit suicide in 66 rather than wait for death at the hands of others.

A second famous school of Greek philosophy was founded by

Zeno, a Greek (with possibly some Phoenician blood); who was born on the half-Greek, half-Phoenician island of Cyprus at about the time of Epicurus' birth.

Zeno, like Epicurus, founded a school in Athens and taught from a place in the marketplace where a porch or corridor was adorned with paintings of scenes from the Trojan war. It was called the "Stoa poikile" ("painted porch") and Zeno's teachings came therefore to be known as "Stoicism."

Stoicism recognized a supreme God and seemed to be on the road to a kind of monotheism. However, it was also felt that divine powers might descend upon all sorts of minor gods and even upon those human beings who were deified. In this way stoics could adjust themselves to prevailing religious practices.

Stoicism saw the necessity of avoiding pain but did not feel that choosing pleasure was the best way to avoid pain. One could not always choose pleasure correctly and even if one did, that merely opened the way for a new kind of pain — the pain that arose when a pleasure once enjoyed was lost. Wealth could disappear, health decay, loved ones die. The only safe way of living the good life, Stoics decided, was to put one's self beyond both pleasure and pain; to train one's self not to be the slave of either passion or fear, to treat both happiness and woe with indifference. If you desire nothing, you need fear the loss of nothing. All that counted lay within a person. If you are master of yourself, you can be the slave to no one. If you live a life that rigidly follows a stern moral code, you need not fear the agonized uncertainty of day-to-day decisions. To this day, the word "stoic" is used in English to mean "indifferent to pleasure and pain."

Naturally such a philosophy could not be as popular as the Epicurean, but to some Romans it seemed that the old Roman virtues of industry, fearlessness, and stern devotion to duty were just those that were valued by Stoicism. Some Romans, therefore, turned to this philosophy even in the most luxurious days of the early Empire.

The best known of the Roman Stoics of this period was Seneca (Lucius Annaeus Seneca), who was born about 4 B.C. in Corduba (the modern Cordova), Spain. His father had been a well-known lawyer and young Seneca was educated to the law himself. He studied at a Stoic school in Rome and became so famous as an orator as to attract the favorable attention of Caligula. After Caligula's death, Seneca displeased Messalina in some fashion, and she had her husband, the Emperor Claudius, banish him from Rome in 41. However, Messalina was executed and Claudius' next wife, Agrippina, recalled Seneca in 49 to serve as tutor to her young son, Nero. Seneca did his best to turn Nero into a Stoic, but, alas, the teaching didn't take.

Seneca wrote essays on Stoic philosophy and a number of tragedies based on Greek myths and imitating the Greek style of Euripides, but so full of emotional sound and fury (odd for a professed Stoic) rather than true feeling and deep thought, that they are not much admired today, even though they are the only Roman tragedies that have survived into modern times.

Still, he was popular enough in his own time to rouse Nero's envy. Nero, who was so proud of his own work, could not bear the thought that Roman society generally thought that it was really Seneca who wrote under Nero's name. Seneca was forced into private life and, in 65, on the grounds that he had taken part in a conspiracy against the Emperor, was made to commit suicide.

The poorer classes in Rome could not, however, be expected to attach themselves either to Epicureanism or Stoicism. They lacked the wealth and leisure to be proper Epicureans, however they might have liked to be, and it was cold comfort to be told to despise pleasures when one had none to despise.

Something warm and consoling was wanted, something a poor man could afford, something that might promise a better life after death in exchange for the miserable one on Earth.

There were, for instance, the Greek mystery religions, where the rites were not open to all, but only to those who were initiated into them. Those who participated were supposed to be close-mouthed ("mystes") about what they experienced and from this comes the phrase "mystery religion" and the present meaning, in English, of the word "mystery" as something secret, unexplained, and even unexplainable.

The mystery rites, whatever they were, were carried on with a solemnity that stirred the emotions; they united those participating in a bond of brotherhood; and they made it possible for the initiates, in their own belief, to enter a life after death. These rites gave life meaning, made people feel the warmth of union with others in a common purpose, and held out the promise that even death was not the end but rather the gateway to something greater than life.

The most revered of the Greek mystery religions were the Eleusinian Mysteries, the center of which was in Eleusis, a few miles northwest of the city of Athens. It centered about the Greek myth of Demeter and Persephone. Persephone had been abducted to the underground realm of Hades, but had been brought out again; and this signified the notion of the death of vegetation in the autumn, followed by its rebirth in the spring and, more specifically, the death of man followed by a glorious rebirth. Another variety of such a form of ritual were the "Orphic mysteries" based on the legend of Orpheus, who also descended into Hades and emerged again.

Even after the decline of Greek political power, the mystery religions retained their importance. So revered were the Eleusinian mysteries that Nero, on the occasion of a state visit to Greece in 66, asked to be accepted as an initiate. This was, however, refused because Nero had condemned his mother to death and this horrible crime disqualified him forever from communion with the other members of the rites.

It is a remarkable tribute to the value placed on the mysteries that those who led them would not bend its rules to admit

Nero, even though in all other ways the Greeks humored him in every possible respect. They held special competitions in which Nero could meet Greek professionals in poetry reading, singing, playing the lyre, chariot-racing and so on, and made sure that he received the prize on every occasion. It is even a more remarkable tribute to the mysteries that Nero, who rarely allowed himself to be thwarted, should not find it expedient to avenge the insult of being rejected by those who were in charge of the mysteries.

The Greek mysteries bore the mark of Greek reason and moderation. As Rome's influence penetrated farther eastward, however, she came into contact with the still more emotional and colorful Eastern religions, many of which also involved the death-and-rebirth motif inspired by the seasonal cycle of vegetation.

In Asia Minor there was an ancient cult of Cybele, the Great Mother of the Gods, who, in some ways, was similar to the Greek Demeter. Her rites spread into Greece at an early time and, in 204 B.C., when the Romans were near the end of their long battle against the Carthaginian general, Hannibal, they, too, made overtures to Cybele. A stone sacred to her which had fallen from the heavens (undoubtedly a meteorite) had been brought with great ceremony from Asia Minor to Rome. At first, the Romans were rather embarrassed at the ceremonies, and at the outlandish priests who had been imported with the stone, but by the time of the early Empire, the worship of Cybele had grown into one of the most important cults in Rome.

Egyptian deities also became popular. In Greek times, the most important Egyptian god and goddess were Osiris and Isis. Osiris had undergone a death and resurrection. He was supposed to exist in physical reincarnation in the shape of the sacred bull, Apis. To the Greeks, Osiris–Apis became "Serapis" and the worship of Serapis and Isis became popular in Greece about 200 B.C. A century later, these rites began to invade

Rome. Augustus, an old-fashioned Roman, disapproved of it, but Caligula gave it official sanction.

Goddesses like Demeter, Cybele, and Isis were particularly attractive to women and to all, indeed, who valued sympathy and love. Male gods were too often gods of wrath and war — and yet soldiers, too, could use the consolations of religion.

From the lands east of the Roman Empire, from Parthia or Persia, came Mithras, a divine figure representing the Sun. He was always pictured as a young man stabbing a bull, and the initiation rites involved the sacrificial killing of a bull. Women were excluded from these rites so that Mithraism was primarily a masculine, and especially a soldier's, religion. It began to make its first inroads into Rome in the time of Tiberius.

CHRISTIANITY

There remain to be mentioned the religions that rose in Judea. The first of these was Judaism itself and this spread outward from Judea along with the Jews who settled in the various cities of the Empire — particularly in the East, although there was also a sizable colony in Rome itself.

In time, indeed, the Jews outside Judea outnumbered those who remained in the traditional homeland. And although they might learn to speak Greek and to forget Hebrew, they did not forget their religion. Their holy book, the Bible, was translated into Greek for the benefit of those Jews who were no longer proficient in the Hebrew original as early as 270 B.C.

There were even Jews who obtained a Greek education and could argue Judaistic beliefs in terms that were comprehensible to the Greeks and Romans of the time. Outstanding among

these was Philo Judaeus ("Philo the Jew") who was born in
Alexandria about 20 B.C. and who, in his old age, headed the
delegation to Rome that was to have pleaded the cause of the
Jews with Caligula.

In the last days of the Republic and the early days of the
Empire, Judaism made converts among the Romans, even including some who were in high places.

It might have spread more widely, too, if it had been willing
to compromise. Other religions had their special rites but did
not try to prevent their members from taking part in the Imperial cult. Judaism did insist that its proselytes abandon even
the most harmless forms of their old worship. This meant that
Romans who wished to become Jewish had to abandon the
state religion, be cut off from society and, possibly, risk the serious accusation of treason.

Furthermore, the Jewish ritual was complicated indeed and
difficult for anyone to undertake if he were not born and educated into it. Parts of it seemed irrational and embarrassing to
those trained in Greek philosophy. Then, too, anyone who
wanted to become a Jew had to submit to the painful opera-
tion of circumcision. Finally, Judaism in its strict sense was
centered in Judea and the Temple at Jerusalem was the one
place where God could really be approached.

The ultimate blow that ended all chance of successful
proselytization for the Jews was the bloody revolt in Judea.
The Jews then became outright dangerous enemies of Rome
and grew more unpopular than ever throughout the Empire.

However, Judaism was not a single religion; there were sects
within it and some of these sects were more congenial to the
various non-Jews ("Gentiles") of the Empire than others.

One sect was established by the disciples of Jesus (see page
33). After the crucifixion of Jesus, it might have seemed that
his following must break up, since his death seemed to make a
mockery of his Messianic pretensions. However, the story
spread that three days after the crucifixion, He was seen again;

that He had returned from death. He was not merely a human Messiah, a king to restore the Jewish monarchy; He was a divine Messiah, the Son of God, Whose Kingdom was in Heaven, and who would return soon (though none knew exactly when) to judge all men and to establish the city of God.

The Christians (as the disciples of Jesus and their followers were eventually called) remained Jewish in their beliefs and rituals at first, and they drew their converts chiefly from among the Jews.

Many Jews, however, remained strongly nationally-minded. They did not want a Messiah who suffered death and left the nation enslaved; they wanted one who would manifest himself gloriously by throwing off the shackles of Rome. This was one of the factors that led to the disastrous rebellion against Rome.

In this rebellion, the Christians took no part. They had their Messiah already; Rome was not going to last long anyway; and to try to anticipate God's plans for the completion of secular history was wrong. The nonviolence preached by the Christians, the duty of turning the other cheek, of loving one's enemies, of rendering unto Caesar the things that were Caesar's, inhibited them from taking part in the rebellion, too.

This failure on the part of the Jewish Christians to join their fellow Jews in the war against Rome made Christianity unpopular with the Jews who survived, and Christianity made no further progress among them. Nor have Jews, in general, accepted Jesus as the Messiah down to the present day, despite the strongest possible pressures.

But if Christianity failed among the Jews, it did not fail elsewhere. That this was so was largely owing to the activities of a Jew named Saul who, in his dealings with the Gentile world, was known by the similar, but more Roman-sounding, name of Paul.

Paul was born in the city of Tarsus on the southern coast of Asia Minor of, apparently, a well-to-do family, for his father (and therefore he himself) was a Roman citizen. He received a strict Jewish education in Jerusalem and was orthodox in his beliefs — so orthodox that on first encountering the teachings of the Christians he was appalled at their blasphemy and was a leader in the persecuting movements against them. He volunteered to travel to Damascus to lead the anti-Christian movement there, but, according to the story in the Bible, a vision of Jesus came to him on the way, and from that moment he was himself an ardent Christian.

Paul undertook to preach Christianity to the Gentiles and, in doing so, he came to the belief that the intricate ritual of Judaism was not essential to true religion and that it might even detract from it by concentrating attention on meaningless details and obscuring the inner essence ("for the letter killeth but the spirit giveth life.")

To become a Christian, then, a Gentile did not need to be circumcized; nor did he have to undertake the full rigor of the Judaic ritual; nor did he have to orient himself about Jewish nationalism and the Temple at Jerusalem.

Almost at once Christianity began to spread in the cities of Asia Minor and Greece, and eventually, in Italy itself. The crucifixion and resurrection of Jesus, and the rites surrounding the commemoration of that event, were reminiscent of the mystery religions. The figure of Mary, the mother of Jesus, lent a softening feminine touch. The strict morals were like those of the Stoics. It seemed to have something to please everyone.

Indeed, Christianity had a flexibility that Judaism never had. As Christianity spread among people who knew virtually nothing of Judaism but a great deal about their own pagan customs, the new creed adapted to its own purposes both Greek philosophy and pagan customs.

Mithraism, for instance — which was Christianity's strongest competitor for a couple of centuries — celebrated December 25 as their prime festival. Mithraism was a form of sun-worship and December 25 was near the time of the winter solstice, when the noonday Sun has declined as far to the south as it ever will and begins its slow return northward. This is, in a sense, the birth of the Sun, the guarantee that winter will some day end and that spring will come and with it new life. This time of the year was celebrated by other religions, too. The ancient Romans held the period sacred to their god of agriculture, Saturn, and the celebration was called the Saturnalia. The Saturnalia was a time of good-will among men (even slaves were allowed to join in the festivities on a temporary status of equality), of feasting and of present-giving.

The Christians, finding the emotions of the season of the Sun's rebirth irresistible, adapted it rather than fought it. They bent the emotions to a new use. Since the Bible does not state exactly when the birth of Jesus took place, it might take place on December 25 as well as at any other time, and that date became Christmas and remains so to this day. And the Christmas celebration even today has a touch of the old saturnalian characteristics.

To the Romans generally, at least in the first half-century after the death of Jesus, the Christians were looked upon as merely another Jewish sect. In fact, they seemed more annoying than other Jewish sects since they worked harder to get converts.

Since Christians would not worship the official Roman gods, they were considered atheists. Since they would not participate in the Imperial cult, they were considered dangerous and possibly treasonable radicals. In fact, the Romans looked upon the early Christians very much as most Americans of today look upon Communists.

This feeling came to a head in 64 (817 A.U.C.) when a great fire broke out in Rome that lasted six days and nearly destroyed the city. It is not hard to imagine how a fire of this sort might have started. The poorer sections of Rome consisted of rickety, congested wooden structures. Modern fire-prevention methods were unknown and modern fire-fighting equipment did not exist. Any fire that might break out could easily go out of control and destroy the city. Large fires had taken place in Rome before Nero and were to take place after him, but this one in 64 was, apparently, the worst on record.

Nero was at Antium (the modern Anzio) on the seacoast about thirty miles south of Rome, when the fire started. When the news of the fire reached Nero, he rushed back and did what he could to organize rescue operations, set up temporary shelters for the homeless and so on.

Apparently, his mania for show business overcame him at one point. Viewing the awful spectacle of the huge city in flames lighting up the horizon all around, he was reminded of the burning city of Troy, and, snatching up his lyre, couldn't resist singing some famous song about that scene. This has been remembered ever since as Nero having "fiddled" (the violin was not invented until many centuries afterward) while Rome burned.

Some attempt was made to correct the conditions that led to the fire. The worst of the slums were utterly gone and attempts were made to regulate the rebuilding, to limit the heights of the buildings, to increase the fireproof nature of at least the lower stories. It might have been a good opportunity to rebuild Rome entirely on a rational plan, but the old owners tended to rebuild where they had been before and Rome was as tangled and planless a city after the fire as before.

Nero seized the opportunity to build himself a new and gorgeous palace out of concrete, faced with bricks; a strong, fireproof construction that came into style thereafter for those who could afford it.

The Roman people suspected arson, of course, and Nero might well have felt that his enemies would spread the story that the Emperor himself had started the fire. Nero beat them to the punch by placing the blame on the Christians. They were a natural scapegoat and, as a result, the first organized persecution of the Christians were initiated.

Many were put to death by being forced to face lions unarmed in the arena, or in other horrible ways. According to tradition, Paul was in Rome at the time, and so was Peter, the chief of the disciples of Jesus and the leader of the Christian fellowship in that city. (Peter is considered the first bishop of Rome and therefore the first Pope, according to Roman Catholic doctrine.) Both Paul and Peter are supposed to have suffered martyrdom in the course of this persecution.

The persecutions were carried to such an extreme, however, even according to the non-Christian historians, that pity was aroused among the Roman populace. Such persecutions did more, in the end, to encourage the growth of Christianity than the reverse.

THE END OF NERO

Nero, like all the early Emperors, was suspicious and even fearful of the Roman aristocracy. He was always afraid that the Senators were dreaming of past power and glory and therefore kept a sharp eye and heavy hand upon them. Nero's cruelty merely served to encourage the Senate to compare present misery with historic glory and to conspire against the Emperor.

In 65, there was a secret movement to remove Nero and replace him with a Senator named Gaius Calpurnius Piso. Unfortunately, the conspirators did not move quickly but managed to dither about long enough for someone to leak the news to Nero. The Emperor reacted fiercely, executing all who were connected (or suspected of being connected) with the conspiracy. Seneca and Petronius were forced to kill themselves at this time and, somewhat later, Corbulo, the successful general against the Parthians, was also forced to commit suicide.

The slaying of Corbulo could not have been popular with the army, or with the other legionary commanders in particular. The execution of a few Senators or aristocrats would not bother a general, but he was bound to be upset when other generals began to be killed.

Then, too, the revolt in Judea was embarrassing to Roman pride, as a few miserable Jewish peasants managed to hold off the flower of the Roman army. It seemed easiest to blame the matter on government mismanagement. It was all the easier to do this since Nero's tour in Greece was a blatant sign of Imperial folly while soldiers were dying. (This was the real "fiddling while Rome burned.") Nero's display in Greece, as he performed at various games, was embarrassing, too, to all those Romans who still believed that the head of the Roman government should be a warrior and statesman, and not a strolling actor.

Legions here and there in the provinces revolted and tried to proclaim their particular commanders Emperor. Nero hastened back to Italy in 68 (821 A.U.C.), but the situation only got worse. The legions in Spain acclaimed their commander Servius Sulpicius Galba as Emperor. The praetorian guard accepted him and declared Nero a public enemy.

There was nothing left for Nero to do but to beat execution by killing himself. After considerable hesitation, he pierced himself with a sword, crying out as he did so (according to the story), "What an artist perishes in me!" He was only thirty-one at the time of his death.

Nero was the last of the descendants of Augustus to serve as Emperor. If we count from 48 B.C., when Julius Caesar had beaten Pompey, the Julio-Claudian house had dominated Rome for over a century and had given it one dictator and five Emperors.

Yet Nero's death did not destroy the tradition of the Julio-

Claudians. There were dozens of Emperors after Nero and though none had a drop of the blood of Caesar and Augustus in their veins, every one of them took Caesar and Augustus as Imperial titles.

The word "Caesar" came, in fact, to be synonymous with "Emperor" so that in modern times the emperors of Germany and Austria-Hungary were called "Kaiser" the German spelling (and the correct pronunciation) of the Latin Caesar. The Russian word "Tsar" or "Czar" is also a form of "Caesar." As late as 1946, Bulgaria was ruled by Tsar Semeon II and until 1947 there was a British Emperor of India whose title was "Kaiser-i-Hind." So for two thousand years after the assassination of Julius Caesar, his name lived on among the rulers of the world.

3

THE LINE OF VESPASIAN

VESPASIAN

The end of Nero was, in a way, a terrible disaster for Rome. It proved to Romans everywhere that the office of Emperor did not belong to a "royal family" like the line of Augustus, but could be bestowed anywhere — on generals, for instance. The lesson was not lost on the army.

Moreover, Galba was particularly poor as the first choice of a general-Emperor. He was an old man of over seventy, so bent with age that he could not walk, but had to be carried in a litter. Then, to top it off, he decided to economize. This is a course of action which may be good in itself, but when he economized at the expense of the soldiers who expected bonuses from each new Emperor and whose support was essential to Galba in particular, he proved suicidally foolish.

Other armies were putting other generals into the fight for

the throne. Marcus Salvius Otho, one of the officers who had served under Galba, raised a rebellion because Galba had indicated someone else to be his successor. Otho won the favor of the praetorian guard, who were angered at not receiving the bonus they had expected, and Galba was killed after he had reigned seven months.

Otho was accepted by the Senate (which could do nothing else) but he reigned only three months, for though the Senate said yes, there were sections of the army which said no.

At the head of the legions in Germany was Aulus Vitellius, who had been appointed to the post by Galba. When news of Galba's death arrived, the legion refused to accept Otho and proclaimed Vitellius Emperor. They marched toward Italy, defeated Otho's troops and when Otho killed himself, the way was open for Vitellius to declare himself Emperor, and receive the Senatorial sanction.

Meanwhile, though, Vespasian, the general who was slowly subduing the rebellious Jews, was also proclaimed Emperor. He occupied Egypt (which gave him control over Rome's grain supply) then returned to Italy and defeated Vitellius' troops. Vitellius was slain after a half-year's reign and in 69 (822 A.U.C.) Vespasian was Emperor.

With Vespasian the fourth Emperor in a little over a year (68-69 is sometimes called the "year of the four Emperors") things settled down. Vespasian's tribal name was Flavius and he was the founder of the "Flavian Line" of Roman Emperors.

Vespasian, like Galba, was advanced in age for he was 61 when he became Emperor. Unlike Galba, he was vigorous of mind and body. He might have established a military despotism for he had the necessary army support for it. However, he viewed himself as the successor of Augustus, and deliberately set about preserving the Principate and its system of government.

His first task was reform. The finances of the Empire were in a state of disrepair as a result of the wasteful extravagance of men such as Caligula and Nero. Vespasian therefore reorganized the tax system once more and set about enforcing rigid economy. He was himself an austere man who believed in the simple life. He would have no pretentions and was not the least ashamed of the fact that he came of a middle-class family of little distinction. (He was the first Emperor who was not of aristocratic lineage.) He was accused of stinginess and avarice by the same Senatorial historians who accused Nero of extravagance, but this can be taken with a grain of salt. There is every reason to believe that Vespasian's economies were necessary and beneficial.

Vespasian also set about reorganizing the army, disbanding some of the legions that had been most disorderly in the civil war that preceded his establishment on the throne.

Army reform was particularly necessary, too, for since the time of Augustus, the armies of the Empire had gradually grown less and less Italian. This was understandable. It was the task of the legions now to remain permanently on guard on frontiers far distant from Rome. It was easy and natural to recruit them from the population of the provinces that were being guarded. Gauls, Pannonians, Thracians filled the rosters and made good soldiers; and they were rewarded with citizenship very often.

This had its good points. It hastened the identification of the outer provinces with the Empire. It made Romanization easier; it spread the Latin language and Graeco-Roman culture through the far reaches of Europe.

And yet the provincialization of the army had its dangers, too. A Gaul might speak Latin and wear a toga and be learned in Greek and Latin literature, but he wouldn't have quite the same feeling for the abstraction of Roman history and tradition. He could not feel the same continuity with the Romans of early times who, after all, were no ancestors of his but who, in fact, had slaughtered and conquered his own ancestors. If he were a soldier, he was much more apt to be faithful to a commander who was capable in war and skilled in handling men than to a distant city and Senate he did not know. If his commander chose to march against that city, he would follow.

That had been proved once and for all in 69 when armies from Spain, Gaul, and Syria had converged on Rome, each fighting for its own commander.

Vespasian couldn't change that; he couldn't fill the legions with Italians for there weren't enough Italians willing to fight, and the provincials were far too good as soldiers to be done without. The praetorian guard, however, which was stationed in Italy and which, as they were on the spot, were the most dangerous, could be taken care of. They, at least, ought to be Italian, and Vespasian saw to it that they were. What's more, he made his son, Titus, its commander as a further method of taming them.

Vespasian also reorganized the Senate, evicting unworthy members, adding good ones, and carefully allowing them no real part in the government. Despite his penchant for economy, he undertook public works for the beautification of the city, knowing that this supplied employment for some Romans and raised the morale of all.

By his firm leadership, he also restored respect for Roman arms, which had rather fallen off under the lackadaisical and self-indulgent Nero. A dangerous revolt of some army corps in Gaul was crushed and Titus completed the mopping up of Judea by taking Jerusalem. Vespasian annexed the last small scraps of self-governing districts in the East and reorganized the provinces of Asia Minor. The Syrian province was extended eastward to include the important trading town of Palmyra. The deck was cleared in this way for any trouble with the Parthians just in case Parthia felt the rebellion in Judea and the anarchy of 68 would make it a good time to start a war. Parthia got the hint and remained quiet.

Titus returned to Rome in 71 with the spoils of the Judean war and a magnificient triumph was held for the father and son. The popularity of the new line seemed assured.

In Britain, the Roman conquest, which had been hanging fire under Nero was renewed in 77. Under a dynamic general, Gnaeus Julius Agricola, Wales was conquered and Roman arms drove northward nearly to the site of modern Aberdeen in 83. A Roman fleet even sailed round the north of Scotland and the invasion of Ireland was projected. After Agricola's campaign, the conquered sections of Britain were quickly Romanized.

But soon after the beginning of the British campaign, Vespasian's allotted time ran out. He knew he was dying and, alluding to the already established Roman custom of voting dead Emperors divine honors, he said wryly, "I feel myself becoming a god." At the last moment, he asked those around him to help him to his feet. "An Emperor," he said, "should die standing."

When he died in 79 (832 A.U.C.) he left the Principate and the Empire standing, too. Ten years of Vespasian had healed the results of Nero's follies.

TITUS

Titus succeeded his father without trouble. Vespasian had planned the succession and had associated his son with himself in the government. For the first time an Emperor was succeeded by his natural son.

Titus had led a gay life but was most popular for his generosity and leniency and settled down, on gaining the Imperial throne, to work hard at it and do a good job. About the only fault the Roman populace could find in him was that he had taken a Jewish sweetheart. While fighting in Judea, Titus had met Berenice, sister of Herod Agrippa II, and the two had fallen in love. When Titus returned to Rome he took Berenice with him and planned to marry her. This the anti-Semitic prejudices of the populace would not allow and Titus was at last compelled, very much against his will, to send her away.

Titus' reign was marked by general peace (except for the campaign in Britain) and prosperity. He refrained from arbitrary acts and was a model ruler. Unfortunately, he lived only two years after becoming Emperor, dying in 81 at the age of about forty.

His short reign was marked by a notable catastrophe. A mountain near Naples, named Vesuvius, was known by scholars to have once been a volcano, but it had never erupted in the memory of man. The towns of Pompeii and Herculaneum were located in its vicinity and farms dotted its slopes. Pompeii particularly was a resort town for wealthy Romans. The Roman orator, Cicero, was one of those who, a century and a quarter earlier, had boasted a Pompeian villa.

In 63, in the time of Nero, there was an earthquake in the area that damaged Pompeii, and Neapolis (Naples), too. It passed and the damage was repaired. In November 79, however, Mount Vesuvius erupted violently and, in a few hours, Pompeii and Herculaneum were overwhelmed and buried under ash and lava.

The tragic catastrophe had its value to modern historians. Beginning in the eighteenth century, Pompeii has slowly been dug out and it is as though a fossilized city had been uncovered; a setting lifted bodily from Roman times and placed in ours. Temples, theaters, gymnasia, homes, shops were uncovered. Artwork, inscriptions, even scrawls scratched by idlers have been discovered. Historians might well want such accidents to take place oftener if it could be arranged without loss of life.

Titus hurried to the scene of the eruption to supervise rescue work and to help the survivors. While he was gone, a three-day fire broke out in Rome and he had to return to attend to matters there, too.

On a happier note, he was able to open new baths (the "baths of Titus") and complete a project his father had started, the first of the large amphitheaters to be built in Rome. Vespasian had started it on the site of Nero's palace, which Vespasian had torn down so that he might turn the site to public use. The amphitheater was stone built and had a seating capacity of fifty thousand which makes it of respectable size even by modern standards. It was the site of the sort of spectacles the Roman populace enjoyed: chariot races, gladiatorial contests, animal fights, and so on.

It might best be called the Flavian amphitheater but standing nearby was a large statue of Nero. These larger-than-life statues were called "colossae" by the Romans (from which our adjective "colossal") and so the amphitheater came to be known as the "Colosseum." It is still known by that name now when, even in a condition of ruins, it is magnificent and tends to dominate the city of Rome.

DOMITIAN

Upon Titus' death, his younger brother, Domitian (Titus Flavius Domitianus) succeeded to the throne. It was as though history were repeating itself. Under Vespasian and Titus, it seemed that the days of Augustus had returned, with good-natured rulers who were thoroughly respectful of the Senators and who therefore got a "good press" from the Senate-favoring historians. With the accession of Domitian, however, it was as though Augustus had been succeeded by Tiberius all over again.

Like Tiberius, Domitian was cold, introverted, and with no knack for popularity. He made no effort to pretend respect for the Senate or to allow them the honors required to save their face. This meant that the historians later described him as cruel and tyrannical. So he may have been to the Senators, but his rule was just and firm otherwise. He tried to encourage family life and traditional religion, forbade the making of eunuchs, rebuilt the temples destroyed in the fire of 80, constructed the Arch of Titus in honor of his older brother, built public libraries and put on lavish shows for the populace. He enforced efficient rule in the provinces and labored to secure the Imperial frontiers.

The Rhine-Danube line that marked the northern boundary of the Empire had as its weakest point the area near the source of the two rivers. There, in what is now Baden and Wurttemburg in southwestern Germany, the line of the rivers formed a bulge thrusting deeply southwestward. German tribes, pushing into that salient, might easily cut between Italy and Gaul and cause enormous trouble.

In Domitian's time, this possibility had to be taken seriously. The German tribes of the area, the Chatti, had been fighting the Romans on and off since the time of Augustus, and Domitian decided to end the danger. At the head of his troops he crossed the Rhine in 83, defeated the Chatti, and prepared for the permanent occupation of the area by Rome.

Like Tiberius, though, he was not interested in an unreasonable (and expensive) extension of foreign conquest. Having removed the menace of the Chatti, he fell back onto a firm defensive. He built a line of forts across the dangerous angle in southwestern Germany, removing the bulge and making the weak point secure. After that, he was content to stand pat in that area.

Furthermore, he called Agricola back from Britain. The

Senatorial enemies of Domitian were quick to maintain that this was done out of jealousy, but it might just as easily be argued that Agricola's long-drawn-out campaign was reaching the point of diminishing returns. The bleak, northern highlands of Scotland, and the wild, barbarous Irish moors were scarcely worth the pains, blood and gold it would take to conquer them. Domitian did not care to bother, particularly when provinces closer to home required military action.

Domitian's introverted nature drove him into solitude, as had been the case with Tiberius half a century before. Since he trusted no one, he was not at ease with anyone. And, naturally, the more he kept to himself, the more suspicious of him the members of the court and the leaders of the army became, for they naturally wondered what he might be up to and it was easy to believe rumors that he was planning wide executions.

Domitian's lack of popularity made it tempting for generals to plan to revolt against him. A general on the German frontier, Antonius Saturninus, had his troops declare him Emperor and rose in revolt in 88. Saturninus counted on help from the German barbarians — a frightful portent of the future and the coming of the day when competing bands of barbarians would be led by opposing Roman factions across the dying body of the Empire.

In this first attempt, the barbarians didn't come through and Domitian crushed the revolt. Domitian's suspicious nature was naturally reinforced by this event and he moved harshly against all whom he felt might have taken part in the revolt or sympathized with it, and his character seems now to have taken a turn for the worse.

He exiled the philosophers from Rome, for he felt they tended to adhere to an idealized republicanism and were therefore automatically against any strong Emperor. He also took action against the Jews scattered through the Empire for he knew they could not be expected to favor any Flavian. Persecution of the Christians is also recorded of his reign, although that may only have been because the Romans were still considering them merely a variety of Jew.

In order to discourage any further military revolts, Domitian instituted the practice of quartering all legions in separate camps at the frontier so that no two legions could combine against the Emperor. This tended to make the legions immobile, however, since any attempt to combine against a threatened attack from without could easily be construed as an attempt to combine with some treasonable activity in mind. Rome's defenses thus underwent a certain hardening and stiffening, a loss of flexibility that made it more and more difficult to ward off the barbarians to the north except under particularly strong Emperors.

Under Domitian, for instance, there was bloody trouble with the Dacians, tribes who lived north of the lower Danube in the region that now makes up the nation of Rumania. In the 80's, the Dacians came under the warlike rule of a chief named Decebalus and they repeatedly crossed the frozen Danube in winter to raid Moesia, the Roman province just to the south.

Domitian was forced to take arms against them. He drove them out of Moesia and then invaded Dacia. For several years, the Romans managed to keep the upper hand. However, the revolt of Saturninus distracted Domitian, a Roman force met disaster in Dacia, and unsuccessful attempts against the German tribes west of Dacia convinced him that further efforts in that direction would not pay.

It was less troublesome, Domitian decided, to accept a nominal submission by Decebalus, who went through the motion of receiving his crown from Domitian, but who remained actually independent. In fact, Domitian agreed in 90 to pay Decebalus an annual subsidy in return for continued peace and freedom from raids. This was cheaper than the continuation of war, but the Senatorial opposition considered it a disgraceful tribute — the first in Roman history.

Finally in 96 (849 A.U.C.), Domitian, whose last years are

described as virtually a reign of terror, came to his end. A palace conspiracy, made up of courtiers and the Empress herself, was organized and Domitian was assassinated.

Thus ended the line of Vespasian. It had ruled Rome for twenty-seven years and had given Rome three Emperors.

4

THE LINE OF NERVA

NERVA

The conspirators who killed Domitian had learned the lesson
taught them by those who had killed Nero a generation before.
They did not leave a vacuum to be filled with quarreling generals; instead they were ready with a candidate. Since they
were not army men (although they had been careful to gain
the support of the leader of the praetorian guard) it was not a
general they chose, but a Senator.

Their choice was an extremely respected Senator named
Nerva (Marcus Cocceius Nerva) whose father had been a well-
known lawyer and a friend of the Emperor Tiberius. Nerva
himself had held positions of trust under Vespasian and Titus
and, in 90, had shared the consulship with Domitian himself.
Later he had fallen out with Domitian and been exiled to southern Italy.

He was in his sixties at the time of Domitan's death and he

was not, in the course of nature, expected to live long. No doubt
those who supported Nerva counted on that and considered
his reign would be a short waiting period in which something
better might be prepared.

Nerva attempted to end the periodic hostility between Emperor and Senate and to put into practice the theory that the
Roman Empire was really ruled by the Senate and that the
Emperor was but the Senate's servant. He promised never to
execute a Senator and he never did. When a conspiracy was
detected against him, he was content to banish the leading
conspirator and to execute no one. He practiced strict economy, recalled political exiles, organized a state-controlled
postal service, set up charitable institutions for the care of
needy children, and in every possible way showed himself to
be a humane and kindly person.

While Nerva's attempt to make his government responsible
for the comfort and welfare of the citizens seems highly praise-
worthy, it nevertheless marks an ominous turning point in ancient society. More and more, local governments were prov-
ing inadequate for their tasks. More and more they turned to
the Emperor. The great ruler in Rome was expected to care
for all. If he did so, that was fine, but if the time came when the
central government was corrupt or incapable, what then would
become of local governments that were no longer able to care
for themselves?

But for now, only the praetorian guard was dissatisfied.
Domitian had been popular among them for he favored them,
knowing well that he depended upon their support to remain
in power. Consequently, he had paid them well and allowed
them many liberties. Nerva's economies and his dependence
on the Senate made things harder for the soldiers of the guard
and, in bitter disappointment, they demanded the death of the
chief conspirator against Domitian and of their own leader,
who had agreed to support the conspiracy. Nerva found himself facing the fate of Galba (see page 75) but bravely

he tried to face down the soldiers of the guard. Nerva did not lose his life as a result but he was badly humiliated when the guard killed those they were after, then forced Nerva to arrange to have the Senate vote them a motion of thanks for the deed.

Nerva realized that he could not control the army himself and that his death might be a signal for serious disorders. He had no children upon whom he might lean as Vespasian had leaned on Titus. He therefore cast about him for some good general whom he could trust to rule well in order that he might adopt him as his son and settle the succession upon him. If he could not have a Titus he might at least have a Tiberius.

His choice fell, most wisely, upon Trajan (Marcus Ulpius Trajanus). Trajan had been born in Spain in 53, near the modern city of Seville and was to be the first Emperor to have been born outside Italy (although he was of Italian descent). He was a soldier all his life and the son of a soldier, serving always with efficiency and ability.

Three months after the adoption had been put through, Nerva died, having reigned nearly a year-and-a-half, and Trajan succeeded peacefully to the throne.

Trajan was to follow Nerva's good example, keeping a promise never to execute a Senator and adopting a capable younger man and making him a successor. Indeed, there were a series of emperors beginning with Nerva, who succeeded one another by adoption. Sometimes they are referred to as the "Antonines" after the family name of the last few.

THE SILVER AGE

Under the new period of peace, security, and prosperity that opened with Nerva, the Roman aristocracy seemed to draw a huge sigh of relief and Roman historians wrote books that described most of the earlier Emperors in the darkest of colors, so as to contrast them all the more with the kindly Senate-favoring Emperors who were now succeeding to the throne and also to exact a kind of posthumous revenge on the previous rulers.

The revenge was more effective than the historians might have imagined, for some of their books survived and have blackened the names of the early Emperors forever. However bad some of those Emperors might have been, there isn't one who doesn't show up far worse in the Senatorial histories (and therefore in men's minds today) than he probably was in real life.

The most important of these historians was Cornelius Tacitus. He prospered under the Flavians but lived through the final years of Domitian's reign with considerable insecurity. He was a son-in-law of Agricola, the general who had extended Roman rule in Britain and had been recalled by Domitian. That, too, increased Tacitus's resentment against that Emperor. He wrote his history of Rome from the death of Augustus to the death of Domitian from the standpoint of Senatorial Republicanism and saw nothing good in most of the Emperors of that period. Tiberius, particularly, met with his displeasure, probably because his character was so like that of Domitian.

Tacitus also wrote a biography of Agricola, a book that is valuable for the light it casts on the Britons of the period. Tacitus was absent from Rome between 89 and 93 and he may have spent part of that time in Germany, for he wrote a book on that country, too, one which is now virtually our only source of knowledge of that region in the time of the early Empire. One can't help but wonder how accurate the book is, though, for Tacitus was clearly trying to draw a moral judgment, comparing the virtuous simple life of the Germans with the decadent luxury of the Romans. To make his point he probably drew the picture a little too brightly in one respect and too darkly in the other.

A younger historian was Gaius Suetonius Tranquillus, born

about 70 on the African coast. He is famous for a book entitled "The Lives of the Twelve Caesars." These were a set of gossipy biographies of Julius Caesar and the first eleven Emperors of Rome down to and including Domitian. Suetonius loved to repeat scandalous stories and included much that would have been dismissed by modern historians as simple gossip-mongering. Nevertheless, he wrote simply and the scandals he retailed made the books popular reading, even to this very day.

The most important non-Roman historian of the period was a Jew named Joseph, who Romanized his name to Flavius Josephus. He was born in 37 and was not only learned in Jewish lore but was worldly-wise enough to pick up a Roman education as well. He had a foot in both camps, visiting Rome in 64 to urge better and more lenient treatment for the Jews while, in Judea, he urged moderation and restraint on the more nationalistic elements.

He failed, and when the Jewish War broke out, he was forced to lead a contingent against the Romans. He fought well, holding out a long time against superior forces. When finally forced to surrender, he did not commit suicide as the other last-ditch holdouts did. Instead, he bowed to the inevitable, made friends with Vespasian and Titus and spent the last quarter-century of his life in Rome as a Roman citizen, dying about 95.

He was not altogether unmindful of his unfortunate compatriots, however. He wrote a history of the rebellion, entitled *The Jewish War,* which was published toward the end of Vespasian's reign. He wrote an autobiography to defend himself against the charge that he had brought about the rebellion, and another book in defense of Judaism against the charges brought by the anti-Semites who, in the wake of the War, had become influential. His masterpiece was *The Jewish Antiquities,* a history of the Jews (including a retelling of the historical books of the Bible) that was carried down to the outbreak of the rebellion.

In this book, a paragraph mentions Jesus of Nazareth — the only contemporary reference to Jesus outside the New Testament. Most scholars, however, consider the paragraph apocryphal, and to have been inserted afterward by some earnest Christian who was made uneasy by Josephus' lack of reference to Jesus in his discussion of Judea in the time of Tiberius.

The period of the Flavians was marked by the production of important literature. Critics do not put it in quite the class of the great products of the Augustan age and are content to refer to the Flavian writings as "The Silver Age."

Three outstanding satirists are included in this silver age; writers, that is, who poked fun at the vices of the day and in this way did their bit to improve public morals. These satirists are Persius (Aulus Persius Flaccus), Martial (Marcus Valerius Martialis), and Juvenal (Decimus Junius Juvenalis.)

Persius was the first and actually preceded the Flavian period, for he wrote in the reigns of Claudius and Nero. He specialized in making fun of the literary tastes of the day which he thought reflected the general decline of morals. He died before he was thirty and would probably have achieved greater fame if he had lived longer.

Martial was born in Spain in 43, came to Rome in Nero's time and remained there for the rest of his life, dying in 104. He is best known for his satiric epigrams, short verses of two to four lines that could be extremely cutting. He wrote about 1500 of them, divided into fourteen books. He made fun of all that was dissolute and wrong in his eyes and it is very likely that his epigrams were on the lips of everyone who counted in Rome just as soon as they were published. Probably anyone made the subject of his biting wit felt the sting for years.

Martial was very popular in his own time and was patronized by Titus and Domitian. This was partly because his wit was genuinely hilarious and partly because he often allowed him-

self to write indecently so that some of his epigrams are almost like "dirty jokes."

A clean epigram which may be used as an example is:

> Non amo te, Sabidi, nec possum dicere quare;
> Hoc tantum possum dicere, non amo te.

This means "I do not love thee, Sabidius, nor can I say why;
but this much I can say, I do not love thee."

The epigram is best known today in the form of a free translation made by Thomas Brown, while a student at Oxford about
1780, concerning his dean, John Fell:

> I do not love thee, Doctor Fell.
> The reason why I cannot tell;
> But this alone I know full well,
> I do not love thee, Doctor Fell.

Juvenal was perhaps the greatest and most bitter of the satirists. He lacked humor and lightness because the faults of
society that he saw all about were so hateful to him that he
could not treat them with anything short of burning indignation. He despised luxury and ostentation, denouncing the
rule of one man or the rule of the mob with equal vehemence.
He found almost every aspect of daily life in Rome hateful and
it was he who said that all Romans cared for was "panem et
circenses" ("food and games"). Still, that doesn't mean that
Rome under the emperors was a worse city than any other in
the world's history. No doubt if Juvenal were alive today, he
could write similar satires, just as bitter and just as true, about
New York, or Paris, or London, or Moscow. It is important to
remember that the viciousness and wrongs of life stick out very
plainly but that even at the worst times there is a great deal of
goodness, kindness, and day-to-day decency that goes unnoticed and makes no headlines.

A poet of an older style was Lucan (Marcus Annaeus
Lucanus). He was born in Corduba, Spain, in 39 and was a

nephew of the Seneca who was a tutor of the young Nero (see page 62). His most famous work was an epic poem about the civil war between Julius Caesar and Pompey. It is the only one of his works that survives.

He was one of Nero's intimates, but it was as fatal a friendship for him as it was for his uncle. Nero became jealous of the acclaim received by Lucan's poetry and forbade him to give public recitations. This was more than a poet could endure. He entered Piso's conspiracy against Nero and when the conspiracy failed, Lucan was taken and forced to commit suicide even though he turned "state's evidence" and betrayed those who had been in the conspiracy with him.

Still another of the "Spanish school" which flourished in the Rome of the Silver Age and which included Seneca, Martial, and Lucan, was Quintilian (Marcus Fabius Quintilianus) who was born in Spain in 35. He served with Galba and came to Rome when that general briefly became Emperor. He stayed in Rome to become the most important teacher of oratory and rhetoric of his age. He was the first teacher to profit by the new Imperial interest in education and was supplied with a government grant by Vespasian. Quintilian was a great admirer of Cicero and labored to rescue Latin style from the tendency to become over-elaborate and poetical.

Rome was never famous for science; that was the forte of the Greeks. In the first century of the Empire, however, several Romans contributed work that must be mentioned in any history of science.

The most famous perhaps was Pliny (Gaius Plinius Secundus) who was born in Novum Comum (the modern Como) in northern Italy, in 23. He commanded troops in Germany in the time of Claudius but it was after Vespasian (whose close friend he was) became Emperor that he really came into his own. He served as governor over sections of Gaul and Spain in that reign.

He was a man of universal interests and universal curiosity, always reading and always scribbling at every spare moment that came his way. His major work was a thirty-seven volume *Natural History* published in 77 and dedicated to Titus, then heir to the throne. It was not an original work, but a digest drawn from two thousand ancient books by nearly five hundred writers. He was quite undiscriminating and selected his items often because they were sensational and interesting rather than because they were plausible and sound.

The book dealt with astronomy and geography but its major concern was zoology and here he quoted voluminously from travelers' tales concerning unicorns, mermaids, flying horses, men without mouths, men with enormous feet, and so on. It was fascinating and the books survived, because so many copies were made, when more sober and factual material did not. Pliny's work remained known throughout medieval and early modern times as a wonder for all, and was generally taken to deal with authentic things.

Pliny came to a tragic and dramatic end. Under Titus, he was placed in command of the fleet stationed off Naples. From his post, he saw Vesuvius erupt. In his eagerness to witness the eruption, study it, and then, undoubtedly, write it up in detail, he went ashore. He delayed too long before retreating and was trapped by the ashes and vapors. He was found dead afterward.

Among other popularizers whose work survived was Aulus Cornelius Celsus. In the time of Tiberius, he gathered together scraps of Greek learning for his audience. The book he devoted to Greek medicine was discovered in early modern times and Celsus then came to be regarded as a famous ancient physician, which was giving him entirely too much honor.

In Caligula's reign, Pomponius Mela (another of the Spanish-born intellectuals of the time) wrote a small popular geography based on Greek astronomy, carefully excluding the mathematics that might have made it too difficult. It was very popular in its time and it survived into the medieval period when, for a while, it was all that was left of ancient geographic knowledge.

In engineering, at which the Romans excelled, important work was done. Vitruvius (Marcus Vitruvius Pollio) flourished in the reign of Augustus and published a large volume on architecture which he dedicated to the Emperor. For many centuries it remained a standard work in the field.

Performing a similar work for other branches of the practical sciences was Sextus Julius Frontinus, who was born about 30. He served as governor of Britain under Vespasian and wrote books on land-surveying and military science which do not survive. In 97, the Emperor Nerva put him in charge of the water system of Rome. As a result, he published a two-volume work describing the Roman aqueducts, probably the most informative work we possess on ancient engineering. He was proud of the practical achievements of Roman engineers and compared them favorably with the spectacular but useless engineering feats of the Egyptians and Greeks.

The fading light of Greek science still shone in the period of the early Empire. A Greek physician, Dioscorides, served with the Roman armies under Nero. His chief interest lay in the uses of plants as a source of drugs. In this connection he wrote five books which formed the first systematic pharmacopoeia and survived through the medieval period.

At about the same time in Alexandria, there lived Hero or Heron, possibly the most ingenious inventor and engineer of ancient times. He is most famous for having designed a hollow sphere with bent arms, within which water could be boiled. The steam, emerging forcefully from the arms, made the sphere whirl about (precisely the principle of many lawn-sprinklers of today). This is a very primitive steam-engine and if the society of the time had been different it is just conceivable that such a device might have led to an industrial revolution of the sort that did not, in actual fact, take place for seventeen more centuries. Hero also studied mechanics and observed the behavior of air and wrote works on each that were far ahead of their times.

And yet, somehow, the light of literature and science that burned quite brightly in the hectic, uncertain times of tyrants such as Caligula, Nero, and Domitian, died down to a flicker under the smooth and enlightened rule of the emperors who followed Nerva.

TRAJAN

The fact that a provincial like Trajan could become an Emperor and remain popular, too, was a sign that the Empire was becoming more than the Italy-dominated realm that Augustus had tried to make it. The force of events was restoring the grand conception of Julius Caesar, an Empire based on the cooperation of all the provinces from end to end and the participation of all in the government.

At the time of Nerva's death, Trajan was inspecting the Rhine-Danube angle, so recently fortified by Domitian and it was not until he was thoroughly satisfied as to its security that he returned to Rome. The fact that his absence gave rise to no disorders showed the eagerness with which Italy had welcomed the serenity of Nerva's reign and its willingness to have that continue.

In 99, Trajan entered Rome in triumph and his forceful personality succeeded in subduing the praetorian guard completely.

Abroad, however, Trajan began to set Roman policy on a new

course. Ever since the defeat of Varus in Germany ninety years before, Rome's policy had been essentially defensive. Territorial extensions had been made at the expense of satellite kingdoms or in isolated corners such as Britain or the Rhine-Danube, but this did not affect the basic decision to seek no trouble with powerful opponents.

Trajan would have none of that. In his view, Rome was getting soft for lack of good enemies; a softness that had reached its climax with the willingness of Domitian to buy peace with the Dacians. This disgrace Trajan was determined to wipe out and then, by hard fighting, to revive the military virtues of Rome. Almost as soon as he had established himself in Rome, then, he set about preparing to settle accounts with Dacia.

First, he ended the tribute, and when Decebalus (still alive and still the Dacian king) responded by raids across the Danube, Trajan led his army eastward in 101. Pouring northward across the Danube, Roman soldiers carried the full force of vigorous war into Dacian territory. In two years, Decebalus was thoroughly beaten and was forced to accept a peace in which the Romans would be permitted to maintain garrisons in the country.

The new state of affairs was as humiliating to Decebalus as the peace with Domitian had been humiliating to Rome. Nor did the Romans take any great pains to spare Decebalus' feelings or save his face. In 105 he began the war anew and in a second campaign the Dacians were beaten worse than before and Decebalus, in despair, killed himself.

This time, Trajan accepted no half-measures. In 107, he annexed all Dacia and made it a Roman province. He then encouraged the establishment of Roman colonies and towns throughout the new province which was rapidly Romanized. The coastal regions north of the Black Sea and east of Dacia were not actually annexed to Rome but they had long contained Greek-speaking cities and they now formed a Roman protectorate. This meant that every inch of seashore inside the Strait of Gibraltar was now under the control of one Government. This had never been true in all human history before the Roman Empire; nor has it ever been true again since the Roman Empire.

Dacia was never an untroubled province. Beyond it, north and east, were hordes of additional barbarian tribes and Dacia was protected by no outstanding natural barriers. It was therefore exposed to perennial raids. For the century-and-a-half that it remained part of the Empire it probably cost Rome more than it was worth, although it did serve as a buffer for the rich provinces south of the Danube.

Oddly enough, traces of the Roman occupation are much clearer in Dacia than in lands to the south that were Roman for much longer periods both before and after. What was once Dacia is now Rumania; or, more correctly, Romania. Its very name is reminiscent of Rome, and the modern inhabitants insist that they are the descendants of the old Roman settlers of Trajan's time. To be sure, the Romanian language is closely related to the Latin. It is classified as a Romance language (along with such tongues as French, Italian, Spanish, and Portuguese) and has maintained itself as such through all the centuries while a sea of Slavic languages washed down from the north and passed around it to the south.

In honor of his Dacian victory, Trajan had erected, in the Roman forum, a magnificent column, 110 feet high; a column which still stands in Rome today. On it, the story of the campaigns in Dacia is depicted in a spiral bas-relief that includes over 2500 human figures. Almost every type of scene from war preparation to actual battles to the capture of prisoners and the final triumphant return to Rome is shown.

At home, Trajan followed Nerva's course of paternalism and humanity. He even extended the care supplied for needy children. This, of course, was not a matter of humanity alone. The

birthrate in the Empire was declining* and the possibility of
a shortage of soldiers was a real threat. To guarantee the care
of poor families with children encouraged the production of
future soldiers, it was hoped.

It is important to remember, incidentally, that the death
rate in the days of the Roman Empire was much higher than
it is in modern technologically-advanced nations, and the life
expectancy was lower. Therefore a drop in birthrate in Rome
was much more serious than a drop in birthrate would be to
the world today. To say that a declining birthrate today would
mean "race suicide" and to use the Roman Empire as an example, is to ignore completely the vital differences in the situation then as compared with now.

But Trajan's long absence from Rome, however it might have
added to the slowly rusting glory of Roman arms, had its dis-
advantages, too. In his absence, government of the provinces
tended to grow corrupt. The cities, particularly in the east,
became more and more incapable of handling their own financial affairs. Interference and supervision by the central government, not only for fiscal reform but for road-building and other
public works as well, was increasingly required.

In 111, for instance, Trajan had to send Pliny the Younger
(Gaius Plinius Cecilius Secundus) to serve as a governor of
Bithynia and reorganize the province. (Pliny the Younger was
a nephew of the Pliny who died in the eruption of Mount
Vesuvius and who is sometimes called Pliny the Elder.)

The younger Pliny was a friend of several of the literary lights
of the period, notably Martial and Tacitus, and he himself tried
his hand at writing now and then. He is best known for his letters which, apparently, he composed with an eye toward pub-

---

* Such a decline is often explained by the selfish luxury of the
upper classes, or the gradual apathy settling over the lower classes.
Theories have recently been advanced that the decline set in after
the large cities of the Empire grew wealthy and sophisticated
enough to develop central water supplies carried through lead
pipes. This slowly subjected many Romans to chronic lead poisoning and helped lower fertility, it is speculated.

lication, so that one wonders how true a light they shed upon his personality.

One letter above all is of importance to people today — a letter he sent to Trajan from Bithynia. It seems that Christians were being punished merely for being Christian and Pliny felt that if people could be persuaded to recant and to stop being Christians they ought to be pardoned, even though they had admittedly been Christian before. Furthermore, Pliny was reluctant to act against people on the basis of anonymous accusations. Then, too, he seemed troubled by the fact that the Christians did not act like criminals but seemed to live according to a high code of ethics. Pliny pointed out that Christianity was spreading rapidly and that it was mildness rather than severity that might halt the spread.

Trajan replied briefly, approved Pliny's actions in pardoning those who recanted, ordered that anonymous accusations ought to be ignored and asserted moreover that Christians ought not be sought out. If legitimately reported and legitimately convicted then they must be punished according to the law, said Trajan, but Pliny was not to go out of his way to find them. (Unquestionably, Pliny and Trajan were, in modern language, "soft on Christianity.")

Pliny the Younger died not long after that letter was written, probably while he was still serving as governor of Bithynia.

The period of peace after the Dacian campaign did not last long, for there was trouble in the east. The Dacians had sought help from Parthia, Rome's old enemy, and Trajan did not forget that. Moreover, Armenia still remained as the disputed buffer land between the two large empires. The last real fighting had been in the time of Nero and since then Armenia had remained delicately balanced.

In 113, however, the Parthian king, Chosroes, set up a puppet over Armenia and broke the fifty-year-old truce. It was a foolish thing to do for Parthia had been distracted for some decades by periodic civil wars between claimants to the throne, while Rome was in a period of strength. In fact, for the twenty years previously, Roman forces had been inching eastward into the Arabian borderlands. The commercial city of Petra, southeast of Judea, together with the Sinai peninsula, between Judea and Egypt, were absorbed in 105 and made into the Province of Arabia. This consolidated the Roman position in the east and made her the more capable of carrying on war against Parthia.

Chosroes must have realized his mistake for he made a quick effort to soothe Trajan. He was too late, however, for Trajan wasn't having any. Trajan marched eastward in 114, took Armenia almost without fighting and made it into a Roman province outright. He next turned southeastward, drove forward to the Parthian capital of Ctesiphon, which he took, then marched the length of Mesopotamia till he stood at the Persian Gulf.

That was the farthest eastward push of the Roman legions and as the sixty-year-old Trajan looked across the gulf in the direction of Persia and India where, four-and-a-half centuries before, Alexander the Great had won such huge victories, he said sadly, "If only I were younger."

At that moment, the Roman Empire stood at its greatest extent. In 116 (869 A.U.C.) Trajan made Assyria and Mesopotamia provinces of Rome and had established the Tigris River as the Empire's eastern boundary.

The land area of the Roman Empire, knit together by 180,-000 miles of roads, was about 3,500,000 miles so that it was roughly the size that the United States of America is today. Its population must have been something in excess of 100,-000,000 and the city of Rome itself had a population of about 1,000,000. The Empire was a large realm even by modern times, and compared to what had gone before in the Mediterranean area (except for the relatively short-lived Persian Empire) it was absolutely monumental. No wonder it made so strong an impression on the men of the centuries immediately

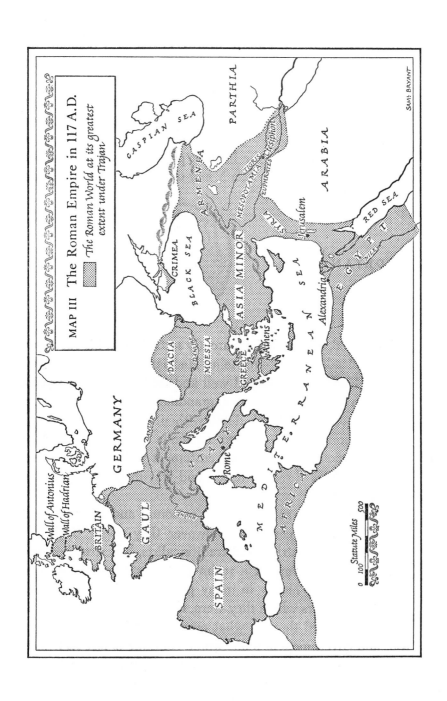

MAP III The Roman Empire in 117 A.D.

The Roman World at its greatest
extent under Trajan

GERMANY

BRITAIN

Wall of Antonius
Wall of Hadrian

GAUL

SPAIN

ITALY

Rome

AFRICA

M E D I T E R R A N E A N   S E A

DANUBE

DACIA

MOESIA

GREECE

Athens

CRIMEA

BLACK SEA

ASIA MINOR

ARMENIA

CASPIAN SEA

PARTHIA

SYRIA

MESOPOTAMIA

TIGRIS

Ctesiphon

EUPHRATES

Jerusalem

EGYPT

NILE

Alexandria

RED SEA

ARABIA

SAM! BRYANT

Statute Miles
0 100   500

after Augustus that not all the disasters eventually befalling the Empire could suffice to wipe out the memory of its greatness.

But it was easier to beat the Parthians than to keep them beaten. Almost at once they renewed the war and Trajan, hearing the news of disorders elsewhere in the realm, was forced to retreat somewhat from the farthest points he had reached. In 117, he died in southern Asia Minor on his way home to Rome.

HADRIAN

About 106, Trajan had apparently settled upon his successor. This was Hadrian (Publius Aelius Hadrianus), a son of Trajan's cousin. Hadrian had served well and faithfully in the Dacian campaign and had married a grandniece of Trajan. He became emperor on Trajan's death without dispute, and through a liberal bonus to the soldiers he made sure there would be none. He flouted the Roman custom of being clean-shaven, one dating back three centuries, and was the first emperor to wear a beard.

The Empire he ruled was not as sound and as great as it seemed. Trajan's conquests, however they might tickle the pride of Roman patriots and traditionalists, had stretched and strained the economy of a realm that was overripe and was turning soft and mushy in many places. If Hadrian tried to keep the frontiers where they were, the army would have to be fed and supplied through what promised to be a long eastern war, and government at home would continue to lose its health.

Hadrian decided not to risk this. If Trajan had tried to play Julius Caesar returned to life, Hadrian intended to play Augustus. He would pull in Rome's horns, establish a firm and secure boundary beyond which it would not budge and within which it would prosper.

With that in mind, he promptly gave up Trajan's eastern conquests and the Roman Empire after two or three years at the peak of its extent began the long pullback that was to last for thirteen centuries and was not to cease until the permanent fall of its last city.

The whole Mesopotamian region was returned to Parthia, and the upper Euphrates, much more easily defensible than the Tigris, was made the eastern boundary again; a boundary, moreover, which exhausted Parthia, its national pride salvaged, was in no mood to dispute. As for Armenia, Hadrian was satisfied to have it a satellite-kingdom again, as before, and made no effort to retain it as an actual province. This meant a pullback of some five hundred miles and an end to the momentary Roman stand upon the Caspian Sea and the Persian Gulf but, really, it was for the best.

Hadrian had to fight off barbarian raids in Dacia, in a war he fought only reluctantly. Indeed, he was anxious to make a clean sweep of Trajan's conquests by giving up Dacia also, but in this he was overruled by his advisers and probably by his own feelings. Dacia was the one recent conquest in which Roman settlers had arrived in numbers and it would have been rather dastardly to leave these to the barbarians.

Hadrian continued and extended the humane and charitable efforts of Nerva and Trajan. He even had laws passed ensuring the considerate treatment of slaves of whom there were still nearly 400,000 in the city of Rome itself, though their numbers were declining, and encouraged the establishment of free schools for the poor. He continued the policy of respect for the Senate and went to great lengths to clear himself of the suspicion that certain conspirators who had been executed by the praetorian guard had been done away with at his instigation. By reorganizing methods of taxation, he managed to increase Imperial revenues while actually lightening the taxes. He also rebuilt the Pantheon, more impressively than ever, after its destruction by fire.

Still, Roman economy suffered, particularly agriculture. When Augustus established the Principate and brought an end to the centuries of spreading conquest, he also brought an end to the influx of thousands of cheap slaves from conquered countries. They were replaced by free tenants who, since they were not property, could move from place to place in search of better working conditions. The percentage of soldiers and city-dwellers (who did not contribute to the raising of food) rose and the population as a whole was declining so that it became more and more difficult to find farm workers and the bidding for their services grew outrageously high (or so it seemed to the land-owners). There was an increasing tendency, therefore, to pass laws designed to keep peasants from moving about, to keep them tied to some particular plot of land. This was the first faint beginnings of what would eventually become serfdom in the Middle Ages.

Although Hadrian treated the Senate with respect, the prestige of that body declined steadily. By now there was no pretense at all that the Senate had anything to do with law-making; only the edicts of the Emperor counted. Of course, a conscientious Emperor such as Hadrian did not issue edicts whimsically or arbitrarily, but made use of a council of distinguished lawyers to advise him.

Hadrian was an intellectual and an antiquarian, and was interested in all the Empire rather than in Italy alone. Indeed, much of his twenty-one-year rule was spent in leisurely travels about the various provinces, letting the people see him and, in turn, seeing them.

In 121, he left for the west and north, traveling through Gaul and Germany and then entering Britain. Britain had been Roman, more or less, for eighty years now, but the northern highlands, inhabited by the wild Picts, were still outside the

Roman grasp. Hadrian was no more enthusiastic about military adventures here than anywhere else. He directed the building of a wall ("Hadrian's Wall") across a narrow section of the island, along just about the line that now separates England from Scotland. The Romans retired south of this wall, which was easy to defend against the unorganized raids of the wild tribesmen, and Roman Britain continued in peace and reasonable prosperity for nearly three centuries.

Hadrian next visited Spain and Africa, then traveled to the East. Affairs with Parthia were clouding over again but Hadrian took the unprecedented step of holding a "summit conference" with the Parthian king and adjusting all differences.

He finally managed to reach Greece, his heart's desire.

By Hadrian's reign, Greece's greatest period lay five-and-a-half centuries in the past. The Athens of the Age of Pericles was as long ago to him, as the Florence of the Renaissance is to us. Learned men already realized that the Periclean period had been something unusual in human history and Hadrian, who had had a thorough Greek education, was very much aware of this.

When he visited Athens in 125 (878 A.U.C.) there was nothing he could find to do that he considered too good for it. He gave it economic and political concessions, he repaired old buildings and built new ones, he tried to reinstitute ancient ways. He even had himself initiated into the Eleusinian mysteries, being accepted where Nero had been rejected (see page 63).

He founded new cities, too, the most important being one in Thrace named Hadrianopolis ("Hadrian's city") in his honor. This has become Adrianople in English and is today part of Turkey, bearing the name Edirne.

In 129, he returned to Athens for a second, prolonged visit, then went on to Egypt and the East once more.

In what had once been Judea, he made a mistake. He ordered the ruined Jerusalem to be rebuilt as a Roman city, and that a temple to Jupiter be built on the site of the Jewish Temple, which had been destroyed a half-century before. At this, the remnant of the Jews left in the land rose in rebellion. The holiness of Jerusalem, even in ruins, was dear to them, and they would not endure its desecration.

The Jews, it must be admitted, had in any case been restless for some time. Even though they were not treated particularly badly under Nerva and Trajan, there were still the old messianic hopes and a continuing resentment over the destruction of the Temple. When Trajan had been fighting his eastern wars, the Jews rose in revolt in Cyrene, west of Egypt. This played its part in forcing an end to Trajan's career of eastern conquest. The Cyrenian revolt was crushed but that merely added to the resentments that finally overflowed with Hadrian's order concerning Jerusalem.

The Jewish leader of the revolt in Judea was Bar-Kochba ("son of a star") a recklessly brave freebooter who was hailed as the messiah by Rabbi Akibah, the chief Jewish teacher of the time. It was a useless fight. Akibah was captured and put to death by torture and after three years during which one Jewish fortress after another was captured despite the stubborn heroism of the defenders, Bar-Kochba was finally taken and killed in 135 (888 A.U.C.).

Judea was virtually cleared of Jews; the site of Jerusalem was forbidden them; and for nearly two thousand years they ceased to have a history as a nation. Their long nightmare began, one in which for many centuries they remained a minority everywhere, hated and despised everywhere, hounded and killed almost everywhere, yet retaining, throughout, their faith in their God and themselves and somehow managing to survive.

Hadrian was particularly interested in literature. Suetonius (see page 88) served for a period as his private secretary. The Emperor also patronized Plutarch, a great Greek writer of the time, making him procurator of Greece toward the end of his life. In this way, Hadrian pleased Greece by placing the land under a native governor.

Plutarch was a living embodiment of the twilight peace of Greece in this period. Under the Empire, Greece had recovered from the long periods of devastations she had experienced as a result of the squabbling among her own cities, followed by the Macedonian and Roman conquests, and then by the various Roman civil wars that were fought out partly on her territory. Her population had declined, her vigor was at a low ebb, but the Greeks lived surrounded by the memory of long-gone greatness and by all the architectural and artistic relics that greatness had left behind. The warmth of Imperial admiration was also a factor that fed Greece's pride.

That pride was embodied in Plutarch's works, the most important of which was his *Parallel Lives*. These consisted of biographical pairs, one Greek and one Roman, the pairs so chosen as to exhibit essential similarities. For instance, Romulus and Theseus formed one pair, since Romulus founded Rome and Theseus organized Athens into its classical form. Julius Caesar and Alexander the Great formed another pair. Coriolanus and Alcibiades (the first a traitor to Rome, the second a traitor to Athens) formed still another. The writing was so attractive and the biographies so filled with interesting anecdotes that it was popular in its own time and has remained popular ever since.

Another Greek writer who flourished under Hadrian was Arrian, who bore the Romanized name of Flavius Arrianus. He was born in Bithynia in 96 and Hadrian made him governor of Cappadocia in 131. He led a Roman army against the Alani, barbarian tribesmen invading from beyond Armenia. It was the first time Roman legions were led by a Greek.

He wrote a number of books of which the best-known is a biography of Alexander the Great. It was supposedly drawn

from contemporary sources, including a biography written by
Ptolemy, one of Alexander's friends and general, who became
king of Egypt after Alexander's death.

Hadrian even dabbled at writing himself and liked to com-
pete with professionals, though not with the offensive vanity of
Nero. In fact, shortly before his death, Hadrian wrote a short
ode to his soul, which he knew was departing; an ode
sufficiently beautiful to be included in many anthologies of
poetry and to be considered a small masterpiece.

In Latin it goes:

> Animula, vagula, blandula,
> Hospes conesque corporis,
> Quae nunc abibis in loca
> Pallidula, frigida, nudula,
> Nec, ut soles, dabis joca.

The translation into English is: "Gentle, fleeing little soul, my
body's guest and comrade, where do you go now, pale, cold
and naked, and not, as is your custom, giving joy?"

ANTONINUS PIUS

Hadrian, like Nerva and Trajan before him, had no sons, but
had taken care to choose a successor before his death. His first
choice did not seem to have been a good one, but fortunately
the chosen successor died before Hadrian did and there was
time for a second choice.

Second time round was fortunate. Hadrian chose Antoninus
(Titus Aurelius Fulvus Boionus Arrius Antoninus) who had
served well in various government offices, including the con-

sulship in 120, and who had also put in a worthy period as provincial governor in Asia. He was already fifty-two, however, at the time he was selected and Hadrian therefore arranged to have Antoninus agree to his own successor as well. Two men were chosen as "grand-successors," one of whom was the nephew of Antoninus' wife, and a youngster of great promise.

Hadrian died in 138 (891 A.U.C.) and Antoninus succeeded without trouble. He was perhaps the gentlest and most humane of all the Roman Emperors. All the paternalistic policies of the previous emperors were continued under him. He extended and intensified the policy of "softness" on Christianity. By now, the distinction between Judaism and Christianity had begun to seem clear to the Roman pagans, as was the fact that the sister religions were increasingly hostile to each other. Since, in Hadrian's time, the Jews were in rebellion against Rome, Christians were automatically looked upon with greater favor on the old notion that "the enemy of my enemy is my friend."

Christianity was far more interested in proselytization than Judaism was, and far more successful at it. It spread most rapidly among the women, slaves, and poorer classes generally. These had little to look forward to in this life, even with the Empire at peace and under stable government. The concentration of Christians on the bliss of the next world, to which life on Earth served but as a temporary trial-period designed to test one's worthiness for the *real* existence, was a deep consolation to such individuals.

For a long time, though, Christianity remained a city religion. The farm population, isolated from the current of new thought and always conservative and set in their old ways, clung to what they were used to. In fact, the very word "pagan," used to identify one who was neither Christian nor Jewish, but adhered to some native religion, is from a Latin word meaning "peasant," one who lives in a "pagus" or village. In the same way, a "heathen" is one who lives in the heath, that is, in some remote countrified district.

Yet we must not think of Christianity as a religion solely of the urban proletariat either. It spread also to a certain degree among the educated. Even some philosophers turned Christian. An example was Justin (usually called Justin Martyr because of the nature of his death). He was born about 100 in what had been Judea. Though born of pagan parents and given a thorough Greek education, he could not help but become acquainted with the holy writings of the Jews and with the story of the death and resurrection of Jesus. He became a Christian convert without abandoning his philosophy. Indeed, he used his philosophic ability to argue the truth of Christianity and thus became an important Christian "apologist" (one who speaks in defense of a cause).

He engaged in a debate of pamphlets with a prominent Jew and opened a school in Rome in which he taught Christian doctrine. His writings are supposed to have reached Hadrian and Antoninus, who were sufficiently impressed to carry on a policy of toleration of Christianity; a toleration that Antoninus extended to the Jews as well despite their recent rebellion.

Although Antoninus was well into middle age at the time of his accession, he reigned for twenty-three years, attaining an age of seventy-five. His reign was one of profound peace; the very height of the Pax Romana; and is almost lost to history, so little took place. (It is the disasters: wars, plagues, insurrections, natural catastophes, that make the headlines and fill the pages of history books.)

Nor did Antoninus share Hadrian's penchant for traveling. He recognized the fact that while Hadrian made himself popular with the provinces by showing himself there, his visits were nevertheless drains on the provincial treasuries. Furthermore, it made Rome itself unhappy to be left without the Emperor for long periods. The Imperial absence seemed a slur on Italian domination over the Empire. Indeed, after Hadrian's death, the Senate, in a petulant display of Italian-centered vanity, balked when it came time to grant the dead Emperor the usual divine honors. Antoninus had to make a strong personal plea before the Senate would consent to act favorably. This was considered a very filial and pious attitude on the part of Antoninus toward his adopted father and as a result he came to be called Antoninus Pius; the name by which he is best known to history.

About the only border troubles that took place in his reign were in Britain. The hostile tribes north of Hadrian's wall raided southward but the Roman governor fought them off. To keep them off, he built another wall across the waist of what is now Scotland, from the Firth of Forth to the Firth of Clyde. This was called "Antonine's Wall." It served as a second breakwater against the barbarians.

Antoninus died in 161 (914 A.U.C.) as peacefully as he had lived. On his last day, when the captain of the palace guard came for the password of the day, Antoninus answered "Equanimity" and died.

MARCUS AURELIUS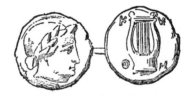

Of the two successors whom Antoninus had adopted at Hadrian's behest, one was confirmed shortly before the old Emperor's death. That was Marcus Aurelius (Marcus Aelius Aurelius Antoninus), Antoninus' son-in-law. The other, Lucius Aurelius Verus, Antoninus had decided proved himself unworthy.

Marcus Aurelius, however, who followed a strict code of behavior felt it was only just to accept Lucius Verus as an equal sharer in the rights and duties of the throne. For the first time in the history of the Empire, two Emperors ruled simultaneously and this set an important precedent for the future.

To be sure, Lucius Verus was not particularly interested in the labors of rule, only in its pleasures and he devoted himself to the latter as far as he could. Marcus Aurelius, who bore the burden of the Empire, is remmembered, therefore, and Lucius Verus is forgotten.

Marcus Aurelius was a model ruler after the pattern of his adopted father. Plato had said, five hundred years before, that the world would never go well until princes were philosophers, or philosophers princes. In Marcus Aurelius that had come to pass for he was a powerful ruler who was at the same time a philosopher whose writings are even today highly regarded.

Marcus Aurelius was, specifically, a stoic. Stoicism had been increasing in favor under the mild rule of the Antonines. Its most renowned exponent in Roman times had been Epictetus, a Greek who was born a slave about 60. He was in poor health and was lame (supposedly because of mistreatment by a cruel master). He had been brought to Rome at an early age and there he managed to attend lectures given by Stoic philosophers and to absorb their teachings. When he was finally freed from slavery, he established himself as a teacher in his own right. In the reign of Domitian, however, when philosophers were expelled from Rome, Epictetus was one of those who had to leave. This was in 89. He retired to Nicopolis, a city which had been founded by Augustus after his final victory over Mark Antony at Actium nearby. At Nicopolis, Epictetus taught for the rest of his life.

Epictetus himself wrote nothing but his teaching was absorbed by his most famous pupil, Arrian (the biographer of Alexander the Great), who recorded them in two books, of which a portion of one survives. Epictetus' philosophy was a kindly and humane one: "Live and let live." "Bear and forbear."

Marcus Aurelius, while young, was attracted to the teachings of Stoicism and himself became the most famous Stoic of all, since he was the Emperor. Marcus Aurelius believed not in happiness, but in tranquillity; he believed in wisdom, justice, endurance, and temperance; he shrank from no hardship that lay in the way of his duty. Throughout his busy life, filled as it was with marches and battles, he recorded his thoughts in a little book that survives under the name "Meditations." This is valued even today as the record of a man who lived a kind and admirable way of life under the most trying conditions.

For Marcus Aurelius was not to have the peaceful life that he deserved. The profound quiet of Antoninus' reign seems to have broken with his death and from all corners, enemies rose against Rome.

On the east, the old enemies, the Parthians, suddenly roused themselves and once again tried to place Armenia under a Parthian puppet. They further made war inevitable by invading Syria. Roman legions, under the co-Emperor, Lucius Verus, hurried eastward.

The Parthians were defeated and the Romans repaid them by invading and ravishing Mesopotamia and burning Ctesiphon their capital. By 166, peace was restored and three years later Lucius Verus died leaving Marcus Aurelius sole Emperor.

The Parthian war might have been looked upon as a triumph for Rome but for a most unlooked-for result —

The human hives of the Far East in India and China have for long centuries been subject to diseases such as cholera or the bubonic plague. In those areas, the diseases are endemic; that is, they are always present at a moderate level of incidence. Every once in a while, however, a disease germ develops a new strain of unusual virulence and then a particular disease shoots upward in intensity and pours out in all directions, carried by travelers, soldiers, and frightened refugees. Every once in a while, such a "plague" advances westward and inundates Europe.

It was such a plague that devastated Athens nearly six centuries before Marcus Aurelius at the beginning of its long war with Sparta. It killed Pericles and probably made it certain that Athens would lose the war. This plague indirectly ended

Athens' glory and contributed to the decay of Greece. Another plague (the famous "Black Death") swept over Europe twelve centuries after the time of Marcus Aurelius and killed one-third of Europe's inhabitants.

Between these two plagues came one, no less important, in Marcus Aurelius' time. It may have been a plague of smallpox. The soldiers fighting in Parthia were exposed to it and their power was greatly weakened by its ravages. They brought it back with them to Rome and to the provinces, too.

The plague struck savagely at the population of the Empire, stripping the land of soldiers and farmers and permanently weakening it. The population of the city of Rome began to decline and it was not until the twentieth century that it was to regain the numbers it had held under Augustus and Trajan.

The depopulation brought the beginnings of another disaster in its wake, for Marcus Aurelius tried to fill the land again by encouraging the immigration of northern barbarians. This was the first swing of the pendulum from the Romanization of the North to the Germanization of the Empire.

The frightened people, finding it necessary to blame someone for the plague, blamed the Christians and a period of persecution began. Among those who died in the witch-hunts was Justin Martyr. Doubtless, Marcus Aurelius disapproved of such persecution on principle, but there was little he could do against the power of a maddened mob.

To be sure, Marcus Aurelius was a great believer in the value of the state religion as a unifying principle among the people of the Empire, who otherwise differed so markedly in language and culture. To him, the Christians must have seemed a dangerously disruptive force. The dangers to Rome were so much greater in his reign than in the immediately preceding ones that he may well have felt he could not afford to tolerate possible rebels, and so he may have reconciled himself to a persecution he knew to be wrong in theory.

The chief outer danger to Rome lay in a coalition of German tribes formed under the leadership of the Marcomanni, who lived in what is now northern Bavaria and who joined with other tribes north of the Danube. Taking advantage of the Roman preoccupation with Parthia, they attacked Rome's northern frontier. For some fifteen years, Marcus Aurelius wore himself out in this Marcomannic War, marching from point to threatened point, defeating the Germans but then having them rise again.

On the whole, Rome might be considered as having won the war, but whereas in earlier centuries, she had conquered and absorbed barbarian lands, now it was a sufficient victory merely to fight them off and keep herself intact. If this was to go on, the next century was bound to see disasters — and it did.

Marcus Aurelius died in 180 (933 A.U.C.) after a reign of nineteen years, while in camp and still embattled against the Germans. His place of death was near the modern Vienna.

THE AGE OF THE ANTONINES

From the accession of Nerva in 96 to the death of Marcus Aurelius in 180, the Empire had witnessed eighty-four years that were mainly peaceful and were marked by sober, conscientious government. There had been foreign wars with the Parthians, the Dacians, and the Britons but they were far away, fought mainly on enemy soil, and left no serious imprint of sorrow on the Roman provinces. There had been rebellions, notably of the Jews under Hadrian, and an occasional uprising of a general, as in the case of the capable head of the Syrian legions who, in 175, was misled by a false report of the death of Marcus Aurelius at the hands of the Marcomanni. These rebellions

were all crushed, however, and represented only pinpricks in
the general peace.

Indeed, the eighteenth-century English historian, Edward
Gibbon, in a famous statement, said that in all the history of
the human race, there was never so long a period in which so
many were so happy as in the Roman Empire under the Antonines.

In a way, he was right. If we think only of the Mediterranean area, it was certainly better off materially under the
Antonines than it had been in the centuries when it was engaged in continual war, region against region. It was also better off than in the following centuries when it was racked by
civil war and barbarian invasions; or still later when it was
again divided among numerous quarreling governments. One
might even say it was better off under the Antonines than it
is now when it (along with the rest of the world) is living in the
shadow of the atom bomb.

Yet if the age of the Antonines represented a period of peace
and rest, it was the peace and rest of exhaustion. The Mediterranean world had worn itself out in the great wars of the Greeks
and Romans, and when the Empire — apparently so great and
strong — was forced to withstand the shocks of disasters afterward, it struggled manfully and almost superhumanly, but it
had become too worn out to win.

The plague of 166 may have been a last straw, breaking what
vitality remained among the population.

The attempt on the part of the Emperors to make the city of
Rome a grand showplace further weakened the economy. Hundreds of thousands of Roman citizens received free food and by
the time of the Antonines, one day out of three was a holiday to
be celebrated by shows, chariot races, gladiatorial fights, and
animal extravaganzas. It was all terribly costly and the long-
term price paid in the weakening of the economy was not worth
the short-term hilarity it occasioned. (Presumably, many of
the Romans of the generations who reaped the benefit of the

fun thought little of what it would mean for their descendants — or cared little, if they thought about it. Our own generation, which is ceaselessly polluting and destroying the resources of the world is equally criminal in its indifference and we have no right to point the finger of scorn at the Romans.)

The weariness of the age of the Antonines is reflected in the slow decline of literature. About the only literary figure of importance in the time of the later Antonines was Lucius Apuleius, who was born in Numidia about 124. He studied in Athens and lived in Rome for a while, but spent the main portion of his life in Carthage.

He is best known for a book usually called *The Golden Ass*; a fantasy of a man who was turned into a donkey and of the adventures he experienced in his animal shape. Included in this tale is the story of "Cupid and Psyche" certainly one of the most attractive of the tales told after the manner of the ancient myths.

Science, too, was fading out. Only two names deserve to be mentioned in connection with the age of the Antonines. One is that of a Greek (or possibly Egyptian) astronomer who lived in Egypt during the reign of Hadrian and Antoninus. He was Claudius Ptolemaeus, better known in English simply as Ptolemy. He summarized the work of the Greek astronomers in an encyclopedic book that survived into the Middle Ages when the works of the earlier astronomers upon whom he had drawn had vanished. It remained the astronomical sourcebook for fifteen centuries. Since the picture of the Universe drawn by Ptolemy placed the Earth at the center, this Earth-centered model is frequently referred to as the "Ptolemaic system."

Somewhat younger than Ptolemy was Galen, a Greek physician born in Asia Minor about 130. In 164 he settled in Rome and was, for a time, court physician to Marcus Aurelius. He wrote voluminously on medicine and his works also survived through the Middle Ages, retaining all their authority and force until modern times.

The burdens of the Empire were increasing and the number
of shoulders willing to bear them was decreasing. Eventually,
these burdens were bound to crush the Empire, and they did.

Yet weariness is only relative, too, and not all endeavors
were attacked by it. In an age when the importance of the
world hereafter was growing in men's minds, discussions of the
nature of that world and its relationship to man grew more
intense. Indeed, it may well be argued that one reason for the
decline in science, art, and literature was the increasing absorp-
tion of the better minds into a new sort of intellectual pursuit
— theology.

Not only did Jews and Christians dispute dogma with each
other; not only did both attempt to defend their beliefs against
pagans; but among the Christians themselves, various competing beliefs arose. (When one particular variety of belief won
out, it became "orthodoxy" — meaning "straight thought" in
Greek — while the others were "heresies" from a Greek word
meaning "choosing for one's self.")

In the first two centuries of the Christian era, for instance,
there were a number of groups of professing Christians who
embraced a system of thought that is usually lumped under the
name of "Gnosticism" and this is one of the most important of
the early heresies. "Gnosticism" is from a Greek word meaning
"knowledge" since the Gnostics claimed that salvation could
come only through knowledge of the true system of the world,
knowledge that was gained by both revelation and experience.

Actually, Gnosticism existed before Christianity and contained many of the elements of Persian religion; notably in
the belief in a principle of good and one of evil, and in the
continuing warfare between the two. With the coming of
Christianity, a number of Gnostics quickly absorbed some
facets of Christian teachings.

Some Christian Gnostics considered God the principle of
good, but felt this God to be so remote as to be beyond man's
comprehension. It was the principle of evil that actually cre-

ated the world and it is the Jehovah of the Old Testament that is this principle. Jesus, the son of the far-off God, comes to Earth to rescue it from Jehovah, by this line of thought. Naturally, Gnostics were strongly anti-Semitic.

On the other hand, those whom we now consider orthodox Christians accepted the divine authority of the Old Testament, and considered Jehovah to be God. They could only be horrified at a system of thought that tried to make Jehovah the Devil. This was the first (but far from the last) of the theological struggles that turned Christian against Christian even more fiercely than it turned Christian against non-Christian.

Individual Christian teachers might also lay claim to special revelations or knowledge and to preach repentance and holiness as Christ himself had done. Thus, a certain Montanus, who first attracted notice during the reign of Antoninus Pius, declared he was specially inspired by God to preach an imminent end of the world and the second coming of Christ.

This is another version of Messianism. The Jews had waited for the coming of the Messiah from generation to generation and every once in a while, some Jewish teachers preached that the coming was imminent and some of those who listened believed them. After Jesus was accepted as the Messiah by some Jews and by increasing numbers of non-Jews, there began new periods of waiting for the second coming of Jesus from generation to generation. Again, there did not fail to be in each generation, some who preached the second coming to be imminent and others who believed. (The sect of "Jehovah's Witnesses" is the contemporary representative of those who believe in the imminence of the second coming.)

Montanus established the sect of "Montanists" who believed that since Jesus was about to come again, men whould be prepared for it by putting away worldly things, avoiding sin, living lives of rigid virtue. He preached what we would today call a "puritanical" way of life.

Thus it came about that increasing numbers of men devoted their energies to disputing the nature of the other world, rather than the development of this one, and increasingly despised this world as something that was worthless at best and evil at worst.

COMMODUS

But all might not have gone as badly as it did, if Marcus Aurelius had followed the precedent set by the four preceding Emperors and had adopted some worthy successor who had proved himself in the civil and military service. He did not and this one disservice to the Empire canceled out all the good that he and his predecessors had done.

Marcus Aurelius had, unfortunately, a son of his own and he made his son his successor. In 177 he had actually made him (a boy of sixteen at the time) the co-Emperor.

The danger is that a son, born to the throne, is almost certain to be spoiled. He encounters too much flattery, finds himself with too much power, and mistakes the accident of birth for the achievements of worth. It had happened with Caligula and with Nero and it was now to happen again.

The son was Commodus (Marcus Lucius Aelius Aurelius Commodus Antoninus), who was nineteen at the time he became Emperor in his own right.

Commodus was no warrior. He made quick peace with the Marcomanni and devoted himself to a life of pleasure. He let the burdens of government fall to his officials. This is dangerous in a way. People are not willing to blame the Emperor himself for misfortunes since they are taught to revere the Emperor (or King or President). It is easy, however, to blame "wicked favorites" (or officials or bureaucrats). Commodus did not have the courage to defend his officials, but sacrificed them to the mob whenever that seemed the easiest way out.

Like most weak rulers, he feared assassination, and it seemed to him that the most likely to conspire against him were the senators. This meant that the long period in which the senators had worked in cooperation with the Emperors came to an end. Once again there was a reign of terror in which the report of a careless word, or the striking of a sudden unreasonable suspicion was enough to herald exile or execution.

The Senate was not what it had once been, of course — not even in the time of Augustus, let alone in the great days of the Republic. It no longer represented the old Roman aristocracy. Much of that had been wiped out in the civil wars that preceded the establishment of the Empire. What was left was killed off by Caligula, Nero, and Domitian. Under the Antonines, the Senate was drawn from a new class of civil servants and its prestige was all the more fallen because of that.

Like Nero, Commodus seems to have been monstrously vain, and to have carried that vanity to still more disgraceful extremes. Nero had at least gloried in feats of the intellect, in his poetry and in his acting and singing. Commodus apparently had the soul of a gladiator in the body of an Emperor. It was his pleasure to kill beasts in the amphitheater (from a safe position) and he is supposed even to have engaged in gladiatorial combats. While the Romans loved the brutal sight of armed men fighting to the death, they still felt that the actual fighters were filling a degraded social position. That an Emperor should play the role of a gladiator was therefore disgraceful.

Once again, Imperial extravagance was emptying the treasury and serious economic distress ravaged the realm.

The end of this new Nero was precisely the same as that of the old one. Those nearest him had the most to fear from his arbitrary impulses and were most eager to make sure of their own safety by putting him out of the way. In 192 (945 A.U.C.) his mistress, Marcia, and certain court officials conspired against him and had him strangled by a professional wrestler, and so, in a way, he died like a gladiator. Like Nero, he was thirty-one at the time of his death.

Commodus was the last of the line (by adoption and descent) of Nerva. It had ruled almost exactly a century and had contributed seven Emperors to Roman history, if one counts the co-Emperor, Lucius Verus.

5

THE LINE OF SEVERUS

SEPTIMIUS SEVERUS

Twice before an important dynasty had come to an end, once with Nero and once with Domitian. The first time, an unprepared Senate had to face a short civil war with, fortunately, a happy ending. The second time, the Senate had been prepared and things had worked out well from the start.

The Senate tried to follow the second precedent exactly. Domitian had been followed by the aged and respected Nerva, and now they arranged to have Commodus followed by the aged, respected Pertinax (Publius Helvius Pertinax).

Pertinax had been born into humble circumstances in 126, during Hadrian's reign. Painfully, he had risen through the civil service until at the time of Commodus' death, he was what today would be called the Mayor of the city of Rome.

Like Nerva, Pertinax felt too old to take on the great task

of the Emperor and pleaded against it. The praetorian guard, however, having been talked into accepting Pertinax by their commander (one of the conspirators against Commodus), insisted. Pertinax agreed with a heavy heart.

The praetorian guard quickly changed its mind, when Pertinax tried to reestablish governmental economy after Commodus' excesses. This was precisely what Galba had tried to do after Nero and it led to precisely the same result. The praetorian guard rebelled and when Pertinax went before them to calm them, they killed him. He had reigned three months.

There then followed a scene which showed exactly how low Rome had fallen; how completely the soldiers ruled; and how little they (or, apparently, anyone) cared for the abstract good of the realm.

The praetorian guard put the Empire on the auction block. Sullenly aware that Pertinax had tried to cut their pay, they determined that the next Emperor would do no such thing. They offered to proclaim as Emperor whoever agreed to pay them the highest sum.

A wealthy Senator, Marcus Didius Julianus, hearing of this, decided to enter the bidding (perhaps just as a joke at first). He won by offering the equivalent in modern money of $1250 per man, and was promptly acclaimed Emperor.

Offices have been bought and sold before and since but never such high office, and never so openly.

However, Didius Julianus had merely bought death in a very expensive manner. After Nero's assassination, the legions had converged on Rome, with each general claiming the throne, and the same was happening now. The legions in Britain, in Syria, and on the Danube were contending for the prize.

The general on the Danube was quickest. He was Lucius Septimius Severus. Like Trajan, he was a provincial, having been born in Africa in 146. He may not even have been Italian in descent, for he learned Latin only comparatively late in life and he always spoke the language with an African accent.

He marched for Rome pell-mell and as soon as he entered Italy in June, 193, the praetorian guard declared for him. (After all, he had some tough legions at his back.) The Senate eagerly did so, too, and poor foolish Julianus was executed after a reign of two months. He kept crying out as they dragged him away, "But whom have I harmed? Whom have I harmed?" No one, of course — but when one plays for top prizes one must be prepared to pay top stakes.

Severus, as Emperor, had then to settle with the competing generals. Once a general has been offered the crown and has accepted it, there is no backing away. A successful candidate cannot allow an unsuccessful one to remain alive, for once the Emperor-fever has struck a man, he can never be trusted again. What's more, the unsuccessful candidate, knowing he can never be trusted, must continue fighting. As a result, what followed after Severus' accession to the throne was the first serious Roman civil war in two hundred years.

The civil war after Nero's death had lasted only a year and the fighting had been minor. This civil war, after Commodus' death, lasted four years and it included major battles. The Pax Romana was seriously jarred!

Severus moved eastward first, to cross swords with Niger (Gaius Pescennius Niger Justus), the commander of the legions in Syria. Niger was an old acquaintance of Severus and the two had once held the consulate together. However, Niger was now the most popular of the contending generals and his position in the east made it possible for him to sieze Egypt and cut off Rome's grain supply. Severus had to prevent that and old friendship was not going to stand in the way.

Niger's popularity was his undoing, for the eastern provinces all declared for him and he felt no urgency about doing anything. He remained in Syria in false security and let the energetic Severus come after him. Severus did so, won several battles in Asia Minor. Niger was captured in 194, while trying to flee to Parthia, and was executed on the spot.

That left the commander of the legions in Britain, Albinus (Decimus Clodius Septimus Albinus.) Oddly enough, where Niger means "black," Albinus means "white," so that Severus had to face Black and White.

Severus had secured Albinus' neutrality at first by declaring him his heir. That gave him time to finish Niger. Albinus, who had hoped for a stalemate between his two enemies, now felt it was only a matter of time before Severus turned on him. He decided to strike first by having himself proclaimed Emperor again and marching south into Gaul in 197.

The energetic Severus sped north to meet him and at Lugdunum (the modern Lyons), the largest city in Gaul at that time, the armies met in the greatest battle of Roman against Roman since the Battle of Philippi a century and a half before. Severus' forces were completely victorious and Lugdunum was sacked so viciously as never to regain its prosperity throughout ancient times. At that price, Severus was finally, in 197 (950 A.U.C.) undisputed master of the Empire.

The Roman realm now settled down under Severus as once it had settled down under Vespasian a century and a quarter before. This time, though, Rome was weaker. It had suffered the devastation of the plague and its population was continuing to decline. It had also suffered the blows, both physical and psychological, of a serious civil war.

Severus could not, therefore, restore the Principate to the Augustan model as Vespasian had tried to do. Perhaps Severus didn't even want to. Instead, he adjusted himself to reality by accepting the fact that it was only as the master of the army that any Emperor could be master of Rome. Neither the Senate nor the people had anything to say about the government.

Severus therefore proceeded to coddle the army. He increased army pay and extended military privileges, allowing soldiers to marry, for instance, while serving, and frequently inducting them into middle class status on retirement. He centralized the army under himself, removing Senators from even nominal control of particular legions. He increased the army's size, allowing it to reach thirty-three legions as compared with twenty-five at the time of Augustus' death. The numbers of auxiliary troops were also increased and by 200, the total number of men under arms in Roman forces may have surpassed 400,000.

Furthermore, Severus disarmed and disbanded the praetorian guard that had sold the Empire and replaced it by one of his own Danubian legions. Thereafter a new praetorian guard was recruited from the legions and it no longer remained particularly Italian in makeup. By stationing a legion in Italy itself, Severus reversed Augustus' policy of two centuries before and in effect, reduced Italy to the rank of the other provinces. From this time on, in fact, there was no real distinction between Italy and the provinces. All parts of the Empire were alike in subjection to the army and its leader.

Under Severus, the centralization of the Empire continued. He subdivided some provinces into smaller units so that individual governors were less powerful and there was a more complicated hierarchy of officials leading up to himself.

On the whole, though, his strength benefited the Empire, which could withstand a military despotism better, at that time, than it could withstand extravagance or anarchy. In Severus' time, in fact, the Roman limits stood firm despite the occupation of the legions in fighting each other while the outer boundaries were left unguarded. Fortunately, Rome's great rival, Parthia, was continuing its own civil wars and was declining in strength so much more rapidly than Rome was that Severus could still face Parthia from an advantageous position.

Thus, when Parthia made a move that seemed calculated to take advantage of Rome's troubles, Severus responded with alacrity. A foreign war was just the thing to unite the realm behind him. In 197, therefore, fresh from his victory over Albinus, he marched eastward again and defeated Parthia handsomely. When he returned to Rome in 202, he celebrated a

triumph and put up an arch (which still stands) commem-
orating his victories.

In the period of peace that followed, Severus reorganized
legal procedures and finances. A close associate of Septimius
Severus was the respected lawyer, Papinian (Aemilius Papini-
anus). It was Papinian who undertook a thorough reorganization of Roman law and, indeed, the commentaries he wrote
formed the basis of that law for three centuries afterward.
The financial reorganization, however, did not heal the under-
lying weaknesses of the Empire for Severus was forced to de-
crease the silver content of coins, a sure sign of continuing economic illness.

Severus' wife, the Empress Julia Domna, was interested in
philosophy and lent the reign an intellectual cast that was quite
foreign to the rough soldierly Emperor himself. She surrounded herself, for instance, with thinkers such as Galen the
physician, who was then in his last years (he died about 200).

Another in her circle was Diogenes, usually called Diogenes
Laertius because he was born in the town of Laerte in Asia
Minor. His claim to fame is that he wrote capsule biographies
of various ancient philosophers of renown. His book was intended for popular consumption and consists very largely
of gossipy incidents in the lives of the philosophers and some
dramatic quotations from their works. It was undoubtedly
wonderful for gentlemen of leisure who wanted to be able to
make small talk about philosophers and philosophy without
having to go through the hard work of actually reading their
works. The book was undoubtedly considered worthless by
the real scholars of the time.

And yet the very popularity of Diogenes Laertius' summary
meant that many copies were made and that some survived into
modern times where the much more worthwhile and much
less popular works of many of the philosophers themselves
did not. It follows that Diogenes Laertius tells us all we know

about many great men and for that we must be thankful to him.

A friend of Severus himself was Dio Cassius (Dion Cassius Cocceianus), a historian of some note. He was born in Asia Minor where his father was serving as governor under Marcus Aurelius. Dio Cassius came to Rome in 180 and served as a Senator under Commodus, surviving the dangers of that reign and living to enjoy high office under Severus and his immediate successors. Dio Cassius wrote a history of Rome and those books survive that deal with the last half-century of the Republic and the first half-century of the Empire. It is through the accident of this survival that we know as much as we do of the times of Caesar and Augustus.

Severus' last years were troubled by conflict in Britain. Mindful of the power of Britain's governor, Albinus, who had almost won the Empire, Severus had divided Britain into two provinces. This weakened the power of the generals there and made them less likely to rebel. It also made them less able to withstand the northern Picts, particularly since Albinus in his bid for the throne had withdrawn quantities of tried soldiers from Britain and brought them to their death at Lugdunum.

In 208, Severus was forced to travel to Britain himself and to press operations with vigor against the hardy highlanders of the wild north. The price was too high, though. Guerilla operations wore down the legions and these could be supplied and reinforced only with difficulty from the main body of the realm. In the end, Severus had to content himself with some nominal gestures of submission from the natives. These masked the real result, which was a Roman retreat. Severus decided the makeshift Antonine's Wall, established a half-century before in mid-Scotland, was too difficult to defend and fell back definitely and finally on the more practical Hadrian's Wall, which he reinforced.

But Severus was never to leave Britain. He was well into his sixties and for years had been suffering horribly from gout. In 211 (964 A.U.C.) he died of the disease in Eboracum (the modern York.)

CARACALLA

Severus, in order to increase his popularity with the people of the Empire and to make his rule seem more legitimate, had indulged in the legal fiction that he was the son of Marcus Aurelius and the brother of Commodus. This shows itself in the name of his older son. Originally, that was Bassianus, but after the father had become Emperor, the son's name was changed to Marcus Aurelius Antoninus.

Like Caligula, however, the older son of Severus came to be known by the name of an article of clothing. He introduced a long cloak after the Gallic style and made it popular in Rome. Such a cloak was a "caracallus" and Severus' son came to be known as Caracalla in consequence.

Caracalla and his younger brother, Geta (Publius Septimius Antoninus Geta) had served in Britain in their father's final campaign and upon Severus' death, the two brothers succeeded as co-Emperors, following the precedent of Marcus Aurelius and Lucius Verus a half-century before.

Caracalla was no Marcus Aurelius, however. The two brothers hated each other violently. They concluded a quick peace in Britain and hastened back to Rome to fight it out one way or the other. It was Caracalla who won out for he had Geta assassinated in 212 and thereafter ruled alone, insuring his own security by wholesale executions of those he suspected of having supported Geta. By lavishing money on the soldiers, he gained their support and he cared not a snap for anything else.

The most distinguished Roman to fall in Caracalla's campaign of execution was Papinian, the lawyer. He had accompanied Severus to Britain and on the Emperor's death, he had been made guardian of Caracalla and Geta, who were still in their early twenties. He tried to keep the peace between them and failed. As so often happens to peacemakers, he gained the enmity of both sides and would probably have been executed just as quickly if Geta had won.

Caracalla, like Caligula, Nero, and Commodus, was spoiled by having been brought up at court, and made a poor Emperor. However, he reigned for only six years.

Under his rule, the enormous "baths of Caracalla," covering 33 acres, were completed. Their ruins still stand in Rome today and are a tourist attraction.

The habit of bathing had increased in popularity through Roman history and under the Empire, it had reached a height of luxury. Public baths were large complexes of rooms in which a bather could move from bath to bath at different temperatures: hot, tepid, and cold. There were steam rooms, exercise rooms, and places where one could undergo anointing or massage. There were even lounges where a patron could rest, read, converse, or hear recitations. The prices were not great and the baths were very popular.

Certainly the popularity of bathing is much more to be admired than the popularity of horrible gladiatorial combats and animal fights. Nevertheless, to the Roman satirists, the Stoics, and, most of all, to the early Christians, the luxury surrounding the baths made the whole practice seem effete and disgraceful. In particular, the practice arose in some places of men and women using the baths simultaneously and this was horrifying to the moralists who imagined that all sorts of wickedness was going on that probably wasn't.

Another important act of Caracalla was his edict in 212 (965 A.U.C.), granting Roman citizenship to all the free inhabitants of the Empire. This was not as wonderful a grant as it might seem for the distinction between citizen and non-citizen had been diminishing for a long time and the practical advantages of being a citizen in an army-run despotism were virtually nil.

In fact, Caracalla is supposed to have had a practical end in view. There were certain inheritance taxes which only Roman citizens had to pay. By extending citizenship, Caracalla increased revenues from that tax.

Caracalla continued an aggressive policy on the frontiers. He fought along the Danube in 214 and kept the German tribes at bay. He then marched east for yet another of the perennial wars against Parthia and, like his father before him, he led a successful raid into Mesopotamia.

However, Caracalla's cruelties were rousing nervousness among his associates. For instance, he had ordered his soldiers to sack Alexandria, the second greatest city of the Empire, for some trivial crime and thousands of people were killed. A man like that would not hesitate to slaughter his associates over some imagined offense if those associates did not act first.

They did. In 217 (970 a.u.c.) Caracalla was assassinated at the instigation of one of his officers, Marcus Opilius Macrinus. Like Nero and Commodus, Caracalla died a violent death at the age of thirty-one.

After the assassination, Macrinus had himself proclaimed Emperor. He was a middle-class citizen of Mauretanian birth and he had never attained the Senatorial rank. He was the first Emperor to reach the throne while still only in the middle class.

Macrinus apparently meant well. He decreased certain taxes and attempted to reduce the pay and increase the discipline among his troops (always a very risky move).

Unfortunately, things did not go well. The Parthians, taking advantage of the disorders that followed the death of Caracalla, invaded Syria and inflicted defeats on the Romans. Macrinus was forced to sign a rather unfavorable peace which at once roused the indignation of the soldiers, and caused them to turn toward other possible contenders for the throne.

ALEXANDER SEVERUS

The logical contender would seem to be one who was related to Caracalla and therefore part of the line of Severus. Caracalla had had no children but he had some female relatives. His mother, Julia Domna, who died shortly after Caracalla's assassination, had a sister named Julia Maesa, who had two daughters, Julia Soemis and Julia Mamea. The two daughters, each a first cousin of the dead Caracalla, had each a young son. The son of the former was Bassianus, that of the latter Alexianus.

Bassianus was living in Emesa, Syria, with his mother. He was seventeen at the time and was serving as priest in the temple of the Sun. The local name for the Sun-god was Elagabal and the young priest was later known as Elagabalus, a Romanized form of that name. (Sometimes, this name is given as Heliogabalus, because "helio-" is from the Greek word for "sun.")

Elagabalus' grandmother, Julia Maesa, wooed the discontented soldiers with a promise of money and spread the story that the young priest was the son of Caracalla. Elagabalus adopted the name of Marcus Aurelius Antoninus and was acclaimed Emperor. Macrinus tried to resist but, after a battle, was forced to flee. He was eventually caught and executed after having reigned for a little more than a year.

Elagabalus went to Rome in triumph and with him went the various Julias, his grandmother, his mother and his aunt, who were the real rulers of the Empire during his reign. He was persuaded to adopt his cousin, Alexianus, as his successor.

Elagabalus proved to be a completely worthless Emperor, a mere figurehead who adopted Syrian customs that shocked the Romans. He introduced the worship of Elagabal into Rome, bringing its image, a conical black stone, with him to the capital for that purpose. He also showed the same arbitrary cruelties that other young Emperors had shown. By 222, (975 A.U.C.) the praetorian guard grew weary of the situation and killed Elagabalus and his mother. The black stone of Elagabal was then returned to Syria.

Elagabal's cousin and successor, Alexianus, was now proclaimed Emperor in his turn. He adopted the name Marcus Aurelius Alexander Severus in order to show relationship to Marcus Aurelius and Septimius Severus. The name Alexander derives from the fact that he was born in Phoenicia, in or near a temple dedicated to Alexander the Great. He is commonly known as Alexander Severus.

Unfortunately, Alexander Severus was no Alexander the Great, or even a Septimius Severus. He was only a seventeen-year-old boy who was completely dominated by his mother and grandmother. The latter died in 226, leaving Alexander's mother, Julia Mamea, as the actual power in Rome.

She ruled mildly and an apparently honest attempt was made to restore the situation as it had been under the Antonines. Alexander's mother established a committee of Senators and lawyers to guide the government. One of these Ulpian (Domitius Ulpianus) had been a colleague of Papinian and had served notably under Septimius Severus and Caracalla. He had been exiled under Elagabalus but was now recalled and served virtually as prime minister in the early part of the reign.

Time, however, could not be turned backward. Economic conditions continued bad and the coinage had to be debased further. New troubles were arising in the East, too.

The Parthian invasion of Syria after the death of Caracalla proved to be that kingdom's last military adventure. It was having increasing trouble keeping its various provinces quiet, and the perpetual wars with Rome and civil wars at home finally brought Parthia to its end. For three centuries it had maintained a more or less equal fight against Rome and now it was forever through.

This did not, however, mean that Rome was to face a vacuum toward its east. In 226, Ardashir, the ruler of Fars (a province on the Persian Gulf, known as Persis to the Greeks and as Persia to us) revolted against the last Parthian king and established himself on the throne.

In the place of Parthia, then, a Persian Empire arose. To distinguish it from the old Persian Empire that Alexander the Great had destroyed five and a half centuries before, the new realm is sometimes called the New Persian Empire or the Neo-Persian Empire. Because the new king traced his descent from a ruler named Sassan, the dynasty came to be known as the Sassanids and the new realm may also be called the Sassanid Empire.

To Rome, the change in the East made little difference. The people to the east of Syria were still the enemy, regardless of who their king was and whether you called them Parthians or Persians. In fact, the enmity grew worse, for the Sassanids thought of themselves indeed as the successors of the old Persian kings and felt that all the land taken from them by Alexander the Great should be restored, and this included Asia Minor, Syria and Egypt.

By 230, then, the Persians were invading the eastern provinces of the Empire and Alexander Severus was forced to travel eastward and lead his armies against the Persians. Details of what followed are uncertain, but although Alexander eventually returned to Rome and celebrated a triumph, alleging all sorts of victories, it seems quite certain that the war was another stand-off.

While he was gone, however, the Germans began to cross the Rhine and raid Gaul. Alexander had to move northward. Unfortunately, he and his mother, in economizing on the army had attracted the gradually gathering hostility of the soldiers. They had mutinied on occasion during his reign and during one of the mutinies, in 228, had killed the old lawyer, Ulpian, in the very presence of the Emperor.

Now they were ready to go further. In Gaul, Alexander was forced to buy off the Germans and this gave the soldiers a kind of pseudo-patriotic excuse. Blaming Alexander's incapacity for the lack of better results (and they were perhaps right in their complaint if not in their remedy) they assassinated him and his mother in 235 (988 a.u.c.)

Alexander Severus' reign was the last in which there was even an attempt to keep up some sort of civilian government. After this, it was military rule only, naked and unashamed.

Thus, the line of Severus came to an end after dominating Rome for forty-two years (minus a year in which Macrinus had nominally ruled). Counting Geta, it had contributed five Emperors to Rome.

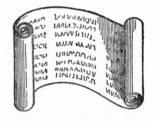

THE CHRISTIAN WRITERS

During the half-century of increasing danger for the Empire that followed the death of Marcus Aurelius, Christianity continued to gather strength, particularly in the cities and most particularly in the Greek-speaking east.

A rising tide of learned writings on Christianity began to pour forth. Those who wrote on Christianity with particular effect during the time of the Roman Empire and the early Middle Ages are sometimes called the "Fathers of the Church" and are divided into the Greek Fathers and the Latin Fathers according to the language in which they wrote. There is no general agreement as to exactly which writers are included among the Fathers, and certainly no decision shall be attempted here. Those mentioned below, however, are all included on the list by one group or another.

In the east, Clement of Alexandria (Titus Flavius Clemens) went even beyond Justin Martyr (see page 110) in turning the full battery of Greek knowledge on the problem of Christian doctrine. He was born about 150 in Athens, of pagan parents, and he was probably indoctrinated into some of the pagan mysteries before his conversion to Christianity. Thereafter he studied and lived in Alexandria where he originated what is sometimes known as the Alexandrian school of theology.

Clement viewed Christianity as a philosophy, one that was not only on a par with the Greek systems but superior. He attempted to show that the Hebrew scriptures were older than the Greek writings and manifested the whole truth where the Greeks had only part. No other of the early Fathers of the Church was so thoroughly learned in Greek philosophy.

One of Clement's students was the still more distinguished Origen (Origenes). Origen, who was born about 185 in Alexandria, came of Christian parents and of a father who died a martyr. He himself lived a life devoted to religious study and even castrated himself in order that he might not be distracted by thoughts of women and marriage. The popularity of his teachings and his writings, together with the fact that he intermingled much of Platonic philosophy in his own beliefs, led to continuing troubles with his superiors.

Nevertheless he wrote voluminously and, in particular, he entered the lists against a Greek writer named Celsus, not the popular science writer of the first century A.D. (see page 93) but a Platonist philosopher who lived a century and a half later. Celsus had written a cool and unimpassioned book against Christianity which was only a minor cult at the time.

It was the first pagan book to treat Christianity seriously. Celsus' arguments were mostly rational ones such as those used by freethinkers today who object to such matters as the virgin birth, the resurrection, and the various miracles as being against reason. He also pointed out how Christian doctrine had been borrowed from Greek philosophy which had been distorted in the process.

The book was far too rational and considered to be much of a popular success and does not survive. It would not be heard of today at all, if it were not that Origen chose to write a book *Against Celsus* to refute it. In his book, Origen quotes about nine-tenths of Celsus' book, thus preserving it for posterity. Origen's work is the most complete and thorough defense of Christianity published in ancient times.

In the period after Marcus Aurelius, Church writers arose in the west, too, though these were farther removed from the Greek centers that served as the fertile soil of philosophy.

The first of these western writers was Tertullian (Quintus Septimius Florens Tertullianus) who was born about 150 in Carthage. He virtually created Christian Latin literature, though he could read and write Greek also. He was of pagan parents and had been intended for a legal career but in Rome, in early middle age, he was converted to Christianity. He returned to Carthage in 197 and remained there the rest of his life. His writings succeeded in reducing the popularity of the Gnostic view (see page 118), which faded rapidly away from this time on.

Tertullian was a Montanist (see page 119) and labored hard to convert Christians generally to the puritan life. In the end he was forced to break away from the Carthaginian Church he had served and to take up his labors in a small Montanist community nearby. He remained always influential, however, down to his death about 222.

Another important African writer was Cyprian. (Thascius Caecilius Cyprianus), born in Carthage about 200. He, too, was born of pagan parents and was converted in middle age. He eventually served as bishop of Carthage, and wrote with a style highly reminiscent of Tertullian. He died a martyr's death in 258.

The growing power of Christianity at this time was so pronounced that the mild Alexander Severus, who tried to placate all the peoples of the Empire by showing an interest in all the major religions, added a bust of Jesus Christ to those of other deities and prophets which ornamented his study.

Naturally, the pagan philosophers reacted to the increasing force of Christian thought. Stoicism, which had never impressed more than a thin layer of the ruling classes, lost its importance with the death of Marcus Aurelius. What succeeded was a new elaboration of the ideas of the Greek philosopher, Plato, made more elaborate and mystical. This Neo-Platonism was an attempt by the philosophers to find an adequate emotional basis for their beliefs without introducing the Christian ritual.

The most important of the Neo-Platonists was Plotinus, who was born in Egypt of Roman parents about 205. He was educated in Alexandria and reached Rome in 244, teaching his complicated and mystical philosophy till his death in 270.

Although Neo-Platonism did not succeed in establishing itself as the dominating philosophy of the Empire, many Neo-Platonic ideas filtered into the Christian church, particularly into that part of it which flourished in the eastern half of the Empire.

6

ANARCHY

THE PERSIANS AND THE GOTHS

Twice before in its history, Rome had seen the extinction of a line of Emperors followed by civil war. After the assassination of Nero in 68, there had been a mild civil war for a year. After the assassination of Commodus in 192, there had been a serious civil war for four years raging over a weaker Empire.

Now after the assassination of Alexander Severus in 235, Rome was still weaker and it was subjected to a series of civil wars and foreign invasions that lasted for fifty years and all but tore the Empire apart.

In that half-century some twenty-six men claimed the Imperial throne with at least some measure of acceptance, and any number of others made an unsuccessful try at it. All but one of these died a violent death.

The basic cause of the anarchy lay in the fact that the army ruled the state and that the army was no longer a unified force under even the vaguest of common ideals. It was increasingly drawn from the provinces and from the poorer classes and lived under conditions that completely alienated it from the civilians of the realm. What's more, an increasing number of soldiers were coming to be recruited from among the German barbarians north of the Roman frontier. They were good fighters who were eager to join for the money and the rise in the standard of living that Army service meant for them, whereas the Romans themselves were increasingly reluctant to serve.

Any legionary commander could use his soldiers as a tool to lift him to the Imperial throne, and though this throne became an invariable form of hard suicide, candidates were never wanting. Indeed, every man who succeeded in grasping the Imperial state labored to apply himself to the serious business at hand with an amazing earnestness considering the almost impossible difficulties that faced them.

The half-century of anarchy began when Maximinus (Gaius Julius Verus Maximinus), a giant Thracian peasant who had led the mutineers who assassinated Alexander Severus in Gaul had himself declared Emperor on the spot. He was the first Emperor who might be considered a soldier of the ranks and almost nothing more. His influence, however, did not extend past the armies he now endeavored to command.

Far to the south, an attempt was being made to imitate the successful choice of Nerva a century and a half before. An honorable and aged man, Gordian (Marcus Antonius Gordianus) was proclaimed Emperor.

Gordian had been born in 159 and claimed descent from Trajan. He had led a virtuous and industrious life, indeed, almost as though he were an Antonine. Under Alexander Severus he became governor of Africa and was still serving in that post when the local legions demanded that he become Emperor.

Gordian remembered not only the successful Nerva, but also the unsuccessful Pertinax (see page 000) and pointed out that he was nearly eighty years old and not fit to bear the burdens of rule. The soldiers threatened him with death if he did not take the throne and, sighing, he associated his son and namesake with himself. They were proclaimed and are known to us as Gordian I and Gordian II, respectively. (Gordian II was notable as a great patron of literature and had a library containing 62,000 volumes.)

Both were accepted by the Senate but ruled for scarcely more than a month. Gordian II died fighting against a soldierly faction in the opposition, and Gordian I, in an agony of grief, killed himself.

Meanwhile Maximinus had also met his death at the hands of his own troops, while the aspiring generals of the troops that brought about the deaths of the Gordians were in their turn killed by other soldiers.

The twelve-year-old grandson and namesake of Gordian I was in Rome and the Senate insisted on considering him as the new Emperor. He is Gordian III and began his reign in 238 (991 A.U.C.).

For a few years, this situation held, but if there was a momentary breathing space internally, the borders suddenly flared with invasion.

In 241, the second king of the Sassanid dynasty, Shapur I, mounted the Persian throne. Eager to prove a conqueror and anticipating no trouble with an empire that was killing its Emperors as fast as they could be enthroned, he invaded Syria and occupied Antioch, the capital of the province.

The young Emperor, Gordian III, was not himself a warrior, of course, but he was already married and his father-in-law, Gaius Furius Timesitheus, supplied the lack. Leading the Roman legions efficiently, he drove the Persians out of Syria. Unfortunately, Timesitheus died of disease in 243 and the army passed under the control of Marcus Julius Philippus, who had

young Gordian III killed and himself declared Emperor in 244
(997 A.U.C.)

Philippus was born in the Province of Arabia and is therefore
known to history as "Philip the Arabian." He bought a quick
and disgraceful peace with Persia, bribing them to stop the
fighting as he had to get back to Rome to confirm his rule.

That rule continued for five years and is remarkable chiefly
for the fact that it was in this reign that Rome passed a notable
milestone. In 248 (1000-1001 A.U.C.) Rome marked the completion of the thousandth year of its existence.

Augustus had begun the custom of holding special elaborate
"secular games" to mark the end of certain epochs of the city's
history. (The word "secular" is derived from a Latin word
meaning a cycle or age of the history of the world, so that the
term has also come to mean "worldly" as opposed to "religious.") It seemed most reasonable to hold these games at the
end of even centuries of the city's existence. Claudius celebrated the 800th year of the city and Antoninus Pius the 900th.
Now Philip the Arabian supervised the most elaborate secular
games yet in order to celebrate the 1000th. Not only was it the
most elaborate, it was also the last. The secular games were
never celebrated again.

The thousandth year brought Philip no luck. In every direction, troops were rebelling. Philip sent one of his supporters,
Decius, (Gaius Messius Quintus Trajanus Decius), to the Danube to quell a rebellion there. On the arrival, the soldiers
hailed Decius as Emperor. Decius didn't want the job and
would have gladly prevented the deed, but once he was acclaimed Emperor he had to move ahead and seize the position,
since execution was the only other alternative. He took over
the leadership of the rebellion, therefore, and led the troops
into Italy. Philip was killed in battle in northern Italy in 249
and Decius became Emperor in fact.

By this time, the growing numbers of Christians were disturbing the Roman government and populace. As misfortunes

gathered they proved a handy scapegoat (as in the fire under
Nero and in the plague under Marcus Aurelius.)

Maximinus, in reaction to the tolerant attitude of Alexander
Severus, the man he had killed, had instituted some measures of
persecution but he did not rule widely enough or long enough
to make much of this. Philip the Arabian, who is supposed to
have had a Christian wife, remained tolerant but under Decius
the storm broke.

The Imperial cult was made obligatory on all loyal subjects
in 250. It was only necessary to drop a pinch of incense and
mutter some meaningless formula of words. Failure to do so
meant one was liable to execution, for this was to the Romans
what a "loyalty oath" has been to some Americans in recent
times.

Many Christians chose martyrdom rather than accept the
taint of idolatry that accompanied the Imperial cult. Origen
was the most noted victim of the Decian persecution. He was
not actually killed but was so roughly handled that he did not
survive long. Cyprian of Carthage was actually killed and so
were the bishops of Rome, Antioch, and Jerusalem.

The Christians of the city of Rome were forced underground
about this time into the now-famous Catacombs, hidden bur-
rows and underground passageways that served as suburban
burial plots and were now used also as churches and secret
meeting-places for illegal worship.

In Decius' time, a new group of barbarians, the Goths, were
beginning to make themselves felt. They were Germanic people who, before the time of Christ, probably occupied sections
of what is now Sweden. (In fact, an island in the Baltic Sea
southeast of Sweden is called Gotland even today.)

About the time of Augustus, they seem to have moved southward to occupy the region that makes up modern Poland.
Gradually, over the succeeding centuries, they drifted southeastward until by the time of Caracalla, they had reached the
Black Sea. They then split into two groups. One dwelt to the

east, along the plains of what is now the Ukraine. These were the East Goths or Ostrogoths ("ost" is German for "east.") A second group remained in the west, pushing hard against the Roman province of Dacia. These were the West Goths or Visigoths ("visi-" possibly being derived from an old Teutonic word meaning "good" so that the name becomes a kind of self-praise, common among all peoples).

Caracalla fought off these Goths in 214, but their incursions grew more and more frequent as the legions in Dacia concentrated more and more on rebelling against Rome rather than on fighting off barbarians. Worse still, with increasing numbers of barbarians in the legions, the temptation grew for them to join in the raiding of Roman provinces. They could then share in the easy loot that followed, rather than risk their lives in an attempt to withstand men who were, after all, their own kin.

In Decius' time, the Goths flooded into Dacia, driving the Romans out of all but a few fortified posts. Then, having reached the Danube, they crossed it and began to visit death and destruction on provinces that had not felt the agony of barbarian raids in a hundred fifty years.

Decius fought against them and won some victories but in 251 (1004 A.U.C.) suffered a defeat and was killed. It was the first time an Emperor had been slain in battle against a foreign foe.

One of Decius' subordinates, Gallus (Gaius Vibius Tribonianus Gallus) was elected Emperor in his place and tried to carry on. He tried to buy off the Goths, for one thing, but although they accepted the money, they would, after a while, be unable to resist a renewal of the raids, penetrating even into Greece and Asia Minor. Athens itself was sacked in 267.

As the Gothic menace forced the legions to concentrate about the lower Danube, the guard along the upper Danube and the Rhine had to be weakened. Other German tribes took advantage of this. The Alamanni of southern Germany drove southward into northern Italy. A new union of west German tribes, calling themselves Franks ("free men") crossed the Rhine in 256, raiding the full width of Gaul and penetrating into Spain. A few contingents even reached Africa.

The despairing cities of the Empire, realizing that they were no longer to be guarded against destruction by an efficient government and a strong army, began to build walls and make ready to withstand sieges.

Gallus had meanwhile died in battle against a rebelling general and was succeeded in 253 by Valerian (Publius Licinius Valerianus), a subordinate of Gallus who had arrived too late to save him. Valerian made his son, Gallienus (Publius Licinius Gallienus), co-Emperor and together they tried to deal with the crisis.

It was a superhuman task. The northern border was in tatters and leaking everywhere. They managed to inflict a defeat on the Goths south of the Danube and to push the German tribes out of Gaul, but then the Marcomanni invaded Italy. As fast as the Emperors turned in one direction, invaders swarmed in from another. Gallienus had as a close friend the Neo-Platonist philosopher, Plotinus, but one can't help wondering whether any amount of philosophy could compensate the Emperor for the problems of the time.

And in all the confusion, Persia struck again. Shapur I was still king. Ten years before he had failed against young Gordian III and his warlike father-in-law, but ten years of disaster had passed for Rome. Now he would try again. Once more he invaded Syria and took Antioch.

Valerian hastened eastward to protect Syria. He managed to drive Persia out of Antioch but his army was weakened by disease. Valerian, only too aware of this, agreed to enter a peace parley with the Persians, who treacherously captured him in 259 (1012 A.U.C.). He was kept in captivity for the rest of his life, concerning which nothing further is known though rumors of ignominies heaped upon him were told and retold. Valerian was the first Emperor to be captured alive by a foreign enemy and this was a tremendous blow to Roman prestige.

Gallienus continued to reign after his father's capture, but to add to his difficulties with the barbarians, so many aspirants to the throne rose here and there that the period is known as the time of the "thirty tyrants" with reference to a well-known period of the same name in Athenian history. It was a slight exaggeration — there were only eighteen — but that was enough, too. Gallienus' temper remained mild under these provocations. Although his father, Valerian, had continued Decius' persecution of the Christians, Gallienus returned to a policy of toleration.

The year 260 was a low point for the Roman Empire. Almost, it seemed, the Empire was collapsing and disintegrating. One Emperor was a captive and the other was fighting perpetually and uselessly. The entire western third of the Empire — Gaul, Spain, and Britain — broke away and shifted loyalty to a competing general. Gallienus, fighting against this general, was wounded and his son killed. He had to abandon his effort to restore the west to its allegiance and the "Gallic Empire" remained in independent existence for fourteen years.

Meanwhile Shapur followed up his capture of Valerian by occupying Syria still again and by raiding deep into Asia Minor. That he was stopped at all was the result not so much of Roman efforts as of that of a desert kingdom which until now had made no mark in history.

In Syria, about 150 miles southeast of Antioch, there was a city which, according to Jewish tradition, had been founded by King Solomon and named Tadmar ("city of palms"). To the Greeks and Romans, this name became Palmyra. In the time of Vespasian it came under the control of Rome and by the time of the Antonines it had grown wealthy because it was a natural stopping place for the trade caravans that traveled across the desert regions. Hadrian visited it and when its inhabitants became Roman citizens under Caracalla they began to adopt Roman names.

Alexander Severus visited Palmyra during his eastern campaign and appointed a leading Palmyrene, Odenathus (Septimius Odeinath), a Senator. His son, of the same name, was similarly honored.

Odenathus, the son, was in control of Palmyra in the period after the capture of Valerian. He held the balance of power in the area and he chose to favor Rome since it was farther away and seemed, at the moment, to be in the process of dissolution, whereas Persia was close by and was united under a vigorous king. Palmyra's chance for independence would clearly be greater under a weak Rome than under a strong Persia.

Odenathus therefore undertook the war against Persia which Gallienus, busy in Europe, could not handle. He defeated Persian troops in a number of engagements and even forced the fight deep into Persian territory. Encouraged by success, he went so far as to race to Asia Minor to counter the invading Goths but they had left before he got there.

Gallienus, grateful for these services, made Odenathus a hereditary prince of Palmyra and deputy over the eastern provinces of the Empire which, but for him, might have been lost completely to the Persian foe.

But in 267, at the zenith of his fortune, Odenathus, together with his oldest son, was assassinated. His forceful wife, Septimia Zenobia, snatched up the reins he had let fall and Palmyrene success continued without letup.

When Gallienus was killed by his troops in 268, Zenobia reacted to that as though she not only considered herself to be the successor of her husband as ruler of the east but as successor (on behalf of her younger son) to the Imperial throne itself. She already controlled Syria and now she moved into Egypt and Asia Minor. In 271, she declared herself Empress and her son Emperor.

The Roman Empire had now broken into thirds. The west and east were both independent and the court in Italy con-

trolled only the central third — Italy itself, Illyria, Greece, and
Africa. Naturally, the economy was at a disastrous ebb, finances were in chaos, and the population was declining faster than
ever. A generation of steady disaster had ruined the Empire
and nowhere did there seem to be any sign of rescue.

RECOVERY

But now there appeared the first of a line of remarkable Emperors from Illyria who snatched the Empire from the jaws of
destruction.

In 268, after the death of Gallienus, the troops acclaimed a
new Emperor, Marcus Aurelius Claudius, usually known as
Claudius II. Of obscure Illyrian birth, he had served well under Decius, Valerian, and Gallienus and now as Emperor, it
was his turn to fight the barbarians.

Results were excellent. He defeated the Alemanni in northern Italy and drove them back across the Alps. He then traveled to Moesia where he faced renewed incursions of the Goths.
In 269 and 270, he won tremendous victories over them and was
therefore acclaimed as Claudius Gothicus (a name honoring
a conquest, as in the great days of the Republic).

He was the one Emperor of this period of anarchy that did
not die by violence. He died of sickness in 270 (1023 A.U.C.)
like any ordinary Roman. But before he died, he performed a
last service for the Empire by nominating a worthy successor,
his cavalry commander and fellow-Illyrian, Aurelian (Lucius
Domitius Aurelianus).

Aurelian found all Claudius' work undone by his death, for
the barbarians, although defeated, assumed that with a new

Emperor there was a new chance. They raided southward again, and Aurelian had to defeat the Goths and Alemanni a second time in order to show them that this time one able Emperor had been succeeded by another.

With the northern boundaries secure in at least a rickety fashion, Aurelian's eyes turned to the East, where Zenobia ruled in splendor. He fully realized that a trip to the East might mean fresh raids from the north and, in 271, he took the desperate measure of beinning the construction of a fortified wall about Rome — a city that had had no use for walls for five centuries. How clearly this showed the extent of the decline that had fallen upon the Empire!

Aurelian further pulled in all the Roman colonists in Dacia, settling them south of the Danube. It had become useless to try to protect that exposed province against the Goths. The cost of such protection was prohibitive and the results disheartening. Thus Dacia was abandoned over a century and a half after its conquest by Trajan.

Now Aurelian felt it safe to turn eastward. He entered Asia Minor, reducing all cities that tried to resist. He invaded Syria, defeated the Palmyrenes near Antioch and finally took Palmyra itself. He tried to impose mild terms at first but when the Palmyrenes revolted and killed the Roman garrison he had left behind, he returned and leveled the city to the ground in 273. Palmyra's prosperity was permanently destroyed and nothing but ruins and a few wretched hovels mark it today.

Aurelian next moved west and found Gaul easy. The Gallic "Emperor" was old and was having troubles of his own with the barbarians. With the conquering Aurelian on his way there was no point in fighting a hopeless battle. The Gallic "Emperor" surrendered at once and the west was reunited to Rome in 274 (1027 A.U.C.).

Aurelian returned to Rome and before 274 was done celebrated a magnificent triumph at which Zenobia was led in chains. He was hailed as "Restorer of the world" and this motto ("Restitutor Orbis") appeared on the coins minted in this year. Nor was it an idle phrase, for Aurelian and his predecessor Claudius II had driven back the barbarians and had recovered both East and West.

What remained for the tireless Emperor now was to teach the Persians a lesson. He headed eastward with that purpose in mind, but the habits of decades could not be shaken. Soldiers rebelled lightly to kill worthless Emperors; they rebelled just as lightly to kill a hard-fighting one. Aurelian was murdered in Thrace in 275 by his soldiers.

Marcus Claudius Tacitus, who succeeded Aurelian, was a surprising throwback to an earlier state of affairs. He was a wealthy, old Italian nobleman who was appointed (against his will) by the Senate, of all things. With unexpected vigor, Tacitus (who claimed descent from the historian, see page 88) tried to be another Nerva. He tried to restore some power to the Senate and to institute some reforms. However, no Emperor in those days could do much of anything except fight the German tribes and old Tacitus was no exception. The Goths were invading Asia Minor again and the army had to be led against them. The Goths were defeated, but Tacitus died in 276, after a half-year reign. The usual story is told — he was killed by his soldiers — but he was an old man and it is possible he died a natural death.

The general in charge of the legions in the East, under Tacitus, was Marcus Aurelius Probus, who had been born in Pannonia, the province north of Illyria, and who had fought well under Aurelian. As soon as the throne was vacant the soldiers declared him Emperor and he continued mopping up the Goths in Asia Minor.

Once the East could breath peacefully again, however, he made a mistake. It seemed to him that the men who were willing to risk death against the Goths should be willing to sweat a bit in the labors of peace. The canals in Egypt needed clearing out if the grain supply of the Empire was to be kept adequate and certainly famine was as dangerous an enemy as the barbarians. So Probus set the soldiers to work clearing the canals, and, in resentment, they killed him in 281.

It was the turn of another Illyrian now (the third), Marcus Aurelius Carus who, like Probus, had fought under Aurelian. He was the first Emperor to feel it completely unnecessary to get the Senate to approve his election and confer on him the various rights associated with the Imperial position. To be sure, such Senatorial approval had long been a pure formality and had frequently been forced out of a most unwilling Senate. Nevertheless, all Emperors had, till then, gone through the motions, however meaningless those motions had been. The fact that Carus felt no need to do so showed how far Senatorial prestige had fallen and close to extinction the conventions of the Augustan Principate had come.

Carus punished the assassins of his predecessor but made no attempt to continue the effort for peace and good works. If it was war the soldiers wanted, he would give it to them. He left his son in charge of the home front and led the army into Persia in 282, taking up the task of Aurelian, which had been left hanging since the latter's death seven years before.

In Persia, Carus was surprisingly successful. Like Trajan, he cleared Armenia and Mesopotamia of the enemy, and pressed on to Ctesiphon. But then, in 283, he, too, was killed by the soldiers who apparently didn't want *that* much war.

Apparently nothing could stop the dreary round. Whether Emperors were old or young, warlike or not, victorious or not, all were regularly slaughtered by their men. For fifty years this had been going on and nothing had come along to stop it.

What was needed was a man forceful enough and creative enough to work out some new system to match the new times. The Principate had finally petered out and another Augustus was required, to put an end to another siege of civil wars, and fashion, once again, a new form of government.

As it happened, another Augustus was at hand in the form of a fourth Illyrian Emperor.

7

DIOCLETIAN

THE END OF THE PRINCIPATE

The man of the hour was Diocles. He came of a poor peasant family and obtained his Greek-sounding name, apparently, from the fact that he was born (in 245) in Dioclea, a village on the Illyrian coast. He did well in the army, serving under Aurelian and Probus. At the time of the death of Carus, he was nearly forty and had risen from the status of an ordinary soldier to that of commander of the imperial bodyguard.

Diocles was acclaimed Emperor by his men at Carus's death and, like Carus, he felt no need to seek Senatorial approval.

His first action was to hold a drumhead court-martial of the general supposed to have masterminded the killing of Carus and then executed him with his own hands. This made it clear where he stood on the subject of killing Emperors — especially now that he was one himself. The average length of the reign of the Emperors over the past half-century (leaving out of account co-emperors, usurpers, and unsuccessful claimants) had been about two years and Diocles was fiercely determined to do better than that.

On gaining the throne, Diocles assumed the royal name of Gaius Aurelius Valerius Diocletianus (he is best known, in English, as Diocletian) and entered the city of Nicomedia in northwestern Asia Minor in 284 (1037 A.U.C.). As often as possible, Diocletian made this city his residence so that it became, in effect, the capital of the Empire during his reign.

This was recognition of an important fact. Italy was no longer the ruling province of the Empire and Rome was no longer the ruling city. In fact, for an Emperor to sit in Rome as in the old days of Augustus or even of Antoninus Pius would have been imprudent. The business of the Emperor was the defense of the Empire and he had to remain within reach of the exposed outer provinces. From Nicomedia, Diocletian was within reasonable marching distance of the Persian frontier to the southeast and the Gothic hordes to the northwest and it was at Nicomedia that he stayed, when not engaged in actual warfare.

Throughout his reign, Diocletian was engaged in the initiation of a top-to-bottom reorganization of the Empire.

His first concern was the protection of the person of the Emperor. It was all very well for Augustus to have played the role of "First Citizen" and to act as though he were simply an ordinary Roman who happened to head the state. He lived in peaceful times and in the midst of a quiet and disarmed Italy. Now, however, Emperors lived in the midst of armies in a disintegrating Empire; fighting barbarians with soldiers who were themselves very often hired barbarians. To walk among the soldiers as merely another Roman was to invite a spear in the belly. Two dozen Emperors had demonstrated this in the previous half-century.

Diocletian therefore withdrew. He made himself more than

a princeps ("first citizen"); he made himself a "dominus" ("lord"). He introduced all the ceremonial of an Eastern monarchy. Men could only approach when invited and then only with deep bows. A variety of rituals were adopted to render unusual and awe-inspiring the position and person of the Emperor and to mark it and him off from the ordinary. This sort of ceremonial had been slowly appearing in previous reigns, notably under Aurelian, but now Diocletian intensified it greatly.

This marks the final end of the principate after it had endured for three centuries. Although Diocletian never called himself king, he was one in fact and the Roman Empire had become a monarchy. The Senate still met in Rome but it had become nothing more than a social club.

Diocletian's system suited his times as Augustus' had suited his. An unapproachable Emperor, about whom a sacred reverence hovered, and whose measured steps were accompanied by incense, trumpets, and the bowing of hordes of flunkies, impressed and overawed the soldiers. Such Emperors were difficult to kill, for a soldier's own superstitions would hold him back. It was for that reason, at least in part, that Diocletian managed to reign for twenty-one years — the longest reign of any Emperor since Antoninus Pius a century and a half before.

What's more, although there were problems enough and disorders enough in the times after Diocletian, the business of Emperor after Emperor being killed by his own troops, in rapid succession and at any trifling whim, ended. The Empire was put back on its feet.

It was back on its feet in rather shaky fashion, however. The Empire was not what it had once been by any means. The destruction of the plague and the devastation of barbarian invasions could not be made up. In fact, Diocletian's stronger effort to counter foreign attack made matters worse in some ways. Diocletian had to maintain an army that was greater in numbers than Augustus' army and do so in a realm that could afford it less.

Diocletian and his successors had to keep the army supplied through heavy taxation. Decent money had vanished over the past century, as the quality of coinage sank, and taxes were collected in goods. The municipal leaders were made responsible for the collection in their areas and had to make up any deficit. They ground down hard on the people and were themselves ground down in turn by government officials. The economic life of the Empire stiffened. Small farmers could not make a living and drifted to the large estates as serfs. Artisans and tradesmen were not allowed to try to search for better ways of making money but were forced by law, and under the threat of severe punishment, to remain in their professions and remain at their labors which were necessary to the economy but which brought them nothing more than a minimal return after taxes. They were not even allowed to enter the army which made up its numbers more and more through the hiring of barbarian bands.

Toward the end of his reign, Diocletian recognized the unbearable difficulties under which the general population was being crushed. In a famous "Edict of Diocletian" in 301 (1054 A.U.C.) he attempted to stabilize matters by setting up a list of maximum prices and maximum wages. This was intended to prevent the large landowners from profiteering at the cost of many human lives in times of food shortages, and to prevent labor from profiteering in times of manpower shortage. Although Diocletian was in earnest and decreed deportation and, under some circumstances, even the death penalty for any refusal to abide by the edict, the effort was a failure. Nothing could stop the slow economic deterioration of the realm.

To the general population of the Empire, there seemed little benefit to be derived from the government. What did it matter whether barbarians or Romans won a battle? Both armies were

barbarian; both were ruthless in their pillaging of the area
they occupied, since both tended more and more to live off the
land. And the devastations of either army were scarcely worse
than that of the tax-collector.

No wonder the Roman populace grew apathetic and could
find little cause for patriotism or for identification with the
realm. If the Roman army were to fall before the barbarians
and if the German hordes were to take over, there was not
likely to be any resistance from the population itself; no guer-
rilla warfare; no people's uprisings. — And when the time
came, there weren't.

Nevertheless, whatever the sufferings of the Empire, Diocletian favored it with two blessings; an army that was once again
reliable and a government that, however harsh, was stable.
Undoubtedly, the Roman Empire lasted longer as a result of
Diocletian's work than it would have if matters had continued
as they had been going before.

THE TETRARCHY

Diocletian's drive toward stabilization was made the easier
by his realization that he could not accomplish the task all by
himself. The problems were too many, the Empire too damaged, the borders leaking at too many places, for one man to
do it all. Consequently, Diocletian determined to take a part-
ner.

This had been done before. Marcus Aurelius had ruled together with Lucius Verus as co-Emperor and the Empire had
been under double rule ("diarchy") for eight years. Since
then, several of the short-reign Emperors had associated sons
or other relatives with themselves.

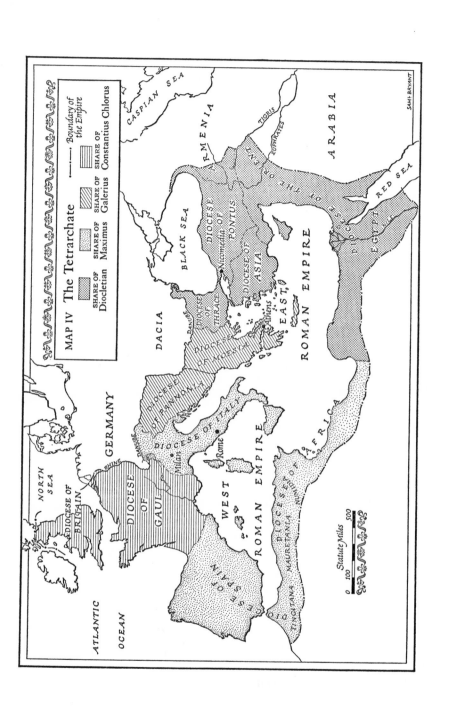

MAP IV The Tetrarchate

SHARE OF Diocletian Maximus

SHARE OF Diocletian

SHARE OF Galerius

SHARE OF Constantius Chlorus

······ Boundary of the Empire

SAM: BRYANT

NORTH SEA

ATLANTIC OCEAN

DIOCESE OF BRITAIN

GERMANY

RHINE

DIOCESE OF GAUL

DANUBE

DIOCESE OF SPAIN

DIOCESE OF ITALY

Milan

Rome

WEST ROMAN EMPIRE

DIOCESE OF AFRICA

DIOCESE OF NUMIDIA

DIOCESE OF MAURETANIA

TINGITANA

DIOCESE OF PANNONIA

DANUBE

DACIA

DIOCESE OF MOESIA

DIOCESE OF THRACE

BLACK SEA

Athens

Nicomedia

DIOCESE OF PONTUS

DIOCESE OF ASIA

EAST, ROMAN EMPIRE

ARMENIA

CASPIAN SEA

TIGRIS

EUPHRATES

DIOCESE OF THE ORIENT

ARABIA

RED SEA

EGYPT

Statute Miles

0 100 500

Such divisions had always been spur-of-the-moment matters and had never been official policy. Now Diocletian tried to make it official. In 286 (1039 A.U.C.) he appointed an old friend, Maximian (Marcus Aurelius Valerius Maximianus) as his colleague. Maximian, a Pannonian, was about Diocletian's age and, like him, was of peasant birth. Like Diocletian, he had risen from the ranks to become a general; but unlike Diocletian he was not particularly bright. Diocletian saw in Maximian someone who could be relied on to take all effective military action and to follow orders without question, but someone who would have neither the nerve nor the ability to turn on his master.

Diocletian took for himself the eastern half of the Empire and left Maximian the western half, with the north-south boundary between the two passing through the narrow strait separating the Italian heel from northern Greece. This division persisted, at intervals, through succeeding reigns so that from 286 on, we can speak of a "West Roman Empire" and an "East Roman Empire." This is not by any means an indication that the Roman Empire had been split into two nations. In theory, it remained an indivisible empire down to its very end in history. The division was purely administrative.

It might seem that Maximian got the better of the deal since the West Roman Empire was larger than the East Roman Empire. Furthermore, the West Roman Empire was of Latin speech and contained Italy and Rome. This, however, was of little moment.

The East Roman Empire was the smaller and it was Greek-speaking and farther removed from the old Roman tradition. Nevertheless, the east was the richer. Nor did Rome have anything but sentimental significance, and Nicomedia was the center of government, not Rome. Even Maximian, who took up his post in the west, did not make Rome his capital. He remained in Mediolanum (the modern Milan), for the most part, since this was a post better suited for guarding against barbarian incursions across the Rhine and the upper Danube. (Nevertheless, certain traditional rights remained to Rome. There were still free food and free games for the populace as a token of the past, and of the fact that Rome had once conquered the world.)

Furthermore the western half of the Empire was no sinecure at this time. Maximian had plenty of internal troubles to deal with. The peasants in Gaul revolted and hordes of them roamed about aimlessly, burning and destroying in a kind of furious desperation at finding themselves part of a society which pillaged them ruthlessly and gave nothing in return.

It did the peasants no good, except for whatever momentary pleasure they could get in seizing the possessions of the wealthy. Maximian fought a regular war with them, facing their barely-armed mobs with his barbarian-laced legions, and slaughtering them till the survivors were cowed into submission.

And while Maximian was pounding the Gallic peasants with one hand, he was trying to save Britain with the other. German barbarians had been taking to the sea and had been raiding the island. Maximian was therefore forced to arrange for the building of a fleet. The thought was fine but the plan backfired. The admiral placed in charge of the fleet came to an arrangement with the barbarians and set himself up as Emperor in Britain. Using the fleet (which was now his) he enforced recognition of himself as master all along the Atlantic shores of the Empire. Maximian was given full Imperial powers and made a complete equal of Diocletian so that he could war against the rebel freely without having to consult Diocletian at every step. Even so, Maximian was out of luck. He built a fleet of his own but lost it in a storm and for the moment, though he might grind his teeth, he could do little more.

It seemed to Diocletian that even two rulers were not sufficient, so in 293 (1046 A.U.C.) he doubled the number. He and Maximian, each with the title of Augustus, each adopted a successor, with the title of Caesar. This would give both Dio-

cletian and Maximian a much-needed assistant and, in addition, would solve the problem of the succession since, in theory,
the Caesars would move up to become Augusti eventually and
be all the better-equipped for top post in view of the experience
they would have gained on the second rung.

For his Caesar, Diocletian chose Galerius (Gaius Galerius
Valerius Maximianus) who married the Emperor's daughter
and thus became his son-in-law as well as his chosen successor.
Galerius, now in his early forties, had a good record as a soldier
and was placed in primary charge of the European provinces
south of the Danube, including Thrace, his own birth province.
Diocletian reserved Asia and Egypt for himself.

Maximian gave his daughter to the man he chose for Caesar.
This was Flavius Valerius Constantius, usually known to us as
Constantius Chlorus (that is "Constantius the Pale," presumably from his fair complexion). He might also be called Constantius I, to distinguish him from a grandson who was to rule
a half-century later as Constantius II.

Constantius was another Illyrian and had been ruling over
his home province before the time of his elevation, not only with
efficiency but with gentleness and humanity as well (qual-
ities rather unusual for the time.) Constantius was given Spain,
Gaul, and Britain as his primary area of interest while Maximian reserved Italy and Africa for himself.

This four-fold division (a "tetrarchy") turned the tide. Constantius found himself face to face with the rebel armies in Britain and Gaul. He secured the Rhine frontier then turned his
concentrated attention on Britain. Building still another fleet,
he used it to land an army in the island. By 300, Imperial authority was restored there and Constantius made Britain his
favorite seat of government, giving it a mild and equitable
rule.

In the East meanwhile, Diocletian marched into Egypt to
suppress the revolt of a general while instructing Galerius to
take care of Persia. Both missions were concluded successfully,

and by 300, there was peace from one end of the Empire to the other, and all the borders were, for a miracle, intact.

In 303 (1056 A.U.C.) Diocletian traveled to Rome so that he and Maximian might be honored with a triumph. It was not, however, a happy occasion. Diocletian didn't like Rome, and Rome returned the compliment. Diocletian ordered baths built in his name in Rome, as well as a library, a museum and other establishments, but this was poor comfort to the Romans. They were sullen at the sight of a Roman Emperor who left the ancient capital untenanted and they made him the object of their jibes and sarcasms. Diocletian therefore left Rome abruptly after having been there but a month. — The world had indeed changed.

In sixteen years, then, Diocletian had performed what must have looked like a superhuman feat. Not only was he still Emperor, but he dominated three other Emperors or near-Emperors.

His internal reorganization was taking hold, too. The Empire consisted now of four "prefectures," so called because they were headed by "prefects" (from a Latin word meaning "to set over"). They were 1) the European provinces northwest of Italy; 2) Italy and Africa west of Egypt, 3) the European provinces east of Italy, and 4) Asia and Egypt.

Each of these was under one of the Caesars or Augusti. Each prefecture was divided in turn into several dioceses (from a Latin word for "housekeeping" which was something a governor was expected to do well, so to speak). The governor of a diocese was a "vicar" (that is, an "underling" of the prefect — we have the same word in an expression such as "vice-president"). Each diocese was divided into provinces and, in the end, there were well over a hundred provinces in the Empire. Each province was small enough for a governor to handle comfortably and all the strings of command went straight up to the Emperor, who made use of an elaborate secret service to keep personal tabs on the various officials.

The organization of the military was made completely independent of the civilian government, but went along parallel lines. Each province had its own garrison in charge of a "dux" (or "leader"). Some army leaders were called "comes" (meaning "companion" — of the Emperor, that is).

The reorganization put through by Diocletian and his successors was cumbersome and rigid and the presence of four Imperial courts and all the officials necessary to keep the four well-coordinated was extremely expensive. Still it held the Empire together for nearly two more centuries and parts of it maintained a continuous tradition for over a thousand years.

Even after the Empire had ceased to exist, the new kingdoms that replaced it kept parts of the traditional organization, and some of the titles have remained to the present day. What the Romans had called "dux" and "comes" became what we call "duke" and "count." What's more, the Imperial organization as it existed under Diocletian and his successors was paralleled by the growing organization of the Christian Church. The Catholic Church, to this day, calls the area under the jurisdiction of a bishop, a "diocese;" and it has vicars, too.

THE BISHOPS

But Diocletian's new system was not the only important power in the Empire. The disorders of the previous generations had led to a vast increase in the strength of Christianity despite the persecutions under Decius and Valerius. Now, in

Diocletian's time, about ten per cent of the population of the Empire was Christian. What's more, it was an important ten per cent for the Christians were well organized and tended to be fervent in their beliefs, while the pagan majority tended to be lukewarm or even indifferent.

The causes for Christian growth were several. For one thing, the imminent disintegration of the Empire made it seem the more likely that the things of the world were indeed coming to an end and that the predicted second coming of Christ was soon to take place. That increased the fervor of those already Christians and convinced those who were hesitating. Then, too, the decay of society and the increasing hardships suffered by men made this world less alluring and the promise of the next world more desirable. That made Christianity the more attractive to many who found the next world it described more convincing than those offered by the various non-Christian mysteries. And again, the Church, which was strengthening its organization and efficiency as the Empire was losing its own, seemed increasingly to be a rock of security in a troubled, miserable world.

On the other hand, the Church, as it grew in numbers, found itself immersed in problems. It was no longer a handful of visionaries, on fire with a zeal for martyrdom. Men and women of all classes and conditions were now Christians, many of them quite ordinary people wishing to lead ordinary lives. Christianity therefore became increasingly sedate and even "respectable."

The pressure on the part of the Christian rank-and-file was always in the direction of greater ceremony and of a multiplication of objects to venerate. A cold, spare, absolute monotheism lacks drama. Drama was therefore supplied by increasing emphasis on the feminine principle in the form of Jesus' mother, Mary, and by the further addition of numerous saints and martyrs. The rites in their honor, often adapted from various pagan rituals, grew more elaborate, and that, too, helped the cause of Christian growth; for as the superficial differences between the rituals of paganism and Christianity decreased, it became easier for people to slip across from the former to the latter.

Yet as the fashion of worship grew more complex and the number of worshippers greater, it became easier for differences in detail to develop. Various differences in ritual could spring up and slowly become more pronounced from province to province and from church to church. Even within a church there might be those who favored one point of view or one sort of behavior over another.

The variations might seem, to those not immersed in the matter, to be minor and unimportant and scarcely worth more than a shrug. However, to those who believed that every item of creed and ritual was part of a chain that led to Heaven, and that any deviation from it meant the doom of Hell, such variations could not possibly be minor. They were not only life-or-death; they were eternal-life-or-eternal-death.

Such variations in ritual, therefore, could lead to a kind of civil war within the Church, reduce it to torn fragments and in the end destroy it. That this did not happen in the long run was due to the fact that the Church gradually built up a complex hierarchy that decided on matters of belief and ritual authoritatively from above.

Thus, the churches and priesthood of a particular region would be placed under a bishop (from the Greek "episcopus" meaning "overseer") who had the authority to decide on disputed points of religion.

But what if the bishop of one area disagreed with the bishop of another? They could, of course, and frequently did, but toward the end of the third century, the custom had grown up of holding "synods" (from a Greek word meaning "meeting") at which the bishops met and thrashed out disputed points. The feeling grew that the agreements reached at such synods ought to hold for all bishops, so that all Christianity would hold a single set of views and follow a single pattern of ritual. There was just one Church, by this line of thought, one Universal Church or, from a Greek term for "universal," one Catholic Church.

The decisions beaten out by the bishops, then, were the orthodox views of the Catholic Church and all else was heresy.

In principle, all the bishops were equal, but this was not so in actual practice. The large centers of population had the largest numbers of Christians and the most influential churches. Those churches attracted the most capable men and it is only to be expected that the bishops of cities such as Antioch and Alexandria would be great men, immersed in literature and learning, writing powerful tomes of their own and leading strong factions among the bishops.

Indeed, there were several important cities in the Eastern half of the Empire, whose bishops were often at odds with each other. The Western half of the Empire, in which Christians were generally less numerous and less powerful had only one important bishop before the time of Diocletian; the bishop of Rome itself.

In general, the west was less literate than the east, had a weaker tradition of philosophy and hair-splitting and was far less involved in the great religious disputes of the time. None of the early bishops of Rome were noted authors or great disputants. They were moderate men who in all the questions of the time never took up lost causes or minority views. This meant that the bishopric of Rome was the only great bishopric that was never tainted by heresy. It was orthodox from beginning to end.

About Rome, furthermore, there clung the odor of world power. Whether Rome was actually the center of government or not, it was Rome that ruled the world in the minds of men, and the bishop of Rome seemed to many to be the Churchly equivalent of the Roman Emperor. This was all the more true since the tradition was strong that the first bishop of Rome had been Peter himself, the first of the disciples of Jesus.

Therefore, although the bishop of Rome did not, in the first few centuries, particularly shine, compared to others in Alexandria and Antioch and even in such cities as Carthage, the future (at least to large portions of the Christian world) was to be entirely his.

Diocletian, then, as he looked about his Empire found that his authority was challenged and rivaled by another authority, that of the Church. This bothered him and, according to some stories, it bothered his Caesar and successor, Galerius, even more.

In 303, at the insistence of Galerius, Diocletian began an intense campaign against all Christians — more against the organization of the Church (which was what Diocletian really dreaded) than against the individual believers themselves. Churches were pulled down, crosses broken up, sacred books forced out of the keeping of the bishops and then burned. On occasion, when pagan mobs went out of control, Christians were killed. Naturally, Christians were fired from all offices, forced out of the army, turned away from the courts and, in general, harassed in every way.

It was the last and fiercest organized physical persecution of Christians in the Empire, but it was not Empire-wide. Constantius Chlorus, the mildest of the four rulers of the Empire, quietly allowed his section of the realm to be free of the persecution even though he was not a Christian himself, but a worshipper of the Sun-god.

Diocletian's action in initiating the persecution was the last important act of his reign. He had grown heartily sick of ruling the Empire. The disappointing trip to Rome soured and depressed him and shortly after returning to Nicomedia, he fell ill. He was approaching the age of sixty, he had been Emperor for twenty years, and he had had enough. Galerius, who was in line for the throne, was perfectly willing, even eager, for Diocletian to step out and he urged the Emperor to abdicate. In 305 (1058 A.U.C.) Diocletian did so. It is most unusual in the history of the world for any ruler to abdicate of his own accord simply because he is old and tired, but it does happen sometimes. Diocletian is an example.

The former Emperor retired to the city of Salona near the village where he had been born, and there built a large palace in which he spent the last eight years of his life. (The palace eventually fell into ruins but when the city of Salona was destroyed by barbarian invasions three centuries after Diocletian's time, some of its people moved into the ruins of the palace and, built homes there. Around these beginnings the city of Spalatum was built up. This came to be known as Spalato to the Italians and Split to the Yugoslavians.)

8

THE LINE OF CONSTANTIUS

CONSTANTINE I

Diocletian had definite ideas as to how the tetrarchy was to work. When he abdicated, he forced his fellow-Augustus, Maximian, to abdicate, too, so that both Caesars, Galerius and Constantius, would move up simultaneously. The next step was to appoint two new Caesars.

Ideally, two good, experienced soldiers, firm, capable, and loyal, should be appointed. Then, someday, they would succeed Galerius and Constantius and appoint good Caesars of their own. If Diocletian's plan could only be worked out there would never be any dispute over the succession and there would only be capable Emperors, one after another.

Unfortunately, human beings remain human beings. The two Augusti are bound to disagree over the selection of the

Caesars and they are bound to consider their relatives before strangers of possibly greater worth.

In this particular case, it was Galerius who succeeded Diocletian directly and who ruled over the Eastern Roman Empire. He could not help consider himself as Emperor-in-chief, as Diocletian had been. Galerius therefore immediately named two Caesars, one for himself and one for Constantius; nor did he bother to consult Constantius in the matter. (Galerius probably disliked Constantius for being "soft on Christianity" which the latter undoubtedly was. Galerius saw to it that persecution of the Christians continued in his half of the Empire all through his reign.)

For himself, Galerius selected one of his nephews, Maximin Daia, as his Caesar and successor, while for Constantius he appointed one of his own men, Severus (Flavius Valerius Severus).

Left in the cold was Maxentius (Marcus Aurelius Valerius Maxentius) the son of the old co-Emperor, Maximian. Maxentius, most indignant at being passed over and feeling he had a hereditary right to his father's crown, had himself proclaimed Emperor in Rome and called back his father to rule again. (Old Maximian, who enjoyed being Emperor, and bitterly resented his enforced abdication, was delighted to come back to the throne.)

Galerius was anything but delighted, however. He sent Severus into Italy with an army, but Severus was defeated and killed and Maxentius remained in control of Italy.

Nor was Constantius pleased by the new arrangement. He, too, had a son for whom no provision had been made. Constantius would undoubtedly have taken action similar to that of Maxentius, but he was busy in a campaign against the northern tribes in Britain. Then, before that was done, he died in 306 at Eboracum where, a century before, Septimius Severus had died.

Before he died, however, Constantius recommended his son

Constantine (Gaius Flavius Valerius Aurelius Claudius Constantinus) to his troops, and the young man, who was only eighteen at the time, was promptly declared Emperor. As Emperor, he may be called Constantine I, for there were to be many Constantines after him.

Constantine had been born about 288, while his father was governing Illyria. His town of birth was Naissus, the modern Nish, in Yugoslavia, so he was another of the great Illyrians. He was of illegitimate birth apparently, his mother being a poor innkeeper who had caught Constantius' fancy. (Because Constantius spent so much of his later life in Britain, the myth arose — carefully fostered by early English historians — that Constantine's mother was a British princess, but this is certainly not so.)

Constantine spent his youth at the court of Diocletian, for the prudent Emperor kept him as a kind of hostage for the good behavior of his father. When Diocletian abdicated, Constantine stayed on under Galerius, although with a certain amount of suspicion on both sides. While Constantius was alive, Galerius would not harm the boy and bring about civil war. When the news reached Constantine, however, that his father was dying, he realized that to Galerius he would be worth far more dead than alive.

Constantine therefore slipped away and raced across the breadth of Europe, evading the pursuit of the Emperor's agents, and reaching Britain just in time to see his father before his death and to be acclaimed as Emperor immediately afterward. (According to another and less dramatic version, Constantius demanded his son immediately after Diocletian's abdication and Galerius, with some reluctance, sent the young man on his way.)

Constantine strengthened himself against Galerius' hostility by seeking allies. In 307, he married the daughter of Maximian, the old Emperor, and the latter promptly recognized his new son-in-law as co-Emperor. Galerius now faced three menaces in the west: Maximian, his son Maxentius, and his son-in-law Constantine. He tried striking into Italy but he was defeated and driven out.

Galerius then called upon the retired Diocletian in 310 and asked him to make some arrangement. Diocletian, for one last moment, took on the cares of the Empire. He declared Maximian out of office, and appointed Licinius (Valerius Licinianus Licinius) as Emperor in the west. Constantine was kept quiet by having his co-Emperorship recognized.

Maximian naturally objected to being forced out of office a second time and tried to carry on against the others. He was promptly defeated by Constantine who had the position he wanted without Maximian, needed the old man no further, and therefore had no compunction about having his father-in-law executed.

Galerius died in 311 (1064 A.U.C.) and was succeeded by Maximin Daia, his Caesar. Maximin Daia continued the persecution of the Christians and tried to strengthen himself by coming to an agreement with Maxentius, who still ruled in Italy.

In this way, the lines were drawn up for a new civil war. Maxentius in Italy and Maximin Daia in Asia Minor stood against Constantine in Gaul and Licinius in the Danubian provinces.

Constantine invaded Italy in 312. It was the third time an army had marched into Italy to fight Maxentius but, unlike the first two armies, that of Constantine was not quickly defeated and thrown out. Constantine defeated Maxentius' forces in the Po Valley and then marched on Rome itself. Maxentius was ready for him and the two armies met near a bridge over the Tiber (the Milvian Bridge). Constantine aimed to cross it and Maxentius intended to keep him from doing so.

Before the battle, Constantine (according to later Christian historians) saw a glowing cross in the heavens and, under it, letters saying "in hoc signo vinces" ("with this sign, conquer"). This is supposed to have encouraged Constantine, who ordered a Christian insignia to be placed on the soldiers' shields, then pushed confidently into the battle. Maxentius' forces were thoroughly defeated and Maxentius himself was killed. Constantine was left master of the west and was declared Emperor by the Senate. He proceeded to disband the praetorian guard once and for all and thus this troublesome band which, in its time, had made and unmade Emperors, came to its end.

The sign of the cross that Constantine had seen in the heavens was supposed to have led him to conversion to Christianity, but that is not so. Constantine, throughout his life, showed himself to be a practical politician and what really happened, most likely, is that he was the first Emperor to come to the conclusion that the future lay with Christianity. He decided that there was no point in persecuting the side that was sure to win. It was better to join them — and he did. But he did not officially become a Christian until late in life when he was sure it was safe to do so. (After all, the Christians of the Empire remained in a minority to the very end of his reign.)

Constantine carefully continued to pay honor to his father's sun-god and did not actually allow himself to be baptized until he was on his death-bed so that his sins might be washed away at a time when he would be in no position to commit more.

But if Constantine did not himself become a Christian at the time of the battle of the Milvian Bridge, he began to take steps to make the Empire Christian, or at least to ensure the loyalty of the Christian portion to himself.

Licinius had beaten Maximin Daia in the East and the two victors met in a kind of summit conference in Milan in 313 (1066 A.U.C.). There, Constantine and Licinius agreed to the "Edict of Milan" which guaranteed religious toleration throughout the Empire. Christians might worship freely and for the first time Christianity was officially a legal religion in the Empire.

In that same year, Diocletian died. Since his abdication he had seen his attempt at arranging an automatic succession degenerate into civil war, and he had seen his attempt to wipe out Christianity fail completely. Very likely, he didn't care. In his isolated palace, he undoubtedly passed the happiest years of his life.

Indeed, when Maximian had written to Diocletian some years before, suggesting they take back the Empire and rule again, Diocletian is reported to have replied, "Were you but to come to Salona and see the vegetables which I raise in my garden with my own hands, you would no longer talk to me of empire."

The foolish Maximian went his own way to a violent death, but Diocletian died in peace and content, a wise man to the end.

THE COUNCIL OF NICAEA

The burden of the Empire was now Constantine's. Licinius shared it with him but with fortunes that declined each year. They remained hostile and as Constantine became more and more pro-Christian, Licinius automatically became more and more anti-Christian. They fought in 314 and again in 324 and both times Licinius was defeated. The second time, Licinius was killed so that Constantine was then left in full control of a united Empire.

Constantine continued and completed the reforms of Diocletian, and much of the system attributed to the latter was really the work of the former. For instance, Constantine continued the trend toward outright monarchy by adopting the symbol of the diadem in 325. This was a narrow white linen headband worn as the symbol of supreme authority by the kings of Persia and of the Hellenistic kingdoms set up on the ruins of fallen Persia. With succeeding Emperors, the diadem grew more elaborate, as did all the paraphernalia and symbolism of royalty.* Before long, the diadem was purple — the royal color and encrusted with pearls.

Constantine went on to alter some of Diocletian's system, however. He removed the artificiality of appointed Augusti and Caesars and returned to the more natural system of the succession within a royal line by appointing his sons to be his Caesars.

He continued Diocletian's practice of welcoming barbarians into the army and even allowed barbarian bands into the Empire to settle depopulated areas. In general, this would have been a wise move if the Empire were healthy enough and its culture vigorous enough to absorb the barbarian infusion and make Romans out of them. — Unfortunately, Rome was not so happily and healthily situated.

Constantine's reign was a time of legal reform, much of it influenced by Christian teachings. The treatment of prisoners and slaves was made more humane, but on the other hand offenders against morals (particularly sexual morals) were treated much more harshly than before. He also established Sunday as a legal day of rest but then it was the Sun's day as well as the Lord's day.

Constantine, having shown himself a Christian sympathizer, if not yet actually a Christian, at once began to take an interest in the affairs of the Church. Previously, the Church, in the quarrels of bishops against bishops had no one to turn to and was forced to fight it out within itself; furthermore the winning

---

* It seems to be almost an invariable rule that as real power declines, the symbols of power multiply and intensify in compensation.

side had no way of forcing the losers to abandon their ideas. Now, however, the bishops had a court of appeal; they could turn to a presumably pious and devout, and undoubtedly powerful Emperor for judgment. And the winning side might hope to use the power of the State against the losers.

In the early years of Constantine's reign, the Church was being torn apart by the Donatist heresy, which received its name from Donatus, a bishop of Carthage who was the best known advocate of the cause. It was in connection with this heresy that Constantine had his first chance for involvement in theological dispute.

The point at issue was whether an unworthy man could be a priest. The Donatists were puritans who believed the Church to be an association of holy men, and that priests in particular could only be priests as long as they did not offend against God. Thus, in the course of the persecutions under Diocletian and Galerius, many priests had avoided martyrdom by giving up the holy books in their care and by repudiating Christianity. When the pressure of persecution passed, they returned to the fold — but could they be priests again?

The more moderate bishops took the attitude that priests were only human and that in the face of death by torture they might flinch. There were ways of atoning for such a sin. Furthermore, if the sacraments of the Church were ineffective if administered by an unworthy priest, how could one rely on the sacraments at any time? When could one be sure that a priest was worthy? They maintained, rather, that it was the Church as an institution that was holy, and its spiritual powers were effective even when wielded by an imperfect man.

In Carthage, the Donatists, who would have none of such moderation, were victorious, but the moderates now appealed to Constantine who called a special synod in 314. The synod declared against the Donatists. In 316, Constantine in person heard the arguments pro and con and he, too, declared against the Donatists.

It did no good. Edicts by pagan Emperors had not succeeded in wiping out Christianity, and edicts by Christian Emperors were not in themselves sufficient to wipe out heresy. The Donatists maintained themselves in Africa although edict after edict was passed against them. They shrank in numbers and power but remained in being until the Arabic invasion three centuries later wiped out all Christianity, Donatist and Catholic alike, in northern Africa.

Nevertheless, although Constantine's interference had not accomplished much, an important principle had been established. The Emperor had acted as though he were the head of the Church, and the Church had accepted that. This was the first step in a battle between the Church and the State that has lasted, in one way or another, down to our time.

Once Constantine became undisputed ruler of a united Empire in 324, he was able to make his Christian sympathies more open. He decided to call a council of bishops to deal with a heresy even more serious and widespread than Donatism.

Synods of bishops were an old custom now, but under pagan Emperors they had been held with difficulty and many found it unsafe to try to make a long voyage. Now the situation had changed. All bishops were urged to come under the official protection and encouragement of the Empire. It was to be an ecumenical ("world-wide") council of the Church, and the first of its kind.

In 325 (1078 A.U.C.) the bishops gathered at the town of Nicaea in Bithynia — a town not far from Nicomedia, which had been Diocletian's capital and was now Constantine's. It was also a place easy to get to from the great Christian centers of the east, particularly Alexandria, Antioch, and Jerusalem. The west was under-represented because of the long distances involved but there were bishops even from Spain.

The chief matter under discussion was the Arian heresy. A certain deacon in Alexandria, named Arius, had in the past decades been preaching a strictly monotheistic doctrine. There was only one God, he maintained, who was marked off from all created objects. Jesus, although superior to any man or any other created thing, was nevertheless himself a created thing and was not eternal in the same sense that God was. In other words, there was a time when God existed but Jesus did not. There were aspects of Jesus that were *similar* to God, but not *identical* with it. (In Greek, the words standing for "similar" and "identical" differed by a single letter, iota, which was the smallest letter of the Greek alphabet. It is amazing the centuries of bitterness, misery, and bloodshed that stemmed from the dispute represented by the presence or absence of that tiny mark.)

The alternate belief, expressed most eloquently by Athanasius, another deacon of Alexandria, was that the members of the Trinity (the Father, who was the God of the Old Testament; the Son, who was Jesus; and the Holy Ghost, or Spirit, which represented the workings of God within nature and man) were all equal aspects of a single God, all of them eternal and uncreated, and all of them identical, and not merely similar.

There grew up in Alexandria, and then in other parts of the Empire, an Arian party and an Athanasian party, and the brawls and disputes grew increasingly bitter as bishop cursed bishop indefatigably.

Constantine viewed the situation with extreme annoyance. If he were going to use the Christian Church as his weapon to keep the Empire whole and strong, he could not allow that Church to disintegrate over doctrinal disputes. The matter would have to be settled at once, and finally.

It was for that reason that he called the First Ecumenical Council at Nicaea. In the course of their sittings from May 20 to July 25, 325, they decided in favor of Athanasius. An official statement was devised (the "Nicene Creed") which upheld the Athanasian position and to which all Christians were expected to subscribe.

This placed the Church on record, so that the Athanasian

position became and remained the official doctrine of Catholicism and the Athanasians can be referred to henceforth simply as Catholics.

The Council of Nicaea did no real good at the time, however. Those who had entered the Council as Arians left it as Arians and continued to maintain their position forcibly. Indeed, Constantine gradually came to incline to the Arian position himself. Or at least Eusebius, the bishop of Nicomedia, and a leading Arian, slowly gained influence over Constantine and Athanasius was forced into the first of a number of exiles. The controversy continued, in the east, in high gear for half a century, with the various Emperors usually on the side of the Arians and against the Catholics.

This served to introduce a new dividing line between the eastern and western portions of the Empire. There had been first the dividing line of language: Latin in the west and Greek in the east. Then there had been a political division, with separate Emperors in east and west. Now there was the beginning of a religious differentiation. The west remained firmly Catholic, by and large, while the east held a large and influential Arian minority. This was only the first in a series of religious divisions that were to become steadily wider and more intense until, seven centuries later, the western and eastern branches of Christianity were to separate permanently.

CONSTANTINOPLE

Even while the Council of Nicaea was going on, Constantine was considering the matter of the capital of the Empire.

Since Diocletian had converted the Empire into an absolute monarchy, the capital could, in a very real sense, be anywhere.

It was not the city of Rome, or any other city, that ruled the Empire, but the Emperor alone. The capital of the Empire was therefore wherever the Emperor happened to be. For more than a generation now, the most important of the Emperors, Diocletian, Galerius, Constantine, had remained in the east, mainly at Nicomedia. The east was the strongest, richest, and most vital part of the Empire and its borders were most vulnerable in that period, thanks to the continuing onslaughts of Persians and Goths, so the Emperor had to be there. The question was, however, whether Nicomedia was the best place in the east.

Constantine considered the matter and his attention was drawn to the ancient city of Byzantium. Byzantium, founded by Greeks a thousand years before (657 B.C. is the traditional date — 96 A.U.C.) had a marvelous position. It was located fifty miles west of Nicomedia on the European side of the Bosporus. This is the narrow strait through which all ships must pass if they wished to carry grain from the great plains north of the Black Sea to the rich and populous cities of Greece, Asia Minor, and Syria.

From the moment it was founded, Byzantium found itself astride this trade route and prospered accordingly. It would have prospered more if it had not been the object of covetous greed by powers greater than itself. Throughout the period of Athenian greatness from 500 B.C. to 300 B.C., Athens had depended on the grain ships from the Black Sea for her food supply, so that she fought over the control of Byzantium first with Persia, then with Sparta, and finally with Macedon.

Byzantium was always capable of withstanding sieges remarkably well for it was strategically situated. Surrounded on three sides by water, it could not be starved out by a land siege alone. If Byzantium were well defended, an assailant had to be strong on land and sea simultaneously to take it — or else have traitors in his pay within the city. In 339 B.C., for instance, Byzantium successfully withstood a siege by Philip of

Macedon, father of Alexander the Great. It was one of Philip's few failures.

Byzantium entered into alliance with Rome, when Rome became dominant in the east and it maintained its position as a self-governing city of the realm right down to the time of the Emperor Vespasian. Vespasian wiped out the last remnants of self-government in Asia Minor and that included Byzantium.

Hard times came to Byzantium after the death of Commodus. It was caught up in the civil wars that followed and fought on the wrong side — for Niger and against Septimius Severus. Septimius Severus besieged it in 196, managed to take it, and subjected it to a savage sack from which it had never fully recovered. It had been rebuilt and was dragging out its life as a minor center when Constantine's eye lighted upon it. He had besieged and taken it in 324 at the time of his last war with Licinius and so he knew its potentialities well.

Soon after the Council of Nicaea, then, Constantine began to enlarge Byzantium, calling in laborers and architects from all over the realm and spending a vast sum on the project. The Empire no longer possessed the necessary supply of artists and sculptors required to beautify it in the manner that the capital of so large and historic a realm had a right to expect so Constantine did the next best thing. He rifled the statues and other art objects of the older cities of the Empire and brought the pick of the lot to Byzantium.

On May 11, 330 (1083 A.U.C.) the new capital was dedicated. It was Nova Roma ("New Rome") or "Konstantinou polis" ("Constantine's city"). The latter name became Constantinopolis in Latin and Constantinople in English. It had all the appurtenances of old Rome, games and all, and Constantine even arranged for free food for the populace. Ten years later, a Senate was set up in Constantinople, one that was every bit as powerless as the one in Rome.

Constantinople grew rapidly, for as the seat of the Emperor

and the court, it inevitably filled up with a large number of government officials. It became the center of prestige in the Empire so that many moved to it from other cities which had suddenly grown provincial. Within a century, it rivaled Rome in size and riches and it was destined to remain the largest, strongest, and wealthiest city in Europe for a thousand years.

Constantinople's existence affected the Church strongly. The bishop of Constantinople gained peculiar importance because he was in the neighborhood of the Emperor at all times. Constantinople became one of the large cities whose bishops were now officially regarded as preeminent over all the rest. These bishops were called "patriarchs" meaning "chief fathers" or, since "father" was a common way of addressing a priest, "chief priests."

The patriarchs were five in number. One of these was the bishop of Jerusalem, respected because of the association of Jerusalem with the events of the Bible. The others were the bishops of the four largest cities of the Empire: Rome, Constantinople, Alexandria, and Antioch.

The patriarchates of Antioch, Jerusalem, and Alexandria suffered through being too closely under the shadow of Constantinople. They tended to wither. Partly out of envy for the greater power of Constantinople, the other patriarchs were easily swayed by one heresy or another, which further weakened their power. It was not long before the Patriarch of Constantinople became in fact, if not in theory, the head of the eastern portion of the Catholic Church.

Standing out against Constantinople was the relatively distant and, therefore, unshadowed patriarchate of Rome. It was the only Latin-speaking patriarchate, the only western patriarchate, and it carried on its shoulders the magnificent name of "Rome." The Emperor had passed from old Rome to new Rome; so had the civil service; so had the representatives of many of the leading families; so had much power and wealth.

But one thing remained, the bishop of Rome. Behind him stood not only actual religious feeling, supporting the strictly orthodox Catholic viewpoint against the subtle, mobile, ever-talking, ever-disputing east, but also the forces of nationalism. There were those who resented the manner in which the Greek east, having been conquered by Rome less than five centuries before, should now come to rule the west.

For centuries, the history of Christianity was to turn more and more upon the battle for overlordship between the bishop of Constantinople and the bishop of Rome. The battle was fated never to end in a clear-cut victory for either side.

Toward the end of his reign, Constantine found himself forced to face a barbarian invasion of the Empire once more. For the most part, the borders had been quiet since the anarchy of the third century. Under Diocletian and Constantine the army had been under sufficiently firm control to guard the frontier adequately and the Empire had even been able to afford civil war.

Now, in 332, the Goths spilled over the lower Danube again and Constantine was forced to face them. This he did effectively. The Goths suffered enormous losses and were forced to accept ignominious defeat and retired behind the Danube again.

Constantine was in declining health, however. He was well into his fifties now and was worn out by a most strenuous life. He did not end it in Constantinople, oddly enough. He retired to his old palace at Nicomedia for a rest and a change of air. There his illness grew serious, so he had himself baptized and died in 337 (1090 A.U.C.).

Thirty-one years had passed since he had first been acclaimed in Britain as Emperor. No Roman Emperor had had so long a reign since Augustus. In Constantine's reign, Christianity was established as the official religion of the Roman Empire and Constantinople became the capital. Admiring Christian historians call him "Constantine the Great" but the declining power of Rome was beyond salvation by any Emperor however great. Constantine, like Diocletian, interrupted and delayed the decline but he did not halt it.

CONSTANTIUS II

Constantine was survived by three sons: Constantine II (Flavius Claudius Constantinus), Constantius II (Flavius Julius Constantius) and Constans (Flavius Julius Contans). The Empire was divided among them.

The Eastern plum went to the middle son, Constantius II, intact. The Western Empire was divided between the older and younger sons: Constantine II got Britain, Gaul and Spain while Constans got Italy, Illyria and Africa.

These were the first Emperors to have been brought up with a Christian education, and it would be pleasant to be able to report that a great change came over the Empire as a result. Unfortunately, that cannot be said. The sons of Constantine were cruel and contentious. Virtually the first act of Constantius II, for instance, was to kill two of his cousins, together with others of the family, who, he felt, might dispute the throne.

As for the other brothers, Constantine II, as the oldest, claimed to be Emperor-in-chief. When Constans resisted this and claimed equal status, Constantine II invaded Italy. Constans, however, was victorious and Constantine II was defeated and slain in 340.

For a while, the remaining two brothers ruled: Constans in the west and Constantius II in the east. In 350, however, Constans was assassinated by one of his generals who claimed the throne for himself. The avenging Constantius II, last of the sons of Constantine, marched west to attack the general and, eventually, defeat and kill him.

In 351 (1104 a.u.c.), then, the Roman Empire was once again under a single rule, that of Constantius II. It was no quiet rule, though, that Constantius had, even as sole Emperor. Almost from the time of his accession to power after his father's death, he found himself facing the Persians.

After the Persians had been defeated by Galerius in 297, there had, indeed, been a period of rest for the Romans that lasted through the reign of Constantine I. In 310, the Persian king died and his three sons were disposed of by the Persian noblemen. They then reserved the crown for the unborn child of one of the wives of the old kings. They looked forward to a king of the royal line, yes, but one who was so young that there would be a long minority during which the noblemen could have their own way.

The child, when born, turned out to be a boy, who was immediately acknowledged as king under the name of Shapur II.

In his helpless youth, Persia was under the control of the noble families and suffered from the raiding Arabs. (The selfish rule of quarreling noblemen is always disastrous for a nation, and even for the noblemen themselves, but somehow this simple fact of history never seems to penetrate the aristocratic skulls of the individuals who hope to profit by national weakness.) In 327, however, Shapur was old enough to seize power for himself. He promptly invaded Arabia and bludgeoned the tribesmen there into a period of sullen quiet.

Then, in 337, with the death of Constantine I and the likelihood of weaker hands at the Roman helm, Shapur struck westward at Rome. In a way, this was but one more of the endless conflicts that had been proceeding between Persia on the east and first Greece, then Rome, on the west; conflicts that had now endured for eight centuries. Now, however, something new was being added; that was Christianity.

Christianity, as a universal religion, was not, after all, intended to be confined within the boundaries of the Roman Empire. Ardent Christian missionaries sought to save souls outside those boundaries, too. One of these was Gregory, called "the Illuminator," who was, according to legend, of Persian birth. Gregory's father died in war while the son was an infant, and the boy was carried into Asia Minor by a Christian nurse and there brought up as a Christian. Eventually, he traveled northeastward to the buffer kingdom of Armenia. This had already been subjected to Christian influences but Gregory's coming completed the job.

By 303, he converted King Tiridates of Armenia, persuaded him to wipe out the last vestiges of paganism in the nation and to establish Christianity as the official religion. Armenia thus became the first Christian nation; Christian even while Rome itself was still officially pagan. Indeed, at the time that Armenia became Christian, Diocletian and Galerius were launching the last and greatest anti-Christian persecutions.

When Constantine I made Rome Christian, this, however, seriously upset the balance of power. Armenia had for four centuries been swinging this way and that between Rome and Persia (or Parthia, before Persia). Now, however, a Christian Armenia was bound to choose a Christian Rome rather than a pagan Persia.

Furthermore, Christianity was filtering into Persia itself. In a war between a Christian Rome and a pagan Persia, on whose side would Persian Christians be? Shapur therefore instituted a thoroughgoing persecution of the Christians and the war between the Roman Empire and Persia became a war not only of nations but of religions.

The war between Shapur II and Constantius II was the first of a long series of wars between a Christian Rome and a non-Christian power to the East.

Constantius II was not very successful against the energetic Persian king. He was continually beaten by Persian forces in

open battle, but the Persians never had the force to conquer
the Roman strong points and occupy the Roman provinces. In
particular, the fortress of Nisibis, in upper Mesopotamia, about
three hundred miles northeast of Antioch, was a tower of Roman strength. Three times Shapur laid siege to it; three times
he had to draw back in failure.

But then, neither king could turn his full attention to the
war. Shapur was being harassed by barbarian raids on the
eastern portions of the Empire and these kept him from turning his full strength on Rome. Constantius, on the other hand,
was distracted by dynastic problems.

JULIAN

Constantius' two brothers had died and left no heirs. Constantius himself had no children and had killed most of the col-
lateral members of the line of Constantius Chlorus. Where
could he turn to find an heir — someone whom he could make a
Caesar and to whom he could turn over a share of the Imperial
burden?

All that were left were a pair of young men who were the
sons of a half-brother of Constantine I, a half-brother whom
Constantius had had executed. These youngsters (children of
different mothers and therefore half-brothers) were grandsons of Constantius Chlorus and cousins of Constantius II.

The two were Gallus (Flavius Claudius Constantius Gallus)
and Julian (Flavius Claudius Julianus). They were mere children at the time of their father's execution and even Constantius felt they were perhaps too young to kill.

Gallus was old enough to be banished from Constantinople
and kept under strict guard, but Julian (only six years old when

his father died) remained for a while in Constantinople. He was given a careful Christian education under Eusebius of Nicomedia, one of the most important of the Arian bishops. (Constantius himself was strongly Arian in sympathies.) Neither Gallus nor Julian knew when the moody and irascible Constantius might not suddenly order their death, so they could not have had a comfortable youth.

In 351, Constantius was in the west, fighting the usurping general who had killed his younger brother, Constans. He needed someone to take care of the East in view of the continuing troubles with Persia. He decided on Gallus, now twenty-five years old, and the young man suddenly found himself whisked from prison to a Caesarship in Antioch. In token of his new position, he was married to Constantia, the sister of Constantius.

Gallus was not equal to the task. Many stories are told of the frivolity and cruelty of Gallus and Constantia. This alone might not have bothered Constantius, but rumors also arose that they were plotting to overthrow the Emperor. That was different. After Constantia died a natural death, Gallus was arrested, brought before Constantius, convicted and executed in 354.

Julian, who had been freed when his half-brother became Caesar, was suddenly exiled and imprisoned. The next year, however, Constantius, plagued with wars against the German tribes in the west, felt more than ever the need of someone to share the burden. Only Julian was left and so he was appointed Caesar in 355 and was sent to take charge of the west while Constantius turned eastward to occupy himself once more with the Persians.

Julian's chief task lay in Gaul, where the German tribes, particularly the Franks, were raiding over the Rhine and were penetrating deep into the province.

Almost like a new Julius Caesar, the young (and aptly named) Julian, who was still only in his mid-twenties and had

had no previous experience with war, attacked vigorously and capably, driving back the Germans, liberating the province and repairing the ravages. He even passed the Rhine himself in three separate successful raids (Julius Caesar had only conducted two.)

Julian maintained his headquarters at the town of Lutetia, where his grandfather, Constantius Chlorus, had been stationed at the time of being elevated to Caesarship. The town's full name was Lutetia Parisiorum ("Lutetia of the Parisians") after the tribal name of its first inhabitants. It was sometimes called Paris and this alternate name happened to come into general use while Julian was there, and thus did this name, which in later centuries was to become so famous, enter history.

Julian gained enormous popularity because of his ability and of his humane character. Since nothing succeeds like success, he became the darling of the army.

The brooding, sullen Constantius, watching this from afar was angered for he was well aware that his own continuing failure against the Persians looked all the worse against the background of his young cousin's successes. Indeed, Shapur had now defeated his own barbarian enemies and had returned to the assault against Rome more ferociously than ever. The Roman strong points began to shake and in 359, Amida, a fortress a hundred miles northwest of Nisibis, fell after a ten-week siege.

Constantius used this as an excuse to weaken Julian by calling part of his army back to the east. Julian objected to the danger into which this would plunge Gaul, but submitted. The army itself, however, refused to leave their commander. They demanded that Julian declare himself Emperor and he had no choice but to accept.

He marched eastward toward Constantinople, and Constantius plunged westward from Syria to meet him while Shapur hugged himself at the thought of the civil war that was to follow. It didn't, though. Before the armies met, Constantius died of sickness in Tarsus, and Julian became ruler over a united Empire in 361 (1114 A.U.C.)

Julian made a most unusual Emperor in one way, for he was no Christian. He had had a Christian education, to be sure, but it had not impressed him. Constantius II, the Christian Emperor, had slaughtered his family and Julian had lived in the constant fear of death for himself. If this was Christianity, how was it to be distinguished from any other religion that fostered tyranny and cruelty?

He found himself attracted instead to the teachings of the pagan philosophers (and half the Empire was still pagan). In the philosophers, he found the memory of an ancient Greece of scholars and democrats which was colored over by the golden haze of seven centuries of history. Secretly, Julian became a pagan and had himself initiated into the Eleusinian mysteries.

Julian longed to recreate the wonderful times when Plato had strolled in his Academy, instructing his students and discoursing with other philosophers. Those times, of course, had been just as brutal as Julian's own times, but there is a kind of selective memory that afflicts men when they view the past. They see the good and overlook the evil.

Once Constantius died and Julian was accepted as Emperor, he openly proclaimed himself a pagan and for this he has come to be known to history as "Julian the Apostate"; that is, one who renounces his religion. (Of course, no one calls the earlier Emperor "Constantine the Apostate" because he renounced paganism and became a Christian. It depends on who is writing the history books.)

Julian did not try to repress Christianity. Instead, he proclaimed religious liberty and the complete toleration of Jews and pagans as well as Christians. Furthermore, he declared toleration of all the various heresies within Christianity and called back all the bishops who had been exiled for one heresy or another.

It was clearly his opinion that outright repression of Christianity was unnecessary. If Catholicism, Arianism, Donatism, and a dozen other "-isms" were merely allowed to fight it out to the end without the power of the state standing behind one or another, Christianity would disintegrate into a large number of weak and competing religions and would no longer be a power. (His estimate was right, for exactly this has happened in many portions of the modern world, but Julian's reign was not long enough to bring this about.)

The humane Julian led a most moral life, attempted to rule sensibly, moderately and justly, treated the Senate with respect and, in general, behaved in far more Christian fashion than did almost all the Christian Emperors that ruled Rome before and after Julian. He even tried to modify paganism in the direction of monotheism and Christian ethics. This did not, however, make him more acceptable to the Christians of the time; rather the opposite. A virtuous pagan is more dangerous than a wicked one for he is more attractive.

Having settled himself in the government and established what he hoped was to be the new religious order, Julian led his army to Syria to take up the quarrel with the Persians. Here he hoped to continue his daring style of warfare. As in Gaul he had successfully imitated the great Julius, so here in the east, he hoped to imitate the great Trajan.

He placed a fleet on the Euphrates River and with a strong army, marched the length of Mesopotamia as Trajan had done. He reached the Persian capital of Ctesiphon and crossed the Tigris, defeating the Persian army at every encounter.

Here, however, Julian made a fatal mistake. His youthful military successes had inflamed him with the notion he was more than Trajan, that he was nothing less than Alexander the Great come back to life. He scorned to lay siege to Ctesiphon but decided to pursue the Persian army as once Alexander had done.

Unfortunately for Julian, there was only one Alexander in history. The wily Shapur had plenty of room in which to retreat and he kept his army intact and out of reach. The Persian force faded away and Julian reduced his own army to exhaustion for nothing. He had to make his way back over hot, desert country, fighting off the raiding Persians every step of the way.

As long as Julian remained alive, the Romans continued to win every battle, but were weakened further each time. Then, on July 26, 363 (1116 A.U.C.) Julian was struck by a spear from an unknown source. The story was put out that a Persian enemy had hurled that spear but it is at least as likely that the hand holding that spear had been that of a Roman Christian soldier. Julian died at the age of thirty-two, after a reign of twenty months.

According to a famous (but very likely, false) story, his last words were "Vicisti, Galileae" ("You have won, O Galilean"). But if he did not say it, he might as well have. The attempt to reestablish paganism, or, at the very least, to establish religious toleration, failed at once with his death. No outright pagan was ever to hold the Roman throne again, and paganism, generally, continued to subside steadily within the Roman dominions, although pagan philosophers continued to teach in Athens for another century and a half.

From the time that Constantius Chlorus became one of the four rulers of the Roman Empire in 293, seventy years had passed, during which he and five of his descendants had ruled all or part of the Empire. Julian, however, had no children, and with him died the last of the male descendants of Constantius.

9

THE LINE OF VALENTINIAN

VALENTINIAN AND VALENS

With Julian dead, the army, on the spot, acclaimed as Emperor, Jovian (Flavius Claudius Jovianus), an undistinguished general, but a Christian. No doubt, the disaster in which Julian's great expedition had ended had convinced many that there was wrath in heaven at Julian's paganism, and only under a Christian Emperor would they now feel safe.

Jovian accomplished two things. He canceled out Julian's religious policy, returning matters to that under Constantius (although without any effort to institute active persecution of pagans). He also canceled out the military policy of both Constantius and Julian by making a losing peace with Shapur. He abandoned Armenia and other areas that Romans had held since the time of Diocletian. Most particularly and disgracefully, he gave up the fortress of Nisibis, which Shapur had never been able to conquer in open fight.

Jovian made the peace in order that he might, as soon as possible, hasten back to Constantinople to assume the full panoply of Empire. However, on the journey back he died and it was only his corpse which, in 364, was brought into Constantinople.

The soldiers chose another Emperor, this time an able officer named Valentinian (Flavius Valentinianus), who had been born in Pannonia. He shared the rule with his brother, Flavius Valens. Valentinian was a Catholic, but tolerant of dissent, while Valens was a fervent and proselytizing Arian. Nevertheless, the brothers got along well together despite the difference in religion and temperament.

Valentinian was the more capable of the two. He was poorly educated and mistrusted the upper classes, but he tried to improve the lot of the general population. Unfortunately his efforts were in vain. All efforts at improving the realm broke against the continuing drain of military necessity.

Valens was left in the East, while Valentinian took over the defense of the West and set up his capital in Milan. After Julian's departure from Gaul four years before, the German tribes had again ventured to cross the Rhine. In Valentinian, however, they found another Julian. Once again they had to withdraw; once again Roman armies struck across the Rhine in reprisal.

Valentinian then swept southward to defend the upper Danube with equal success, while his able general, Theodosius, capably performed the same service in Britain, clearing the Picts and Scots out of the Roman portion of the island.

Unfortunately, Valentinian died of a stroke in 375 when he fell into a passion during a parley with the head of certain barbarian tribes. As for Theodosius, he was falsely accused of treason by officials whose corruption he was exposing and he was executed that same year.

Valentinian was succeeded by his eldest son, Gratian (Flavius Gratianus), who ruled in association with a half-brother, Valentinian II (Flavius Valentinianus). Since the latter was only four years old, Gratian, in effect, ruled the West.

It was in the East, however, that somber events were gathering. For a century and a quarter now, the Goths had inhabited the regions north of the Danube and the Black Sea. They had been at more or less constant war with the Romans but had been defeated over and over again by a series of capable Roman Emperors.

But now the Goths faced an even more terrifying adversary than the Romans, an adversary approaching from the recesses of Asia.

The vast tracts of central Asia have, throughout history, periodically belched forth horsemen. Ordinarily, central Asia offered pasture to nomads, hardy men who ate, slept, and lived on horseback; who were at home nowhere and everywhere, but who followed the grass from season to season. The nomads gradually increased in numbers through successions of good years with ample rainfall, but every once in a while, the rains would fail for several years in a row and the land would no longer support the population.

Out from the steppes, then, would pour the horsemen. They carried all they needed with them, their flocks, their families. They could live on next to nothing, on horse's blood and mare's milk, if necessary, and had no need to worry about lines of supply. On their fleet horses, they could cover ground almost as rapidly as a modern army, so that they could fall like thunderbolts where least expected. It was the terror of their whirlwind advance and their impetuous charge that destroyed their enemies, as well as their frustrating ability to fade away from firm opposition only to return from another direction.

The succession of peoples who lived north of the Black Sea in ancient times were probably the products of a series of out-pourings from the central Asian steppes. In Homer's time, the Cimmerians had lived there; in Herodotus' time, they had been succeeded by the Scythians; in Roman times by the Sarmatians.

It was unusual, indeed, that the Goths who came thereafter emerged from the European north rather than from the Asian east. But now, in the time of Valentinian and Valens, the old order was reestablishing itself. A new wave of nomads was pouring westward.

These nomads had been throwing themselves southward and eastward against China for centuries. The Chinese had called them the Hsiung-nu and, in the third century B.C. (when Rome was battling Carthage) had built the Great Wall, a huge rampart stretching over a thousand miles, in an attempt to keep them off.

It was perhaps unfortunate, for Europe, that the Chinese were as successful as they were, for the Hsiung-nu, frustrated in the east, turned westward. To the astonished and terrified western world, the new invaders were called Huns.

In 374, the Huns had reached the territory of the Ostrogoths, north of the Black Sea, having conquered and forced into al-liance the tribes they had met en route. The Ostrogoths were defeated in their turn and compelled to submit. The Huns then passed on to assault the Visigoths north of the Danube.

The Visigoths, too terrified to attempt to fight, fell back on the Danube and, in 376, petitioned their old enemies, the Ro-mans, to allow them haven within the Empire. The Romans set hard conditions: the Goths were to come over unarmed, and their women were to be transported to Asia as hostages. The Goths had no choice but to agree and some hundreds of thou-sands flooded into the Empire while the Huns advanced to the Danube.

All might yet have gone reasonably well if the Romans had

been able to resist exploiting the Gothic refugees. The Goths were sold food at exorbitant prices and in other ways made to feel like cowards and weaklings being saved by Roman charity. (In a way, they were, but that doesn't mean they liked to be treated that way.)

The result was that they found arms somehow and began to pillage as though they had invaded the Empire, rather than having been allowed in as refugees. They even teamed up with some of the Huns before whom they had fled, since the Huns were perfectly willing to share in the Roman loot.

The news reached the Emperor Valens in Syria, where Roman armies were once again fighting the aged Persian king, Shapur. (Shapur II was now approaching his seventieth birthday and had been king all his long life.) The Romans had won some victories, but now they were forced to patch up an unfavorable peace. Valens, after all, had to take care of the Goths.

In 378, Valens marched impetuously west from Constantinople to encounter the Gothic hordes in the neighborhood of Adrianople, the city founded by the Emperor Hadrian two and a half centuries before. Valens' forces were inferior in numbers to those of the Goths, and he might have waited for his nephew, Gratian, who was hastening eastward to join him, but he didn't think he needed the reinforcement. He was quite mistaken; indeed, even the reinforcement might not have helped, since a new era in warfare was opening up.

All through history, the foot soldier had been the king of war. It had been the foot soldiers of the Macedonian phalanx who had conquered vast stretches of the east for Alexander the Great. It had been the foot soldiers of the Roman legions who conquered the Mediterranean world for Rome.

There had been horsemen and chariots, too, but these were few and expensive and had rarely been decisive in the long run in Greek and Roman times. They could be used to support the foot soldiers and, skillfully handled, could turn a retreat into a rout, or conduct useful raids against an unprepared enemy. They could not be used in direct battle against determined and disciplined foot soldiers, however.

One possible reason for this is that the early horsemen did not have stirrups, and their seat was always unsteady. A thrust of a lance could easily shove them off the horse and this forced them to keep their distance and reduced their effectiveness.

It had been the horsemen of the steppes who had invented the stirrup. Their seats were firm and they could veer and swerve at will as long as their feet were well planted. A man on horseback, well-stirruped, could withstand a lance thrust and could, in his turn, wield a lance or swing a sword with force.

The Roman foot soldiers had to adapt to the need to fight increasing numbers of increasingly effective barbarian cavalry. Roman armor was lightened to increase mobility and an end was made to the rigid rule whereby Roman armies built fortified camps every evening. Swords grew longer and lances came into use, for the length was needed if a foot soldier was to reach a horseman. Rome was even beginning to reverse a thousand years of military tradition by making increasing use of cavalry herself, and multiplying their numbers to the point where they nearly rivaled the foot soldiers in numbers and importance.

Nevertheless, it was still the foot soldier upon which Rome relied. The legions had always conquered before and surely they would conquer to the end of time.

At Adrianople, the Roman legions met the Gothic-Hunnish cavalry, stirruped, and skillful as never before. The footmen, indifferently led, were helpless. They were penned together by the charging horsemen and slaughtered. The entire Roman army was destroyed; the Roman Emperor, Valens, with them.

In 378 (1131 A.U.C.) at this battle of Adrianople, the era of the foot soldier came to an end. The legions that had so long supported Rome were destroyed as a useful fighting force. For a thousand years, horsemen were to rule Europe and it was not until the invention of gunpowder that foot soldiers were to come into their own again.

THEODOSIUS

With the death of Valens, Gratian became virtually sole ruler of the Empire, since the boy-Emperor Valentinian II could scarcely count. This was more than Gratian could bear — he was still only twenty years old — and he sought someone with whom to share the rule.

His choice fell on Flavius Theodosius, who was then about thirty-three years old. His father had been the able and successful general who had pacified Britain and then been unjustly executed a few years before.

Theodosius tackled the victorious Goths not by outright battle (the affair at Adrianople was not something to be repeated) but by diplomacy. He got rid of the Goths not by destroying them but by playing one faction against another, and inducing them to join the Roman army. He also agreed to let them settle south of the Danube as Roman allies (in theory) but under their own ruler and their own laws.

Little by little, in this way, the border was sealed and the provinces pacified — but at a great cost, for the precedent was set for the existence of barbarian kingdoms within the boundaries of the Empire. In addition, the Roman armies had now become almost completely barbarized. Indeed, if the Romans were going to fight in the new fashion, with cavalry as the army's mainstay, they were going to have to depend more and more on barbarian horsemen. Barbarians of one sort or another came to fill the highest military offices of the state. Only the Emperor himself — still Roman in the sense that he was descended of those peoples who were native to the regions within the boundaries of the Empire — was higher. If the time came when a weak Emperor ruled, it would be German barbarians who would be the real rulers of the Empire and that time was soon to come.

Under Gratian and Theodosius, the tide finally and definitely turned against paganism. Christian proselytization was more successful than ever and pagans were turning Christian in flood-like proportions now that preferment under Christian Emperors automatically went to Christians. And if the converted pagans often paid mere lip service to Christianity, their children, educated in the Church, were sincerely Christian. The final night began to close in on the culture of ancient Greece and Rome.

One of the chief of those who presided over the deathbed of paganism was Ambrose (Ambrosius) who was born about 340, the son of a high government official. He himself entered government service but was caught up in the wordy conflicts between Catholics and Arians occasioned by the death of the old Bishop of Milan and the consequent quarrels over the identity of the new appointee. Ambrose delivered so successful an address in favor of the Catholic viewpoint that he found himself nominated to the bishopric in 374.

During the fourth century, when the Western Emperors held court in Milan, that city became the most influential bishopric in the west, quite overshadowing — at least temporarily — the various bishops of Rome. This was most true under Ambrose, a fearless and dynamic churchman.

Ambrose gained great influence over Gratian and forced him to abandon his earlier policy of toleration. The weight of the Empire was now brought down hard upon what remained of paganism. In 382, Gratian gave up the title of Pontifex Maximus, in which he served as "high priest" on behalf of the pagan portion of the population of the Empire. He also removed the pagan altar of victory from the Roman senate, forbade property to the vestal virgins extinguished the "eternal flame" they had tended for centuries; and, in general, made it clear that the pagans were second-class citizens.

Ambrose won the Emperors over to a policy of repression not only of pagans but of Arians as well. For the first time, since the Council of Nicaea a full half-century before, the Emperor in the East, Theodosius, was an ardent Catholic. From that time on, the Arian heresy began to fade within the Empire. Not only Christianity, but Catholic Christianity, was to reign supreme.

Gratian lost his popularity, however, as he grew more interested in the pleasures of power rather than in the responsibilities thereof. He gave himself over to hunting game in the company of barbarian horsemen and usurping generals were bound to step into the breach. The British legions proclaimed their general, Magnus Maximus, as Emperor and he seized Gaul, killing Gratian in 383 (1136 A.U.C.).

Theodosius was not yet done with pacifying the Goths in the East and was forced to recognize the usurper on condition that Valentinian II, Gratian's half-brother, be recognized as controlling Italy. This wasn't exactly ideal, either, for Valentinian II (now twelve years old) was under the control of his mother, a convinced Arian, and she did her best to strengthen the heresy.

When, some years later, Maximus invaded Italy, Theodosius had his chance. He had just married a new wife, Galla, the sister of Valentinian II and daughter of Valentinian I. This made him a member of the family, so to speak, and gave him another motive to avenge the death of Gratian. Theodosius made still another disadvantageous peace with Persia and marched into northern Italy. There he defeated Maximus in 388 and had him killed.

Theodosius now controlled the entire Empire, in effect. He celebrated a triumph in Rome and granted the young Valentinian II nominal rule over Gaul, under the guardianship of one of his own generals, a Frank named Arbogast, who had cleared

Gaul of Maximus' adherents. Here was the first example of an Emperor in nominal command with a German general as the power behind the throne. This was to become the rule in the West over the next century.

Arbogast, finding he could not control Valentinian II, who was beginning to display independence and ability as he grew older, had the young co-Emperor assassinated in 392 (1145 A.U.C.) Once again, Theodosius had to avenge the death of a western colleague.

He succeeded in doing so, defeating the Frank in 394. Arbogast killed himself and the entire Empire was united — for the last effective time — under a single rule. The experience with Arbogast did not persuade Theodosius, however, to abandon the use of Germans in positions of great influence. Actually, he had no choice. Only the army could protect an Emperor, particularly a young one, and the army's generals were Germans. It was as simple as that.

One of Theodosius' most trusted officers, toward the end of his reign, was Flavius Stilicho. He was the son of a Vandal (according to the accepted account), one of the German tribes who had harried the Empire in the recent past and were to do so again in the near future. And yet Stilicho was and remained a stalwart prop of the Empire.

With the Arian Valentinian II gone, and with the Catholic Theodosius ruler of the entire realm, the movement in favor of total victory for Catholic Christianity was even further accelerated. For his services in this direction, the gratified Church historians gave him the title "Theodosius the Great." In 394, for instance, Theodosius put an end to the Olympian Games which had been conducted in Greece since 776 B.C.; that is, for nearly twelve centuries. The tradition was not to be renewed for another fifteen centuries.

The most famous incident in Theodosius' reign came in 390, however, while Arbogast and Valentinian II still ruled in Gaul. In that year, the officers of the army garrison in Thessalonica, a city in northeastern Greece, were lynched by a mob in the course of a local dispute of no great importance.

Theodosius, in a moment of blind rage, ordered Thessalonica to be given over to an army sack and some seven thousand people died. Ambrose, bishop of Milan, was horrified at this act and notified Theodosius that he would not be admitted to the rites of the Church until he had performed public penance for this deed. Theodosius held out eight months — but finally gave in.

This was the first grand example of the manner in which the Church could act independently of the State and even, in a fashion, prove itself superior to the State. It is significant that this happened in the Western Empire and not in the Eastern, for as the centuries passed it was the Church in the west that was to prove more and more independent of the State.

Theodosius died in 395 (1148 A.U.C.) and, amazingly enough, the Empire still stood virtually intact. For a century and a half it had managed to fight off the steady incursions of barbarians from the north. It had fought periodically against the Persians on the east and insurgent generals within. It had had to endure being torn apart by religious disputes of Christian against pagan and Christian against Christian. Its economy was blasted; its people worn out; its armies defeated numerous times and finally slaughtered at Adrianople; its administration put into the hands of the Germans.

And yet the borders of all the Empire were virtually intact. To be sure the provinces captured by Trajan in the last period of Imperial conquest had been given up — Dacia, Armenia, Mesopotamia — but nothing else was.

That this was so was due, in part, to the fact that the barbarians were unorganized. They never united themselves under a single leader for a coordinated attack on the Empire. They specialized in rapid raids which were really successful only when Rome was caught off guard or preoccupied by civil war. They could only rarely withstand the Roman army when competently led. In short, before the barbarians could destroy the Roman Empire, or any major part of it, that Empire had to be eaten away from within. Even the disasters of a century and a half had not quite rotted the Empire sufficiently for that. Not yet. Not at the moment of Theodosius' death.

But the Empire had never been quite so near the ragged edge, either. All the efforts of Emperors and generals for a century and a half; all the superhuman labors of Aurelian, Diocletian, Constantine, Julian, Valentinian and Theodosius had succeeded only in holding the line. Persia still nibbled hungrily in the direction of Syria, the Germans still raided across the Danube and the Rhine, whenever they could (with the Huns waiting ominously behind them), and usurpers still rose at every opportunity.

To be sure there were places in the Empire where conditions had improved over the appalling ruin that had overlaid them during the half-century of anarchy before Diocletian. Egypt and Syria were almost prosperous and some landowners everywhere grew rich even while the general population grew poorer.

On the whole, though, the Imperial ship was sinking and with every decade, the Empire's fight to remain barely afloat drained it of a bit more strength — its population declined a bit more, its cities fell a little farther into impoverishment and ruin, its administration sank a bit deeper into corruption and ineffectiveness.

The life of the intellect was also declining. Pagan literature (naturally) died down to its last feeble glimmer of light, as represented by Quintus Aurelius Symmachus, born about 345 and almost the final representative of virtuous and prosperous paganism in Rome. He held numerous high offices and was distinguished by his honesty and humanity. He was the last of the great pagan orators and did not fear to put his rhetorical writings on the line before the irresistible advance of Christianity. He represented the dwindling contingent of pagan Senators

and when Gratian removed the altar of Victory from the
Senate, Symmachus addressed a letter to Valentinian II, titu-
lar ruler of Italy, asking that the symbol of the old Rome be
reinstated. It wasn't and he was banished from Rome instead.
He was later pardoned and he continued to serve Rome in high
office, dying in peace at last.

The Roman poet, Decimus Magnus Ausonius represented a
kind of semi-paganism. He was born in Burdigala (the modern Bordeaux) about 310 and established a very popular school
of rhetoric in that city. His father had been private physician
to Valentinian I, and the son was called in to serve as tutor to
the young Gratian. In order to accept the office, he paid lip
service to Christianity. In Gratian's reign, he attained high
honors, even the consulship, but after Gratian's death, he retired to his native city and continued producing quite bad poetry until he died at the ripe age of 80.

MONASTICISM

Christian Latin literature was, however, flourishing. Ambrose of Milan wrote extensively, but even more important was
the work of Jerome (Eusebius Sophronius Hieronymus).
Jerome was born in Illyria about 340 and despite the fact that
he was a Christian of Christian parents, he found himself
strongly attracted to pagan literature and learning, and what
is more he found himself repelled by the scriptures because
of the clumsiness and poor style of the Latin in which they were
couched.

He determined to prepare a proper Latin rendering of the
Bible and with that in mind, he traveled to the East and studied not only Greek, but also Hebrew. Eventually, he translated

the Bible into literary Latin, not scorning the help of learned Rabbis. The result of his labors was the version of the Bible commonly called the "Vulgate" (that is, in the "vulgar" tongue, the language of the common people of the west — which was then Latin — rather than in the Greek or Hebrew which were the original languages of the New Testament and Old Testament respectively.) The Vulgate has remained the standard Bible in use by the Catholic Church ever since.

Jerome returned to Rome for a while, but then traveled east again and died in Bethlehem in 420. He was a strong advocate of celibacy and monasticism; a fashion which was arising and growing strong in fourth-century Christianity.

Monasticism (from a Greek word meaning "alone") is the habit of withdrawing from the world in order, usually, that the cares and corruption and luxury of everyday life not distract one from the pursuit of the good life or from devotion to God. Before the establishment of Christianity, there were groups of Jews who would form separate communities in isolated areas where they might worship God in peace and concentration. There were also some Greek philosophers who withdrew, in some ways, from society. Diogenes the Cynic was one of them.

Usually, the monastics (or "monks") tended to lead very simple lives, partly because that was all that was available in distant, isolated communities, and partly because they felt it to be an absolute good since the more they disregarded the needs and desires of the body, the more they could concentrate on service to God. This disregard of bodily comfort is called "asceticism," from a Greek word for "exercise" since the Greek athletes had to forgo luxury when in training for athletic competition. An ascetic, in other words, is someone who is "in training."

The early Christians tended to be ascetic since many of the pleasures of ordinary Roman society were considered by them to be immoral or idolatrous. However, as Christianity grew more successful, it also grew more worldly and for many ascetically-minded people, merely being a Christian was no longer enough.

The first notable Christian monk was an Egyptian named Anthony, who was supposed to have lived a hundred years, from 250 to 350. At the age of twenty, he withdrew into the desert to live alone in very simple fashion, and numerous dramatic stories are told of him by later writers (such as Athanasius, who much admired Anthony's zeal against Arianism) as to the manner in which he withstood temptations thrown in his way by the devil in the form of all kinds of luxurious and lustful visions.

Anthony's example was very popular and the Egyptian desert came to contain many monks. The popularity is not hard to understand. To the truly pious, it might be a sure way of avoiding temptation and sin and ensuring passage to heaven. For many of the less pious, it was still a way of unburdening one's self of a wearisome world.

This type of solitary monasticism, although it fitted the word literally, had its dangers. For one thing, each monk, left to himself, might see his role in almost any fashion, and some were most eccentric in their activities. For instance, a Syrian monk named Simeon (who lived from 390 to 459) practiced almost unimaginable austerities. He built pillars and lived on them, scarcely ever descending, a day or night, in all weather for thirty years. He is called Simeon Stylites (from the Greek word for "pillar") in consequence. What his life on such a pillar must have been like is most unpleasant to think of and many men could not help but doubt whether this sort of thing could be truly pleasing to God.

Then, too, solitary monks who withdrew from the world might shun its temptations and wickedness, but they also shunned its responsibilities and labors. Was it altogether righteous to forsake so many souls who needed salvation in the overriding concern for one's own soul alone?

An alternative form of monasticism was therefore first established by Basil, bishop of Caesarea, the capital city of Cappadocia in Asia Minor.

Basil was born about 330 of a family that contributed many notables to church history. He was very interested in monasticism and traveled throughout Syria and Egypt to study the monks and their way of life.

He thought he saw a better and more useful way of turning the energies of man toward God. Instead of living entirely alone, a monk should live as part of a separated community. He forms part of a group, but the group itself is withdrawn from temptation.

Moreover, instead of indulging in asceticism as the one goal of life, the group should work as well as pray. What's more, the work should not merely be another form of asceticism; it should be directed to the good of humanity. This meant that the group should be located near centers of population so that the value of their work could overflow into those centers. While avoiding the sins of the world, the monks could contribute to the good of the world.

While such Basilian monasticism has always remained most popular in the east, it spread into Italy, too, in the fifth century.

ARCADIUS

On Theodosius' death, his two young sons inherited the throne. Arcadius, the elder, seventeen at the time, ruled the East Roman Empire from Constantinople. Honorius, the younger, only eleven, ruled the West Roman Empire from Milan.

In theory the Empire was still one and undivided and merely had two Emperors sharing the administration, as had been true,

on and off, throughout the century since Diocletian. For instance, laws and edicts were issued in the name of both Emperors. Then, too, the venerable institution of the consulate
whereby every year since 509 B.C., the Roman realm had elected or appointed two consuls continued in a special way: one
consul held office in Rome and one in Constantinople. (The
consulate continued till 541, so that, all told, the institution
lasted for over a thousand years.)

In actual fact, though, the two halves of the Empire
remained distinct and separate after the death of Theodosius
and there was even hostility between them. The rulers of one
were often quite ready to contribute to the harm of the other,
if their own short-term good could be gained in that manner.

One particularly irritating dispute between the two halves of
the Empire was a territorial one. Illyria lay west of the north-
south line separating the two halves of the Empire and was
usually considered part of the West. Nevertheless, the court
at Constantinople coveted it and seized part of it. This action
was resented by the West and Illyria served as a perpetual
reason for enmity between them. It was this dispute, ex-
acerbated by the ambitions of ruthless, hard-driving men on
either side that really divided the Empire — not merely the
existence of co-Emperors.

Furthermore, there was the gathering force (still mild at
the time of Theodosius' death) of religious dispute between
East and West — the slowly growing fight for precedence between the bishop of Rome and the patriarch of Constantinople.

Signs of this showed up in connection with a religious dispute that convulsed the Eastern Empire at this time. It centered about a man destined to become the most famous of the
Greek Fathers of the Church — John, known as Chrysostom
("golden-mouth") because of the skill of his oratory and of its
effect on his audience.

John Chrysostom was born in Antioch in 345, of a noble and

wealthy family and was educated in the law. There is no question but that with his worldly advantages and his natural tal-
ents he would have made a marvelous lawyer. About 370, however, he got religion and decided to become a hermit. For years
he buried himself in the desert areas east of Antioch and it was
only illness that compelled him to return to the world. He then
entered the priesthood and soon became extremely popular
with the audiences who gathered to hear his stirring sermons.
Nor was it skilled oratory only that made him popular. He led
a life of exemplary morality, using his wealth and influence to
establish hospitals, extend charity to the poor, and in other
ways make himself a well-deserved favorite of the people.

In 398, three years after the death of Theodosius, the patriarch of Constantinople died and John Chrysostom was appointed to the post. He could now extend his influence over a
broader sphere and did so.

The thunder of his sermons, denouncing luxury and im-
morality, grew louder. He insisted on strict celibacy among
priests and his sharp tongue spared no one, once his anger was
aroused (and if he had a fault, it was that his anger was easily
aroused). Naturally, this made him enemies among those
churchmen whom he denounced and among those who were
jealous of him. The bishop of Alexandria, Theophilus, was a
particular opponent for he was both luxurious and jealous.

Theophilus happened to be a favorite of Eudoxia, the empress, who was the daughter of a German chieftain, and
a strong-willed person who completely ruled her weak husband.
Furthermore, John Chrysostom was anything but a favorite of
this very same Eudoxia for the reproaches of the golden-tongue
did not stop short of the palace. Eudoxia led a gay life and
John Chrysostom denounced her in strong terms.

A special synod was arranged in 403 at which Theophilus
was to accuse John Chrysostom of heresy, and a verdict of
guilty was prearranged. John Chrysostom refused to appear

before it and he was therefore removed from the patriarchate and sent into exile. A storm of protest arose among the populace and Eudoxia, in panic, had to recall him after two days. That, however, was only a gesture; Eudoxia began to lay the groundwork for a better-arranged exile.

A new synod was gathered in 404 and this time a detachment of German mercenaries was brought into Constantinople. These soldiers did not care a bit as to whether John Chrysostom or Theophilus was to win; they were there only to follow orders and if the orders were to slaughter the population they would do so. The people, well aware of this, could do nothing.

John Chrysostom was sent to a town in the eastern stretches of Asia Minor, some 400 miles from Constantinople, in a second exile that was not reversed. While there, however, he remained in constant communication with his followers all over the Empire. What's more, he fearlessly sent letters to the bishop of Rome and to Honorius, the Western Emperor, in an effort to get them to have his case reopened.

For the court at Constantinople, both the State and the Church, this was the worst thing he could do. It made it seem that John recognized the priority of the Western Emperor and the supreme religious position of the bishop of Rome.

Eudoxia had died, but the remainder of the court were convinced that the fierce old man would have to be silenced. He was ordered removed to a still more remote spot, at the extreme northeastern corner of the Empire. On his way there, he died in 407. The next year he was joined in death by Arcadius, the Eastern Emperor.

Even John's death did not wipe out the attachment of the people of Constantinople to their old patriarch. Large numbers of them refused to accept the new patriarch of Constantinople until John's memory had been cleared and eventually this had to be done. John's dead body was brought back to Constantinople with full honors thirty years after his death. His conviction was reversed; he was eventually made a saint;

and the son of Arcadius and Eudoxia, who was then on the throne in Constantinople went through a careful ceremony of repentance in the name of his parents.

Nevertheless the affair could not help but weaken the prestige of the office of patriarch at Constantinople, and later quarrels between Church and State were to weaken it further. And, inevitably, as the prestige of the patriarch of Constantinople declined, that of the bishop of Rome increased. The latter was particularly true, since the prestige of the competing Western bishopric, that of Milan, underwent a sudden eclipse as we shall see.

ALARIC THE VISIGOTH

While the ups and downs of John Chrysostom engaged the attention of the court, the bishops, and the people of Constantinople, dire events had been transpiring at the borders from nearly the moment the strong Theodosius had been removed from the throne by death.

His sons, Arcadius and Honorius, were both of them, young, weak, and incapable. Both, at the time of their accession were, by Theodosius' instructions, under the guardianship of military protectors. In charge of Arcadius was the Gallic general Rufinus, while in charge of Honorius was the Vandal-descended Stilicho. The two men were at bitter odds from the first for Rufinus had seized eastern Illyria and Stilicho was determined to regain it.

Unfortunately, they were not allowed to work out their quarrel between themselves. Interference came from the Visigoths. Nearly twenty years had passed since the battle of Adrianople and the Visigoths still occupied the province of Moesia. They were not, of course, quite the barbarians they had been when they first appeared on the Roman horizon a century and a half before and killed the Emperor Decius. To some extent they had been Romanized.

They were, for instance, rapidly adopting the Roman religion thanks to the activity of a man who was himself a Visigoth. His name, Wulfila ("little wolf") is known to us in its Roman version — Ulfilas.

He was born somewhere north of the Danube, in what had once been Dacia, about 311. When in his early twenties he had visited the newly established Constantinople, either as part of a Gothic mission there or as part of a captured group of hostages. In either case, he was converted to Christianity in those hectic days when that religion was enjoying its first years of official favor, and he burned to carry his new religion to his own people. For the rest of his life he labored at this task as missionary among the Goths.

In the course of his efforts, he translated much of the Bible into the Gothic language. To do that, he had to work out an alphabet and create a written language where one did not exist before. Indeed, those fragments of his translation that still exist (mostly portions of the New Testament) are almost all the written records of the Gothic language that remain today.

Ulfilas did not succeed in making an instant mass conversion of the Goths, but he sowed the seed. He gathered an increasing flock of Christians about him and their power grew steadily.

Ulfilas, however, in becoming a Christian convert had gained his beliefs from the Arian groups in Constantinople and was, therefore, himself an Arian. Indeed, he is supposed to have returned to Constantinople in 383 to take part in a synod of Arian bishops who were facing their final fate at the hands of the Catholic Emperor, Theodosius. Ulfilas died before he could actually begin his labors.

The missionary to the Goths left behind him Arian Christianity among his people and, eventually, among the other German tribes as well. While Arianism was largely extinguished within the Empire, it flourished widely outside it. This was a matter of considerable importance, actually. When the day came that German war bands controlled large sections of the Western Empire, it was their religion that separated them from the people. It was German Arian rulers versus Roman Catholic subjects and religious hostility was an important factor in preventing an amalgamation of peoples and in helping bring about a more thorough destruction of ancient culture in consequence.

At the time of Theodosius' death, a leading Arian was Alaric, a Visigothic chieftain who had been born about 370 on an island at the mouth of the Danube. He was one of Theodosius' generals, loyally leading a Gothic contingent into battle.

Apparently, he felt himself to be sufficiently in the Emperor's graces to be sure of high office under his successors and was indignant at being passed over for Rufinus and Stilicho. In revenge, he decided to take by force what he had not been given by law.

Had the Empire stood against him firmly there is probably little Alaric could have done and he would have gone down in history as just another raiding chieftain committing a nuisance. His chance came, however, through the fact that the courts in East and West saw only each other as the enemy. Powerful influences, both in Milan and in Constantinople, in their blind struggle over Illyria, were each perfectly ready to make use of a barbarian, provided they could get him to raid and ravage the other side. As a result, Alaric moved into the chaos of internal enmities and became the first of the great barbarian destroyers of the Roman Empire.

He went about matters in as straightforward a fashion as possible, marching straight for Constantinople, in the hope that in terror of his approach, the Eastern court would let him have his way at once.

To be sure, the rulers at Constantinople seemed far more interested in turning back Silicho's attempt to regain Illyria than in stopping Alaric's incursion into Thrace. Stilicho was in position to block Alaric but Constantinople implacably ordered the Western general out of its dominions. Seething, Stilicho returned to Italy but got his revenge by engineering the assassination of Rufinus. This didn't help, however, as other ministers, equally absorbed by short-range goals, took his place in Constantinople.

Alaric's bluff against Constantinople didn't work. He knew he couldn't storm its fortifications, so he veered off instead and marched into helpless Greece, with no one daring to stop him.

Greece had known almost nothing but profound peace for four hundred years. It was no longer the old Greece, of course, for it had been sleeping for all those centuries, dreaming of past greatness. Many of the old statues, temples and monuments still stood but much had fallen to the tooth of time, much to those who had rifled the land to enrich the new city of Constantinople, much to the anger of the new Christian rulers of the land.

The temples were deserted and Delphi itself was a ruin. The Eleusinian mysteries, to be sure, were still feebly carried on under the hostile eyes of Christians, but now the Gothic bands of Alaric, firm Christians even though of the Arian variety, entered Eleusis. The temple of Ceres was destroyed in 396 (1149 A.U.C.) and the age-old mysteries came to their end.

Thebes remained safe behind its walls and Athens was spared when even the Goths avoided it in respectful memory of its long-gone greatness. Alaric passed on into the Peloponnesus and remained there through the winter while not a hand was raised against him.

In the west, however, Stilicho was again on the move. Feeling that Constantinople was in too desperate a position to try to stop him, he saw the possibility of a successful attack on Alaric leading to a union of both halves of the Empire under himself.

His campaign began well. In defiance of Constantinople, he marched into the Peloponnesus and drove Alaric back, penning him up in what seemed a neat trap. Nevertheless, Alaric managed to escape. Some speculate that Stilicho, having shown his superiority over the Eastern Empire in handling Alaric, now deliberately let him escape in order to use him as blackmail against Constantinople and force the recognition of himself, Stilicho, as undisputed master of the whole Empire.

If so, the Eastern Empire outsmarted Stilicho, or, to put it more accurately, out-treasoned him. Constantinople established Alaric as governor of the disputed Illyria. It was a clever move from the short-range point of view for not only did it bribe Alaric to cease hostilities in the east but by placing him in charge of a province Stilicho claimed as that of the Western Empire, it ensured continuing hostility between Alaric and Stilicho. The tables had been neatly turned.

For a while, Alaric and Stilicho eyed each other, each waiting for the proper moment to attack. Alaric finally thought the time had come and in 400 (1153 A.U.C.) struck westward into northern Italy. Stilicho reacted slowly but eventually moved north to meet him and the two armies (both German, actually) collided at Pollentia, in what is now the northwestern corner of Italy. Stilicho attacked on Easter Sunday in 402 (1155 A.U.C.) and found Alaric unprepared for he had assumed that no battle would be fought on the holy day. The result was a narrow victory for Stilicho, followed by a more definite one at Verona farther east. Alaric had to evacuate Italy in 403 and retire into Illyria to catch his breath and recover.

Considerable damage had, however, been done. Milan, which had been the capital of the Western Empire for a century, had been placed in danger by the Goths and the government no longer felt safe there. In 404 (1157 A.U.C.) the young Emperor — who, like his brother Arcadius, was, and remained, a complete nonentity) moved to Ravenna, some 280 miles southeastward on the shores of the Adriatic. It was a strong position which, for three and a half centuries, was to remain the center of Imperial power in Italy. With the passage of the Capital from Milan, the bishop of Milan lost his prestige and ceased to be a competitor for Churchly power with the bishop of Rome.

Then, too, the immediate danger to Italy and the Imperial court led to the near-panic recall of some of the distant legions. The forces stationed in Britain had been weakened twenty years earlier at the time of Gratian's assassination. In the short civil war that followed, legions from Britain had been used and many of them had never returned to the island. The weakened Roman forces remaining in Britain had to fall steadily back from Hadrian's Wall. In the emergency caused by Alaric's invasion of northern Italy, what troops could be scraped out of Britain were called back to Italy to fight at Pollentia.

Some returned to Britain after Pollentia, but the Picts were swarming southward from the Scottish highlands and German raiders were striking westward across the North Sea into Britain. The Roman soldiers could do little but amuse themselves by proclaiming their generals to be Emperors and by 407 (1160 A.U.C.) the legions left Britain permanently. After three and a half centuries of Roman civilization, Britain fell back into barbarism and paganism under Germanic invaders.

The loss of Britain was not, by itself, fatal to the Empire. It was as much an outlying province as Dacia had been, almost as late an addition to the Empire and, even worse than Dacia, was the one large province separated from the rest of the Empire by the sea.

But the loss of Britain was the least of it. The preoccupation of the Western Empire with Alaric gave the other German tribes their chance. Those east of the Rhine and north of the upper Danube were feeling the steady pressure of the Huns to their east. A confederation of tribes from above the upper Danube, referred to collectively by the Romans as Suevi ("Schwaben" in German and "Swabian" in English) poured south across the Alps and invaded northern Italy once more just as soon as Alaric had been pushed out. Stilicho defeated them, too, in 405, but only at the cost of virtually stripping the Rhine frontier of its defenses.

On the last day of 406, therefore, the Suevi, together with several groups of Vandals (Stilicho's ancestral people) and a contingent of Alani, a non-Germanic tribe from the Caucasus, crossed the Rhine. They encountered no opposition to speak of and moved completely across Gaul and into Spain. By 409, they had settled themselves there, the Suevi in the northwest, the Vandals in the south, and the Alani in between. (The stay of the Vandals in southern Spain has left its mark to this day for that section of the land is still called by the name of the tribe. With the initial V gone, that section is "Andalusia.")

At the time, it might not have been recognized just at first that this westward and southward push of the Germans was something new. After all, for nearly two centuries now, the Germanic tribes had been periodically spilling over into Gaul, pushing against a steadily weakening Empire. Always until now, though at a steadily increasing cost, the Romans had managed to throw them back. Just half a century before under Julian (see page 189), the Romans had managed to do so with considerable glory.

The invasion of the last day of 406 was different, however, because it was permanent. One Germanic tribe might defeat and replace another, but never again were the western provinces to be cleared of those peoples altogether.

It is just possible this might not have been so if Stilicho had remained in charge. He had defeated first the Visigoths and then the Suevi in northern Italy. He might have organized an offensive against the Germans in Spain — but he didn't get the chance. His enemies were winning at home.

They told Honorius that his warlike minister was planning to raise his own son to the throne. The imbecilic Honorius believed this and gave the order for his general's execution, legalizing what would otherwise have been merely an assassination. Stilicho was beheaded in August, 408 (1161 A.U.C.). This was an act of incredible folly and it sealed the fate of the Western Empire.

The Goths in Stilicho's army, loyal until now, were outraged at this, and were further infuriated by strong anti-Arian measures taken by the new ministers who now came to power. The Goths deserted by tens of thousands to Alaric who still hovered just outside Italy.

Once again Alaric crossed into Italy and this time there was no Stilicho and virtually no army to stop him. He marched southward without noticeable opposition and within one month of the Roman government's suicidal execution of Stilicho, Alaric stood at the gates of Rome. For the first time in six hundred years, Rome saw the foreigner at the walls — something that had not happened since the time of Hannibal of Carthage.

Alaric had no intention, however, of destroying Rome. The very conquerors of the period couldn't bring themselves to believe that the Western Empire was fatally ill. The Empire had lasted so long it seemed almost a natural law that it would last forever, and it seemed almost blasphemy to seek to destroy it. All Alaric wanted was to be a great part of this eternal Empire, to govern a province, to be in command of its armies, to have land and loot for his troops.

Rome itself capitulated helplessly, but Alaric had to have the consent of the Emperor to make matters legal and this he could not get. The well-fortified and nearly inaccessible Ravenna was safe from Gothic sack and while that was so, Honorius was prevailed upon by his ministers to refuse to yield to Alaric's demands. (*They* were safe, and therefore brave.)

Alaric had to return to the siege of Rome a second time, to force a temporary agreement and when the government backed away from it, he returned a third and last time in 410 (1163 A.U.C.). This third siege he continued to the climax. Rome surrendered in August, just two years after Stilicho's execution, and for the first time since 390 B.C. (exactly eight centuries before) a barbarian army actually occupied and sacked Rome, the city of Scipio, Caesar, and Marcus Aurelius.

Yet Alaric only held Rome for six days, then marched southward. The sack was mild and the damage done the city was slight, but the prestige of Rome and its empire was irretrievably damaged. The terror of the Roman name vanished.

Alaric on his southward march had, apparently, the intention of sailing across the Mediterranean and invading Africa where, in an outlying portion of the Empire he might make himself lord of a province as the Suevi, Alani, and Vandals were doing in Spain. But a greater enemy than the Romans stopped him. His ships were destroyed in a storm and soon after that he died of fever in southern Italy. He was succeeded by his brother-in-law, Atawulf (or Ataulf, in the Latin version).

10

THE GERMANIC KINGDOMS

THEODORIC THE VISIGOTH

Like Alaric, Atawulf aspired to high position within the Roman Empire, but considered as visionary any attempt to replace it by a Gothic Empire. He marched into southern Gaul, where he found loot enough and forced a high price for keeping at least a reasonable peace. He arranged to marry Galla Placidia, the half-sister of Honorius. This placed him within the royal family and allowed him to remain in southern Gaul under the color of legality.

Meanwhile, the Imperial court had finally found a competent replacement for Stilicho; a Roman named Constantius. He was one of the few non-barbarians in the West who could serve efficiently at the head of troops and even, on occasion, win.

Constantius felt the most economical way of fighting the German invaders was by pitting one tribe against another. He

persuaded Atawulf that, as brother-in-law of the Emperor and
ally of the Romans, he ought to lead his Visigoths against the
Germanic invaders in Spain. Guided, perhaps, by the thought
of further loot and greater power, Atawulf led his Gothic army
into Spain. He was murdered in 415 but his successor, Wallia,
continued the war, and just about destroyed the Alani. The
Suevi were penned into the northwestern angle of Spain, and
a remnant of the Vandals were pushed against the sea in southern Spain.

The Visigoths might have completed the job and cleared
Spain altogether, but the great problem of using one enemy
against another is that a too-complete victory for either side is
dangerous. The Imperial court did not dare let the Visigoths
become too lopsidedly victorious and persuaded them to leave
Spain with their task unfinished.

Wallia died in 419 and it was under his successor, Theodoric I, that the Visigothic army emerged from Spain and returned to Gaul.

Even so, the results of the adventure of German-against-
German were bad for the Romans. The Visigoths under
Theodoric now settled down in southwestern Gaul. In 418
(1171 A.U.C.) they established what came to be known as the
kingdom of Toulouse, after the capital city in which they
made the seat of their power. Toulouse, about sixty miles north
of the Pyrenees, remained the seat of the Visigothic kings for
a century.

The kingdom of Toulouse was the first of the Germanic successor kingdoms. Unlike previous settlements of German war
bands within the borders of the Roman realm, this kingdom
acknowledged no Roman overlordship. It was an independent
power. And it was permanent, for in one form or another, the
Visigothic kingdom was to remain in being for over three centuries.

To be sure, it remained in alliance with Rome and was, usually, friendly to Rome. However, the Visigoths became the land-owners in southwestern Gaul. The pattern was established that was to dominate the west of Europe more and more as the century wore on. A land-owning aristocracy of Germans and their descendants was to rule over a peasantry of descendants of Romanized natives.

The rise of the Visigoths was remarkable. In 376, they had entered the Roman Empire as suppliants, crossing the lower Danube in advance of the Huns who would otherwise have enslaved them. Now, merely forty years later, they had traversed over a thousand miles of Roman land and had established themselves as masters under a king, Theodoric I, whom the Western Emperor was forced to treat as an equal.

GAISERIC THE VANDAL

The Vandals in Spain, bruised and battered by the Visigothic onslaught, held the southern extremity of the province with some difficulty, but fortunately for themselves circumstance pointed out to them a new field of activity — a new area in which they attained a century of greatness and power.

That area was Roman Africa, which included the North African coast west of Egypt and which had Carthage as its metropolis. Africa had been rich in its contributions to early Christian history. It had been the center of Puritan heresies such as those of the Montanists and Donatists and it had been the home of such early Christian writers as Tertullian and Cyprian. Now, toward the end of the Roman stage of its history, it was the home of the greatest of the Latin Fathers of the Church, Augustine (Aurelius Augustinus).

Augustine was born in 354 in a little African town about 150 miles west of Carthage. His father was a pagan and his mother a Christian but he himself was uncertain at first as to his own course of belief. During his youth, he inclined to a new form of religion called Manichaeism.

Manichaeism is named for a religious leader, Mani, who had been born in Persia about 215. He developed a form of religion somewhat akin to the older Mithraism that borrowed strongly from the Persian beliefs in the equal strength of the forces of light and darkness, of good and evil. (The Jews themselves had picked up this "dualism" during the time they were part of the Persian Empire, and it is only after that period, that Satan, as "Prince of Darkness" becomes important as an adversary of God — although neither the Jews nor the Christians that followed ever allowed Satan to be considered the equal of God in either power or importance.)

To the Persian dualism, Mani added the strict moralism that he borrowed from Judaism and Christianity. Although it underwent persecutions in Persia itself, Manichaeism began to spread into the Roman Empire just before Christianity became Rome's official religion. Diocletian viewed Manichaeism with dark suspicion for he felt that Manichaeans must be agents of Rome's great adversary, Persia. In 297, therefore, he began an official campaign to repress it — six years earlier than his similar campaign against Christianity. Neither campaign succeeded.

The legal establishment of Christianity actually helped the spread of Manichaeism for a while. Once Christianity became official, the Emperors tended to lend their support to one particular sect of Christianity, first Arianism, then Catholicism. The minor heresies that had flourished when all sorts of Christian beliefs were equally illegal and persecuted now found themselves worse off than before for they were singled out for suppression. Many of them tended, therefore, to abandon

Christianity which had now become the persecuting enemy and join Manichaeism.

There is, after all, something dramatic about the cosmic clash of good versus evil. Men and women who supported what they considered the good felt themselves to be part of this universal battle while their enemies became part of a vast darkness which, however dominant they seemed now, were inexorably doomed to a final overthrow. To those who adopt a conspiratorial view of history (in which the world is believed to be in the power of a secret conspiracy of evil men or forces) Manichaeism has its natural attractions.

Manichaeism reached its peak in Augustine's time and he succumbed to it. He was also interested in Neo-Platonism, reading the works of Plotinus with great interest.

Manichaeism and Neo-Platonism turned out, however, to be mere stages in Augustine's development. His restless seeking for philosophic security, combined with the ceaseless pressure of his strong-willed mother, led him to Christianity at last. He had gone to Milan in 384 (then the capital and religious center of the Western Empire) and had been converted by Bishop Ambrose. In 387, he finally allowed himself to be baptized.

He returned to Africa and in 395 became bishop of Hippo Regius, a small seaport just north of his birthplace (and now known as Bone, a city in what is now Algeria.) Augustine remained there for thirty-four years and Hippo, otherwise completely inconsequential (except possibly as the birthplace of the historian, Suetonius, three centuries before) became famous because of Augustine.

Augustine's letters were sent over all the Empire, his sermons were collected into books, and he wrote numerous formal works on various theological questions. He was an ardent battler against the various African heresies, and he believed (perhaps because of his shame at his own youthful experiences) in the essential depravity of humanity. Each individual was born with an inheritance of the "original sin" that stained man when

Adam and Eve disobeyed God in the Garden of Eden. This was removed only by baptism and infants who died before baptism were eternally damned. He also believed in "predestination"; that is, in the careful design of God, existing from the beginning of time, that guides every phase of history so that nothing happens that is not predestined to happen.

In his early years as bishop, Augustine wrote his *Confessions,* an intimate and apparently honest autobiography, not sparing his own early faults. The book has remained popular ever since.

After the sack of Rome by Alaric, Augustine wrote *Concerning the City of God,* a defense of Christianity against the new attacks of the pagans. Rome had risen to world mastery and had been invincible, said the pagans, as long as she had kept faith with her ancient gods. Now that she was Christian, the displeasure of those gods was clearly seen in the fact that now the city was sacked. And where, by the way, was this new Christian god; how was it he did not defend his city?

Augustine reviewed all of history known to him, pointing out how it passed in cycles of the rise and fall of states, as part of the great divine predestined plan. Rome was no exception; it, too, having risen, must fall. But Rome, when sacked by Alaric, had been treated mildly and its religious treasures had been respected. When had the gods of any pagan city so protected it from the consequences of a barbarian sack? In any case, the decline of Rome was only a prelude to the rise of a heavenly City of God, a final City that would not fall but would stand as the grand climax of the divine plan.

One of Augustine's disciples was Paulus Orosius, who had been born in Tarragona in Spain. At the suggestion of Augustine, he wrote a history of the world — *History Against the Pagans* — which he dedicated to Augustine. He, too, tried to prove that the Roman Empire was falling for faults and sins of the pagan era and that Christianity was not destroying Rome, but was merely saving what was left of it.

Augustine's great book was finished in 426, and the few remaining years of his life saw still greater calamities than those that had preceded; calamities that began with intrigues in the court of Ravenna and that involved the Vandals waiting at the southern tip of Spain.

In Ravenna, Honorius died in 423 (1176 A.U.C.) after a dim reign of twenty-eight disastrous years as Roman Emperor. He lived uncaring that in his reign Rome was sacked and that his provinces were stripped from him. He was a complete figurehead.

His general, Constantius, had married his half-sister, Galla Placidia, the widow of Atawulf the Visigoth, and for a few months was acclaimed as Constantius III, co-Emperor of the West. There was a fatality hanging over the Western Empire which killed its strong men and let its weaklings live. Constantius III died after ruling only seven months in 421, and when Honorius died two years later, the son of Constantius III and Galla Placidia came to the throne.

He was a boy of only six years and he reigned as Valentinian III. He was the grandson of Theodosius I and on his maternal grandmother's side the great-grandson of Valentinian I.

Valentinian III, as a child, was a nonentity, of course, and intrigues were constant within the court for control over him. The prime influence was the queen mother, Placidia, and the battle grew hot as to who was, in turn, to influence her.

Vying for that privilege were two generals, Flavius Aetius and Bonifacius. Of the two, Aetius may possibly have been of barbarian descent. In any case he spent some years of his life as hostage in Alaric's army and later additional years with the Huns, so that much of the barbarian must have rubbed off on him. In 424, he rode into Italy at the head of an army of barbarians, including Huns (although, to be sure, all armies were barbarian in those days) and placed himself in a position of power which he was to maintain for a generation.

Bonifacius, also a successful general, faded before Aetius.

Bonifacius was given the governorship of Africa, but this was a kick upstairs, for it removed him from Ravenna and left Aetius in charge there, with full access to the queen mother.

In Africa, Bonifacius realized his disadvantage and his thoughts turned to rebellion. In his anger, he was ready to grasp any weapon to fight his enemy in Italy and he made the horrible mistake of calling a barbarian war band to his aid.

The nearest were the Vandals in southern Spain. Their position was precarious and Bonifacius judged, rightly, that they would be ready to hire themselves out to him. What Bonifacius did not, and could not, foresee was that the Vandals had just gained a new leader, Gaiseric (or Genseric), who was now nearly forty and who was one of the most remarkable men of the age.

In 428 (1181 A.U.C.) Gaiseric accepted Bonifacius' invitation and some 80,000 Vandals made use of the fleet supplied them by Bonifacius to sail to Africa. Gaiseric, however, had no intention of engaging himself as a mercenary when a wide province seemed open to him for the taking.

The situation was made to order for him, too. There were native African tribesmen in the hilly and desert areas of Mauretania and Numidia who were never entirely reconciled to the Roman rule from the cities on the coastal strip. In addition there were the Donatists and other heretics, whom the strong hand of Augustine, bishop of Hippo, was holding under, and who were quite ready to make common cause with an Arian barbarian against the Catholic orthodoxy.

Too late, Bonifacius recognized his error and was reconciled with the court (Aetius being away in Gaul). By that time, however, Gaiseric had swept up Africa, leaving only Carthage, Hippo, and Cirta (the last a hundred miles west of Hippo) in Roman control.

Gaiseric laid patient siege to Hippo, which endured for nearly two years because supplies could be, and were, brought in from the sea. The Eastern Empire, for once joining with the west, sent a fleet and helped carry supplies. All was to no avail, however, for twice armies led by Bonifacius were defeated on land by Gaiseric. In 431, Hippo was taken. Its bishop, Augustine, did not live to see the surrender. He died while the siege was in progress.

Bonifacius returned to Italy and there was engaged in battle by his implacable enemy, Aetius. Bonifacius won, but was wounded at the hand of Aetius and died soon after.

In 435, Gaiseric arranged a treaty with the court at Ravenna, whereby the Vandal kingdom was recognized and his position was made legal. The Romans were anxious for such a peace since, with Egypt in the firm control of the Eastern Emperor, Africa was the chief granary of Rome. Gaiseric might occupy the land, in their view, if only he would continue regular grain shipments.

By the terms of the treaty, Gaiseric also agreed to allow Carthage (which he had not yet conquered) to remain Roman. Gaiseric agreed — until it suited his purpose to agree no longer. In 439 (1192 A.U.C.) he marched on Carthage and took it, making it his capital and the base of his newly-built navy that made him the terror of the Mediterranean for twenty years.

ATTILA THE HUN

While the Vandals had taken the southern province of the Western Empire and the Visigoths had ensconced themselves in the western provinces, a still more barbaric menace threatened from the north.

The Huns were on the move again.

It had been their westward migration, nearly a century earlier, from central Asia to the plains north of the Black Sea, that had driven the Visigoths into the Roman Empire and had begun the long assault that had now brought the Western Empire to the brink of ruin.

While the Goths and Vandals had been winning their victories, the Huns had remained relatively quiet. They had looted across the Roman border now and then but no substantial invasion had been made.

In part this had been because the Eastern Empire had remained in a more healthy condition than its Western sister. After the death of Arcadius in 408, his seven-year-old son, Theodosius II (sometimes called "Theodosius the Younger") came to the throne. When he came of age, he proved stronger than his father and there was even a sort of amiability and goodwill about him that made him popular with the people. In the course of his long forty-year reign, the Eastern Empire retained a certain stability. He enlarged and strengthened Constantinople, opened new schools, and had the law summarized in what was called the Theodosian Code in his honor.

The Persians (an old enemy almost forgotten in the terrors of the new dangers from the northern barbarians) were held off in two reasonably successful wars, and while the borders of the Western Empire were crumbling, those of the Eastern held intact.

In 433, however, two brothers, Attila and Bleda, succeeded to the rule over the Huns. Attila, who was the dominant member of the pair, at once took a threatening attitude toward Rome and forced Theodosius to agree to pay him a tribute of 700 pounds of gold a year in return for a promise to keep the peace.

And Attila kept the peace — for a while. He used the interval to strengthen himself elsewhere, driving his horsemen northward against the primitive Slavs who then occupied the plains of east-central Europe. He also moved westward into

Germany, which was weakened and in part depopulated by the migrations of so many fighting men into the western provinces of the Empire.

The westward drive of the Huns pushed additional German tribes across the Rhine. Among them were the Burgundians, some of whom had been included in the earlier Suevian advance into Gaul. Now, in 436 and the years after, additional groups of Burgundians entered Gaul and settled in the southeastern corner of the province after a defeat by Aetius had discouraged any plans they might have had for a wider sway just at the moment.

Another Germanic tribe pushed into Gaul by the Huns were the Franks. They had tried a Gallic adventure nearly a century before but had been so badly beaten by Julian that they had remained quiet since. Now they occupied the northeastern section of Gaul and this occupation also was limited by a defeat at the hands of Aetius.

Still other German tribes — the Angles, Saxons, and Jutes — dwelling north and northeast of the Franks on the coasts of what are now Denmark and western Germany, were forced across the sea in the 440's. They raided Britain, which had fallen back into barbarism, and in 449 the Jutes made their first permanent settlements in what is now Kent in the southeastern corner of England. For centuries thereafter the "Anglo-Saxons" slowly expanded their holdings westward and northward against the fiercely battling Celtic Britons. It was this Celtic defense that eventually gave rise to the legends of King Arthur and his knights.

Some of the Britons eventually fled to the northwest corner of Gaul, establishing themselves in what is now known as Brittany.

After the death of Bleda in 445 (1198 a.u.c.) Attila was relieved of a moderating influence and found himself ruler of a vast Empire stretching from the Caspian Sea to the Rhine River and covering the northern frontier of the Roman Empire from end to end.

He decided on a still more adventurous foreign policy and invaded the Eastern Empire until bought off by the increased tribute of a ton of gold a year.

Theodosius II died in 450 (1203 A.U.C.) and succeeding him was his sister, Pulcheria, granddaughter of Theodosius I. She felt the need of masculine support in the evils that pressed about her and so she married Marcian (Marcianus), a Thracian of humble birth, but an able general.

The change in rule made itself felt at once, for when Attila sent to demand the latest installment of the annual tribute, Marcian refused and declared himself ready to go to war.

Attila refused the challenge. Why bother with Marcian, who might well give him some trouble, when to the west was a region ruled by a feeble Emperor, quarreling courtiers, and competing barbarian kingdoms? There is a story that Honoria, the sister of Valentinian III, having been imprisoned for some misdeed, had smuggled her ring to Attila, and urged him to come to Italy and claim her as his bride. This might have served the Hunnish king as an excuse for an invasion he would have planned anyway.

Almost immediately after the accession of Marcian and the refusal of the tribute, Attila made ready to cross the Rhine and invade Gaul.

For a generation now, Gaul had been the scene of fighting between Aetius, representing the Emperor, and the various Germanic tribes. Aetius had been performing prodigies. He kept the Visigoths confined to the southwest, the Burgundians in the southeast, the Franks in the northeast, and the Bretons in the northwest. Large tracts of central Gaul remained Roman. Indeed, because Aetius won the last important victories that could be ascribed to the Romans in the west, he is sometimes called "the last of the Romans."

But now it was not German tribes fleeing from Huns whom Aetius had to fight, but the Huns themselves. When Attila and his Hunnish hordes crossed the Rhine in 451 (1204 A.U.C.) Aetius was forced to make common cause with Theodoric I the Visigoth. Indeed the Germans in Gaul recognized the overriding danger and Franks and Burgundians flocked to Aetius' army.

The two armies, that of Attila, which included auxiliaries from among those German tribes conquered by the Huns, notably the Ostrogoths; and that of Aetius with its strong Visigothic contingent; met in northern Gaul in a region that had been inhabited by a Celtic tribe called the Catalauni. The region is therefore called the Catalaunian Plain and the chief city of the area is now called Châlons, about ninety miles east of Paris. What followed is called either the battle of Châlons or the battle of the Catalaunian Plain, but by either name it was to a certain extent a battle of Goth against Goth.

Aetius placed his own troops on the left of the line and the Visigoths on the right. Weaker allies were placed in the center where, Aetius hoped, Attila (who always remained in the center of his own line) would launch the chief attack. So it happened. The Huns struck at the center and drove inward, while the ends of Aetius' line closed upon them, surrounded them, and wreaked havoc.

Had the victory been properly pursued, the Huns might have been wiped out, and Attila killed. However, Aetius was even more an intriguer than a general and he was concerned not to allow the Visigoths to grow too strong as a result of a victory over the Huns. Theodoric, the old Visigothic king and the son of Alaric, died in this battle, and Aetius saw his chance. He had been holding Theodoric's son, Torismund, as a hostage in order to keep the old Goth from suddenly changing his mind as to whose side he was supporting. He now urged the young prince to rush back to Toulouse with his army to make sure of his own succession. With the disappearance of the Visigothic contingents, Attila and what was left of his army could escape, but Aetius could count on the Visigoths being absorbed in a civil war. Aetius was right. Torismund mounted the throne but within a year was killed by his younger brother who mounted the throne in his turn as Theodoric II.

This dubious affair at Châlons did keep Attila from conquering Gaul but it did not end the Hunnish menace and does not merit the honor of being the "decisive victory" succeeding ages have viewed it as.

Attila reorganized his army, caught his breath, and in 452 invaded Italy, still using as his excuse his demand for the hand of Honoria who had promised herself to him. He laid siege to Aquileia, a city at the northern tip of the Adriatic Sea and, after a three-month beleaguerment, took and destroyed it. Some of the inhabitants, fleeing from the devastation, took refuge among the swampy lagoons to the west. This, the story goes, served as the initial nucleus of what later became the famous city of Venice.

Italy was prostrate now before the advance of this barbarian who boasted that "the grass never grew again where my horse trod." He was proclaimed by Churchmen as the means by which God punished a sinful people. He was "the scourge of God."

Attila's advance toward Rome was unopposed. As Honorius had cowered in Ravenna forty years before while Alaric assailed Rome, so now Valentinian III cowered in Ravenna.

The only leader in Rome who might oppose Attila was the bishop of Rome who, at this time, was Leo, a man of Roman birth who had become bishop in 440. (Because of his history he is often referred to as "Leo the Great.")

It was under Leo that the bishop of Rome first achieved an undoubted position as the greatest churchman in the west. The shift of the Western capital from Milan to Ravenna had ruined

the prestige of the bishop of Milan, while the barbarian grip on
Gaul, Spain and Africa had lessened the prestige of the bishops
in those areas.

The word "papa," meaning "father," had been applied in
various languages and still is ("pere," "padre") to priests generally. In the later Roman Empire it came to be applied to bishops, particularly, and to the important bishops even more particularly.

When Leo was bishop of Rome, it became the increasing
practice in the West to confine the word "Papa" with the capital
letter to him. Leo (and succeeding bishops of Rome) was the
"Father" par excellence; he was *the* Father, *the* Papa; or, as
we now say in English, the Pope.

While it is customary to list all the bishops of Rome, from
Peter himself, as among the Popes, it is in Leo's reign that the
name came into common use, and Leo is therefore considered
by some to be the founder of the Papacy.

Leo took a strong line in all the religious disputes of the day.
He did not hesitate to act as though he were the premier
bishop of the Church, and his opinion of himself was adopted
by others. He showed his strength by a severe repression of
the Manichaeans, which meant the beginning of the end of
their attempt to dispute with Christianity for the allegiance of
the populace. (Nevertheless, Manichaeism did not die, but was
driven underground, and streaks of it appeared throughout
the Middle Ages, and influenced the development of certain
medieval heresies, particularly in the south of France.)

Leo's prestige was still further increased by his action with
respect to Attila. Rome, having been deserted by her political
leaders, could turn only to Leo.

Meeting the challenge with firm bravery, Leo set out northward to meet the oncoming conqueror. At the Po River, 250
miles north of Rome, the two met. Wearing his papal
robes in their full magnificence and surrounded by all the pomp

he could manage, Leo urged Attila to forbear venturing against the holy city of the Empire.

According to tradition, Attila was abashed and taken aback at the firmness of Leo, his imposing appearance, and the aura of the papacy. His awe, or superstition, was touched, and he turned back. After all, Alaric had died only shortly after sacking Rome. Then, too, it is also possible that Leo's words were accompanied by the offer of a generous dowry in lieu of the hand of Honoria, and that gold, as well as awe, persuaded Attila to turn back.

Attila left Italy and back in his own barbaric camp in 453 (1206 A.U.C.) he married again, adding one more wife to his numerous harem. He partook of a vast feast, then retired to his tent and, during the night, died under mysterious circumstances.

His empire was divided between his numerous sons and broke up almost at once under the impact of a German revolt that erupted as soon as news of Attila's death spread over his realm. In 454, the Germans defeated the Huns and the Hunnish hordes dissolved. Their danger was done with.

Attila's great adversary did not long survive, either.

In the eyes of the Roman court, Aetius had been entirely too fortunate. He had won out over his rival, Bonifacius; he had won out over Attila. His army was devoted to him and bands of protecting barbarians surrounded him everywhere.

The do-nothing Emperor, who had been a quarter-century on the throne, and had reached unheroic manhood only because of the feats of his general, resented having to cower before that same general. It annoyed him that he had been forced to agree to let his daughter be promised in marriage to Aetius' son. As, a half-century before, his uncle Honorius was easily made to believe that Stilicho aspired to the throne, so now Valentinian III was easily convinced of the truth of the same accusation against Aetius. And, in a sense, Aetius brought the result upon

himself by his arrogance and the cocksure way in which he
ignored precautions.

In September, 454, he presented himself, alone, before Valentinian, who was visiting Rome at the time. Aetius was trying
to make final arrangements for his son's marriage to Valentinian's daughter which was, of course, the most suspicious factor
of the situation as far as the Emperor was concerned. Suddenly
drawing his sword, Valentinian stabbed at Aetius and that was
the signal for the court functionaries to surround the general
and hack him to pieces.

It saved Valentinian not at all. Not only did the act prove
unpopular throughout Italy — which relied on Aetius as a
shield against the barbarians — but it was a form of suicide
for the Emperor. A half-year later, in March 455 (1208 A.U.C.)
two men who had, at one time, served in Aetius' personal guard,
found their chance at last and stabbed Valentinian to death.

Valentinian was the last male ruler in the direct line of descent from Valentinian I. The line had lasted, with increasing
feebleness for nearly a century. The last ruler of this line in the
east, had been Pulcheria, wife of the Emperor Marcian, and
first cousin of Valentinian. She had died in 453, and Marcian in
457.

GAISERIC THE VANDAL

Both halves of the Empire had now to select new rulers.

In Constantinople, the most powerful man was Aspar, a German who was commander of the barbarian troops who
patrolled the capital. He might easily have made himself
Emperor but he was an Arian and he knew that as ruler

he would have to face the constant and unwearying opposition of the monks and the people. It clearly would not pay! It would be easier to arrange to have some nondescript Catholic on the throne and rule through him. Aspar's choice fell upon Leo of Thrace (after the province in which he was born), an elderly and well-respected general.

Leo's assumption of the throne marked another important change. Once it had been the Senate that had officially made a man into an Emperor, then it was the Army — and now it was the Church. Leo I had the purple diadem placed on his head by the Patriarch of Constantinople and the crowning of the head of the State by the head of the Church has remained habitual ever since.

Like Marcian before him, Leo I did better than was expected. For one thing, he did not prove to be Aspar's puppet. Indeed, Leo carefully set about undermining Aspar's position, and one way of doing this was to exchange the Imperial bodyguard of Germans for one of Isaurians — tribesmen from eastern Asia Minor. Such a substitution meant that Leo did not have to fear assassination the moment he crossed Aspar. Moreover, it gave him a reliable group to pit against Aspar's Germans in case of any violent dispute. This was especially so since he gave the general of the Isaurian troops (who adopted the Greek name of Zeno) his daughter's hand in marriage.

This was a development of key importance and marked a crucial difference in the development of the histories of the Eastern and Western Empires. The West, ever since the death of Theodosius I, over half a century before, had fallen more and more into the hands of German troops and German generals until there remained no Romans to resist the complete Germanization of the realm. In the East, however, the Germans were effectively resisted. After the assassination of Rufinus (see page 216), successive German king-makers found their powers increasingly limited until, under Leo I, recruits were found among the Isaurians and other peoples within the realm.

These formed a native army that could fight off the outer enemy and keep the Eastern Empire reasonably intact and at least culturally continuous for a thousand years.

In the West, a Roman patrician, Petronius Maximus, was raised to the throne following the death of Valentinian III. To cast a glimmer of legitimacy over the situation, Petronius forced Eudoxia, Valentinian's widow, to marry him. According to the story, Eudoxia resented this partly because she was not particularly fond of the aged Petronius as a person and partly because she suspected him of having maneuvered the assassination of her late husband. She therefore sought some help in order to escape from her position.

At the time, the most powerful individual in the West was Gaiseric the Vandal. He was now in his sixties and he and his Vandals had been ruling over the African province for a quarter of a century, but his vigor had not in the least diminished. The other powerful barbarians of the time — Theodoric the Visigoth and Attila the Hun — were dead but Gaiseric the Vandal remained.

What's more, he alone of the fifth-century barbarians built a fleet. His rule over the African mainland was not as extensive as the Roman rule had been, for the native tribesmen of northern African once more controlled Mauretania and sections of Numidia, but with his fleet, Gaiseric was able to make up for that elsewhere. He controlled Corsica, Sardinia, the Balearic Islands, even the western tip of Sicily. He raided, almost at will, the northern coastline, both west and east. Under Gaiseric, the old sea empire of Carthage was seemingly reborn, and Rome faced him now as it had faced that city seven centuries before.

But Rome now was not the Rome of seven centuries before. Not only was it incapable of resistance, but Eudoxia, the Empress, invited Gaiseric to come to Rome, assuring him of its weakness and guaranteeing his success, perfectly willing to arrange her personal rescue at the cost of general misery.

Gaiseric did not require the invitation to be repeated. When

June, 455 (1208 A.U.C.) arrived, so did Gaiseric's ships at the mouth of the Tiber. The Emperor Petronius tried to flee but he was murdered by a panicky population who hoped to appease the enemy in this fashion and the Vandals entered the city un-opposed. Forty-five years after Alaric's entry into Rome, the city on the Tiber was sacked a second time. This time the situa-tion was particularly ironical for the invaders came from Carth-age. One might almost imagine the implacable ghost of Han-nibal urging them on.

Pope Leo tried to use his influence with Gaiseric as he had with Attila, but the situation was different. Attila had been a pagan who could be impressed with the general aura of the su-pernatural; Gaiseric was an Arian to whom a Catholic bishop meant nothing.

However, Gaiseric was an efficient man. He had come for spoils and that alone. For two weeks, he systematically and al-most scientifically removed all that was movable and valuable for carting off to Carthage. There was no useless destruction, no sadistic carnage. Rome was impoverished but, as after Alaric's sack, she remained intact. It is ironic, therefore, that the bitter Roman denunciation of the thefts of the Vandals have made the term "vandal" today synonymous with one who sense-lessly destroys — something which was precisely what the Van-dals on this occasion did not do.

Among other things, Gaiseric removed the holy vessels of the Jews, which Titus had brought to Rome from the destroyed Temple of Jerusalem nearly four centuries before. They, too, were carted off to Carthage.

As for Eudoxia, she received the treatment she might have ex-pected. Far from rescue and the restoration of her dignity, the cool and unsentimental Gaiseric had her jewelry stripped from her and ordered her and her two daughters carried to Car-thage as prisoners.

The sack of Rome was a source of melancholy reflections on the part of some historians of the time, notably Gaius Sollius

Apollinaris Sidonius. He was a Gaul who was born in 430 and who lived through the final stages of the Roman Empire in the West.

He called attention to the manner in which, according to legend, Rome had been founded. Romulus and Remus had watched for a portent in the morning.* Remus had seen six eagles (or vultures) and Romulus twelve. It was Romulus who had the better of it and who founded Rome.

Throughout Roman history, there had been a superstition to the effect that each eagle represented a century. Had Remus built the city, it would have lasted six centuries according to the superstition — until 153 B.C. (600 A.U.C.) That was actually just about the time when Carthage had been finally destroyed by the victorious Romans. Could it have been that a Remus-founded Rome would have been defeated by Hannibal after the battle of Cannae and then have lingered on for another half-century before its final destruction at the hands of the Carthaginians?

Since Romulus built the city, it was allotted twelve centuries, one for each eagle. The twelve centuries were up in 447 (1200 A.U.C.) and it was not long after that time that Gaiseric had come — and from Carthage, as though Rome, early or late, could not avoid its fate, "Now, O Rome, thou knowest thy destiny," wrote Apollinarus Sidonius.

RICIMER THE SUEVE

What was left of the Roman realm of the West was now once again disputed between two generals, both of whom had fought under Aetius. One of these was Marcus Maecilius Avitus,

* See my book *The Roman Republic* (Houghton Mifflin, 1966).

who was descended from an old Gallic family. The other was Ricimer, the son of a Suevian chieftan.

Avitus carried on the policies of Aetius in his native Gaul, trying to use the barbarians as tools with which to salvage as much of the Roman tradition as possible. He formed an alliance with the Visigothic king, Theodoric II, who made use of peace in Gaul to concentrate on Spain. There in 456 he began to expand his holdings at the expense of the Suevi. Eventually, virtually all of Spain was Visigothic. From Brittany to Gibraltar, the Visigoth ruled everywhere but in the mountains of northern Spain where some Suevi and the native Basques maintained a precarious independence.

Meanwhile, the news that Gaiseric had sacked Rome and that the Imperial throne was vacant tempted Avitus. He had the backing of the powerful Theodoric and he obtained the assent of the Eastern Emperor, Marcian. For a short while in 456, Avitus ruled as Western Emperor.

Opposing him, however, was Ricimer. Since he was of Suevian descent, he could scarcely be expected to be fond of the man whose alliance with the Visigoth had led to the virtual extinction of the Suevi in Spain.

And Ricimer's opposition was not to be taken lightly. In 456, he had defeated a Vandal fleet off Corsica and anyone who could, at that time, present the spectacle of a Roman victory over the hated Vandals was bound to be the darling of Rome. When Ricimer ordered Avitus off the throne, Avitus had to obey.

For sixteen years, thereafter, Ricimer was the real ruler of Rome, appointing a series of nominal Emperors, through whom he ruled.

The first he placed on the throne was Majorian (Julius Valerius Majorianus) who had also fought under Aetius. The first order of business was the war against the Vandals. A troop of Vandals ravaging the coast of Italy southeast of Rome was surprised and set upon by Imperial troops and driven with slaughter to their ships.

Heartened by this, Majorian now made ready a strong fleet with which to invade Africa itself. He needed the help of the Visigothic king, Theodoric II, for this. At first, Theodoric II, mindful of the fate of his old ally, Avitus, was in no mood to do this. When the Visigoths lost a battle in Gaul to the Imperial troops, it seemed better to Theodoric to join in the common cause against the Vandals as eight years before his father had joined in the common cause against the Huns. The allied Roman-Gothic fleet gathered at Cartagena in Spain.

But Gaiseric was not sleeping. His own fleet, in a lightning strike, surprised the yet-unready Imperial fleet and destroyed it in 460. The discomfited Majorian was forced to make peace and return ingloriously to Rome, where Ricimer, deciding he had outlived his usefulness, forced him to resign in 461 (1214 A.U.C.). Five days later, he was dead, possibly poisoned.

Ricimer's attempts to name further Emperors were weakened by the fact that Leo I, the Eastern Emperor, withheld the necessary assent. Leo's own gathering strength made him consider the possibility of uniting the entire Empire under himself as once it had been united under Theodosius I, nearly a century before.

To begin with, Leo needed someone on the Western throne whom he could consider a safe puppet. After considerable negotiations with Ricimer, the two came to an agreement and Ricimer accepted Leo's candidate Anthemius, who was the son-in-law of the Emperor Marcian, Leo's predecessor on the throne at Constantinople. Anthemius became Western Emperor in 467 (1220 A.U.C.) and his position was strengthened when Ricimer, the true ruler of Rome, married Anthemius' daughter.

The next step for Leo was to launch a fleet of his own against the Vandals, and to accomplish what Majorian had been unable to do. With the glory that would bring and with the addition of conquered Africa to his throne, there seemed no limits to what else might lie in store. A tremendous fleet of over 1100 ships was prepared; manned, according to the account, by 100,000 men.

Sardinia was taken from the Vandals by means of this fleet and an army was disembarked in Africa. For a while, matters looked bad for the aged Gaiseric, now in his late seventies. Gaiseric, however, noticed that the Imperial fleet was so negligently guarded and so crowded in the harbor by the very superfluity of its numbers that it offered a tempting target.

At night, Gaiseric sent fire ships drifting into the huge fleet, which was quickly reduced to a shambles. The Imperial troops were forced to escape as best they could and the whole expedition was a farcical failure.

Leo was able to garner a crumb of positive action out of this, however. He managed to shift the blame for the fiasco on his general, Aspar, and to maneuver his execution in 471. This put a final end to German influence in the Eastern Empire.

In the West, Ricimer tried to salvage the situation by placing the blame on Anthemius and deposing him in 472 (1225 A.U.C.). He then chose a puppet all his own since Leo was no longer in a position to throw his weight about in the West. The puppet was Anicius Olybrius, who had married Placidia, the daughter of Valentinian III and therefore carried some of the aura of the great Theodosius I. However, both Olybrius and Ricimer died that same year.

The way was clear for Leo I to try his hand at selecting puppets and in 473, he chose Julius Nepos (a relative of Leo by marriage) to serve as Western Emperor.

Leo himself died in 474, however. His grandson, who was also the son of the general of his Isaurian bodyguard, succeeded as Leo II, reigned for a few months, then died. The Isaurian general, Zeno, father of Leo II, now became the Eastern Emperor.

At the death of Leo I, the East Roman Empire was still completely intact. Its borders remained virtually those that had existed at the death of Theodosius I, eighty years before or, for that matter, those that existed in the time of Hadrian three and a half centuries before.

Not so the West Roman Empire. In 466, Theodoric II of the Visigothic kingdom had been killed by his brother Euric and, under Euric, the kingdom reached the peak of its power. Euric published codifications of the Roman law, adapting it to the Gothic traditions, so that his rule was by no means mere barbarian outlawry. Under the settled regime of the Goths, indeed, the peasantry might well have been better off than under the feeble rule of the Romans before the coming of the Visigoths. The natives lived under their own laws and their rights were respected. The Goths took over two-thirds of the land, cattle, and slaves and the dispossessed Roman land-owners suffered, of course. Then, too, the general populace resented the Arian Christianity of their Gothic overlords. Still, day-to-day life showed no sudden descent into a dark age.

The southeastern third of Gaul had come under the firm control of the expanding Burgundians, whose border now marched along that of the Visigoths. And in the southeast of Britain, the Anglo-Saxons now had a firm hold.

In northern Gaul, a section of the native population still retained a hold. They formed the kingdom of Soissons, centered about the city of Soissons, some sixty miles northeast of Paris. It was governed by Syagrius, the last ruler of any sizable section of Gaul who might be considered Roman, even though he had revolted from Rome and maintained himself quite independent of the Imperial court.

In Africa, Gaiseric still ruled. He did not die till 477, at which time he had reached the grand age of eighty-seven. He had ruled over Africa for nearly half a century and had been victorious always. Of all the barbarians who brought the Roman Empire to ruin in the fifth century, he was the most capable and the most successful.

Virtually all that was left to the Imperial court at Ravenna was Italy itself and Illyria.

ODOACER THE HERULIAN

After Ricimer's death, the remaining fragments of the dominions of the West fell to another general, Orestes. He forced the abdication of Julius Nepos and placed his own son, Romulus Augustus, on the throne in 475.

The name Romulus Augustus seemed to be a remarkable omen, since Romulus had been the founder of Rome and Augustus the founder of the Empire. It was not to be a good omen, however. Romulus was only fourteen at the time he came to the throne and his name was therefore distorted into its diminutive and made Romulus Augustulus ("Romulus, the little Emperor") the form by which it is commonly known to history.

Romulus was to remain Emperor for less than a year, for trouble began almost at once with the barbarian mercenaries who served the Imperial cause in Italy. They were restless at the thought that in other provinces such as Gaul, Spain, and Africa, their fellow Germans ruled rather than served. The German mercenaries therefore demanded the cession of one-third of the land of Italy.

Orestes, who was the real power behind his young son, refused this. The mercenaries grouped themselves under a leader named Odoacer (a Herulian, that is a member of one of the less famous Germanic tribes) and decided to take all since they had not been granted part. Orestes was forced to retreat to Ticinum (the modern Pavia) in northern Italy. The city was taken, and Orestes executed.

On September 4, 476, Romulus Augustulus was forced to abdicate and disappeared from history. Odoacer did not bother to choose a puppet of his own. Indeed, no Emperor ruled with his capital in the West for centuries, and when one came again (the famous Charlemagne) it was to rule over a realm that had nothing in common, except its name, with the Roman Empire of Augustus and Trajan.

It is for this reason that 476 (1229 A.U.C.) is usually taken as the date of the "fall of the Roman Empire."

The date, however, is a false one. No one at this period of time considered that the Roman Empire had "fallen." Indeed, it still existed and was the most powerful realm in Europe. Its capital was at Constantinople and the Emperor was Zeno. It is only because we ourselves are culturally descended from the Roman west, that we tend to ignore the continued existence of the Roman Empire in the east.

In the thought of the time, it was true that some of the western provinces of the Empire were occupied by Germans but those provinces were still, however, part of the Empire — in theory at least — and often the German kings ruled as Roman officials of one sort or another. To be given the title of "patrician" or "consul" was an honor greatly valued by the barbarian kings, who themselves accepted the almost mystical concept of the indestructible Empire.

Zeno himself had never recognized Romulus Augustulus as Western Emperor. He, the Eastern Emperor, considered the boy a usurper and Julius Nepos his own legal colleague. Julius Nepos, after his deposition, had fled Rome and dwelt in Illyria and there he maintained himself as West Roman Emperor and was recognized as such by Zeno.

The Western Empire remained in being in a legal sense till 480 (1233 A.U.C.) when Julius Nepos was assassinated. Only then, was there no Emperor in the West in the eyes of the court at Constantinople.

In theory, thereafter, the Empire was reunited as it had been in the days of Constantine I and Theodosius I. Zeno became sole Emperor. He bestowed the rank of patrician on Odoacer, who ruled Italy (in theory) as Zeno's deputy. Odoacer sent the Imperial insignia to Constantinople, thus acknowledging Zeno as Emperor. He never called himself king of Italy, but only the king of the German tribes who now began to assume ownership of the land of the peninsula.

After the assassination of Julius Nepos, Odoacer invaded Illyria on the pretext of avenging the deed. This he did, to be sure, executing one of the assassins. However, he also annexed Illyria to his own holding and this made him uncomfortably powerful and uncomfortably close, from Zeno's viewpoint.

Zeno began to look about for some method of neutralizing the dangerous Odoacer.

THEODORIC THE OSTROGOTH

His eyes fell upon the Ostrogoths.

The Ostrogoths had fallen under Hunnish rule a century before, when the Visigoths, further to the west, had managed to avoid the same fate by entering the Roman Empire as refugees. The Ostrogoths remained in subjection for eighty years, fighting on the Hunnish side at the Battle of the Catalaunian Plains.

After Attila's death and the collapse of the Hunnish Empire, the Ostrogoths were once more their own masters. They raided the Eastern Empire periodically and settled south of the Danube where they were a constant nuisance and threat to Constantinople. In 474, the Ostrogoths came under the rule of a competent leader, Theodoric.

It seemed to Zeno that he could kill two birds with one stone. He could deputize Theodoric the Ostrogoth and send him after Odoacer the Herulian. In this way, he could, to begin with, get rid of the Ostrogoths. And in the fight between the two Germans, he reasoned, both would be weakened.

In 488 (1241 A.U.C.) Theodoric set out westward with Zeno's satisfied blessing. He marched around the head of the Adriatic Sea and into Italy, where he defeated Odoacer in two separate battles. By 489, Odoacer was under siege in Ravenna.

Theodoric carried on the siege patiently and relentlessly and in 493 (1246 A.U.C.) Ravenna was finally forced to capitulate. Theodoric, violating the conditions of surrender, killed Odoacer with his own hand.

Theodoric then ruled from Ravenna as undisputed monarch over Italy, Illyria, and regions to the north and west of Italy. His position was recognized by Anastasius, the new Emperor at Constantinople, who had succeeded to the throne on Zeno's death in 491.

Theodoric remained king for a full generation and so capable was he, so just and mild was his rule, so prosperous his dominion, that he is sometimes called "Theodoric the Great."

Indeed, the first quarter of the sixth century was a most unusual time for Italy. Compared to the nightmarish century that had begun with the invasion of Alaric, Italy under Theodoric seemed heaven. It had not been so well ruled in fact since the time of Marcus Aurelius three centuries before.

Theodoric was a self-conscious guardian of the Roman heritage. Although his Goths took over much of what had been state-controlled land in Italy, this was done with a minimum of injustice to private landowners. The Roman population was not unduly oppressed and Romans could reach high rank under the Goths as Germans had reached high rank under the Romans. Corruption among officials was minimized, taxes were lowered, harbors were dredged, marshes drained. The state of agriculture prospered in this time of profound peace. The city of Rome lived in comfort, unharmed by the two gentle sacks of the fifth century, and the Roman Senate remained respected. Although Theodoric was an Arian, the Catholics among his subjects were tolerated. (In the dominions of the Arian Vandals and Visigoths, however, Catholics underwent periods of persecution.)

It even looked as though Roman culture might again gleam forth. Cassiodorus (Flavius Magnus Aurelius Cassiodorus Senator) was born in 490 and survived to the patriarchal age of ninety-five. He served as treasurer under Theodoric and his successors. He devoted his life to the acquisition of learning and founded two monasteries in order that worthwhile books of all sorts might be collected and copied. He himself wrote voluminously in the fields of history, theology, and grammar. He wrote a history of the Goths which would undoubtedly be invaluable if we had it, but it is lost.

Boethius (Anicius Manlius Severinus Boethius) born in 480 was the last of the ancient philosophers. He served as consul in 510, and his two sons served as consuls together in 522. The feeling that Rome was still what it had been was so strong that Boethius felt he had reached the summit of happiness at seeing his sons achieve the eminence of a title which was, in truth, quite meaningless, except for the honor it conferred or seemed to confer. (Unfortunately, Boethius was imprisoned in his later life by an aging Theodoric who had grown suspicious and who feared that the philosopher was intriguing with the Eastern Emperor. And, in the end, Boethius was executed.)

Boethius was supposedly a Christian but this does not clearly appear in his philosophical works, which retain an aura of the stoicism of the great days of the pagan Empire.

He translated some of the works of Aristotle into Latin and wrote commentaries on Cicero, Euclid, and others of the ancients. It was his works, rather than the originals, that survived though the first half of the Middle Ages, so that Boethius served as the last bit of ancient light to illuminate the darkness that was to come.

Indeed, it might have been possible to hope in those opening years of the sixth century that Rome might yet absorb the ef-

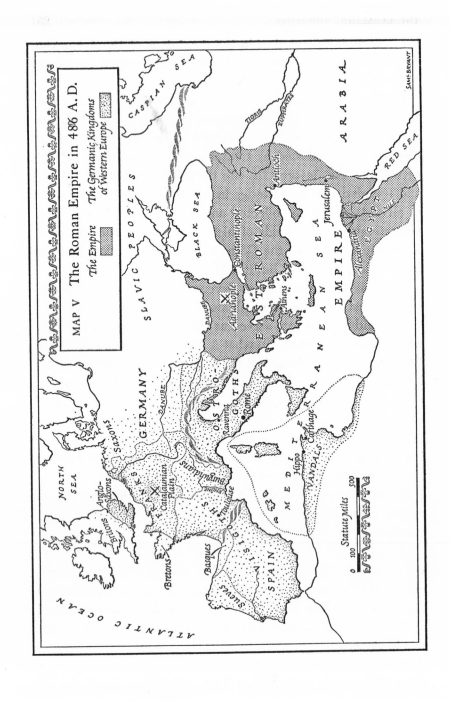

MAP V   The Roman Empire in 486 A.D.

The Empire

The Germanic Kingdoms
of Western Europe

fect of the barbarian invasions and that German and Roman might melt together to form a rejuvenated Empire, stronger than ever before.

Unfortunately, the German leaders were Arian and though German and Roman might mix, Arian and Catholic would not.

Unfortunately, too, the influx of German tribes had not yet ended and the situation as it was in Theodoric's early reign was not to be allowed to remain so.

In northeastern Gaul, the Franks, who for half a century had remained reasonably quiet, now came under an energetic chieftain named Clovis. In 481, when he came to power, Clovis was only fifteen, but by the time he had spent five years consolidating his power over his people, he had become quite old enough to take on a program of expansion.

Clovis' first target was Syagrius, the ruler of Soissons Syagrius was attacked, defeated, and killed in 486 (1239 A.U.C.) and thus vanished the last piece of territory in what had once been the West Roman Empire which was still being ruled by the native peoples of the Empire.

A long era had come to an end. Twelve hundred and thirty-nine years had passed since a little village named Rome had been founded on the Tiber. It had built itself into the greatest nation of the ancient world, had established an Empire that had brought peace to a hundred million people and had given a system of laws to succeeding generations. It had taken an Eastern religion, placed the Roman touch upon it and passed that on, too.

But now, in 1239 A.U.C., no one ruled anywhere in the west who could consider himself a true and direct descendant of the Roman tradition.

To be sure, the eastern half of the Empire was still intact, and it was yet to have great Emperors, but the Eastern Empire was moving beyond the horizon of the developing West. It would play little part in the slow development of a new civilization that was to rise in place of the Roman Empire.

With the last bit of the Western Empire gone, Europe had turned an important corner. Who was to build the new civilization on the ruins of the old? The Franks and the Goths were on stage. Others, now unheard of, were to follow: Lombards, Northmen, Arabs. Even the Eastern Empire itself was to attempt a comeback.

But it was the Franks who were to be the true heirs of Rome in the west. Clovis' victory at Soissons was the first whisper of a new Frankish Empire to come and a new Frankish culture — centered in Paris rather than Rome — that was to lead on to the High Middle Ages and, eventually, to our world of today.

GENEALOGIES

I. THE LINE OF AUGUSTUS (27 B.C.–68)

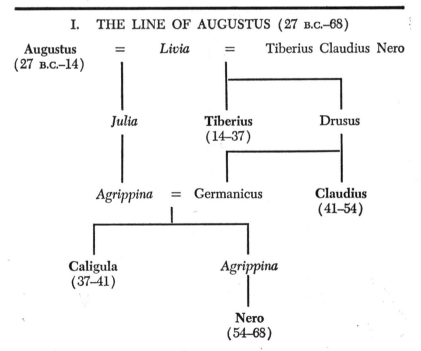

Augustus = *Livia* = Tiberius Claudius Nero
(27 B.C.–14)

Julia **Tiberius** (14–37) Drusus

Agrippina = Germanicus **Claudius** (41–54)

Caligula (37–41) *Agrippina*

Nero (54–68)

II.   THE LINE OF VESPASIAN (69–96)

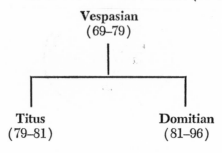

Vespasian
(69–79)

Titus   **Domitian**
(79–81)   (81–96)

III.   THE LINE OF NERVA (96–192)

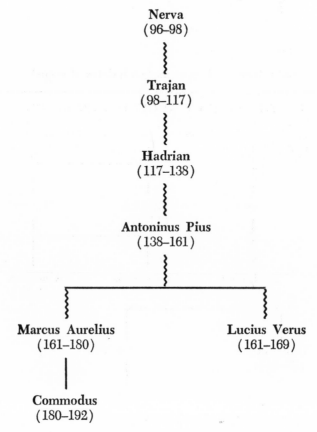

Nerva
(96–98)

Trajan
(98–117)

Hadrian
(117–138)

Antoninus Pius
(138–161)

Marcus Aurelius   **Lucius Verus**
(161–180)   (161–169)

Commodus
(180–192)

IV.   THE LINE OF SEPTIMIUS SEVERUS (193–235)

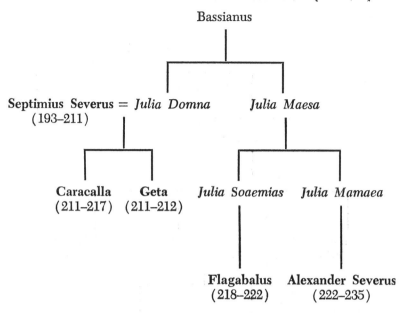

Bassianus

Septimius Severus = *Julia Domna*   *Julia Maesa*
(193–211)

Caracalla   Geta   *Julia Soaemias*   *Julia Mamaea*
(211–217)   (211–212)

Flagabalus   Alexander Severus
(218–222)   (222–235)

V.   THE LINE OF CONSTANTIUS I CHLORUS (293–363)

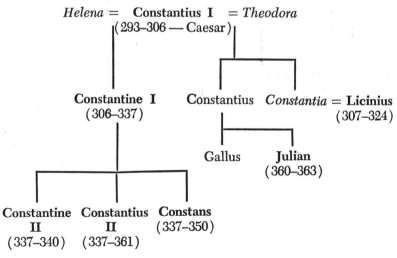

Helena =   Constantius I   = *Theodora*
(293–306 — Caesar)

Constantine I   Constantius   *Constantia* = Licinius
(306–337)   (307–324)

Gallus   Julian
(360–363)

Constantine   Constantius   Constans
II   II   (337–350)
(337–340)   (337–361)

VI.   THE LINE OF VALENTINIAN I (364–472)

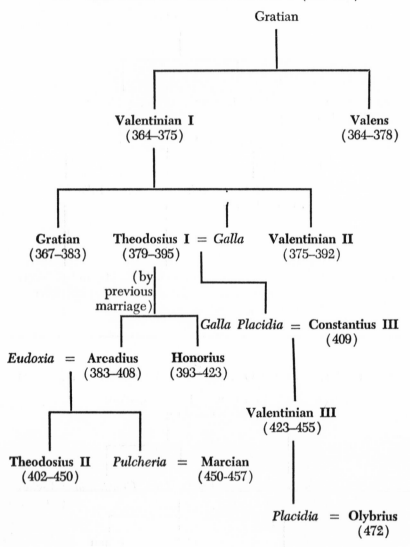

Gratian

Valentinian I
(364–375)

Valens
(364–378)

Gratian
(367–383)

Theodosius I = *Galla*
(379–395)

Valentinian II
(375–392)

(by
previous
marriage)

Galla Placidia = Constantius III
(409)

Eudoxia = Arcadius
(383–408)

Honorius
(393–423)

Valentinian III
(423–455)

Theodosius II
(402–450)

Pulcheria = Marcian
(450-457)

Placidia = Olybrius
(472)

A TABLE OF DATES

NOTE: B.C. *represents the number of years before the birth of Christ* A.U.C. *represents the number of years after the founding of Rome. Birth-years are usually in doubt.*

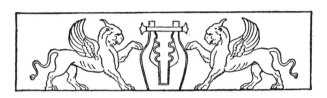

OUR DATE	A.U.C.	
753 B.C.	1	Founding of Rome
509 B.C.	244	Establishment of Roman Republic
390 B.C.	363	Gauls occupy Rome
270 B.C.	483	Rome controls all Italy
216 B.C.	537	Rome loses battle of Cannae to Hannibal
202 B.C.	551	Rome defeats Carthage
133 B.C.	620	Rome virtually controls Mediterranean world
101 B.C.	652	Marius destroys German invaders
70 B.C.	683	Birth of Vergil
65 B.C.	688	Birth of Horace
63 B.C.	690	Birth of Octavian (Augustus)
59 B.C.	694	Birth of Livy
44 B.C.	709	Assassination of Julius Caesar

OUR DATE	A.U.C.	
43 B.C.	710	Birth of Ovid
42 B.C.	711	Birth of Tiberius
29 B.C.	724	Octavian in control of Rome
27 B.C.	726	Octavian becomes Augustus; Roman Empire established
19 B.C.	734	Death of Vergil
9 B.C.	744	Roman forces reach Elbe
8 B.C.	745	Death of Horace
4 B.C.	749	Birth of Jesus
9	762	Rome loses battle of Teutoburger Wald, retreats to Rhine River; birth of Vespasian
14	767	Death of Augustus; Tiberius becomes Emperor
17	770	Death of Ovid and Livy

OUR DATE	A.U.C.		OUR DATE	A.U.C.	
29	782	Crucifixion of Jesus			Rome; Nero refused entrance into Eleusinian Mysteries
35	788	Birth of Nerva			
37	790	Death of Tiberius; Caligula becomes Emperor; Paul converted to Christianity	68	821	Suicide of Nero
			69	822	Vespasian becomes Emperor
41	794	Assassination of Caligula; Claudius becomes Emperor	70	823	Titus takes Jerusalem and destroys Temple
43	796	Roman army begins conquest of Britain	76	829	Birth of Hadrian
52	805	Birth of Trajan	79	832	Death of Vespasian; Titus becomes Emperor; Destruction of Pompeii; Death of Pliny
54	807	Death of Claudius; Nero becomes Emperor			
58	811	Corbulo defeats Parthians	81	834	Death of Titus; Domitian becomes Emperor
60	813	Birth of Juvenal			
61	814	Revolt of Boudicca in Britain	83	836	Agricola completes conquest of Wales and southern Scotland; Domitian occupies the Rhine-Danube salient.
64	817	Great fire in Rome; first organized persecution of Christians; martyrdom of Peter and Paul			
			86	839	Birth of Antoninus Pius
65	818	Death of Seneca and of Lucan	90	843	Domitian agrees to pay annual ransom to Dacians
66	819	Outbreak of the Jewish rebellion against	96	849	Assassination

OUR DATE	A.U.C.		OUR DATE	A.U.C.	
192	945	Assassination of Commodus	235	988	Assassination of Alexander Severus
193	946	Septimius Severus becomes Emperor	238	991	Gordian III becomes Emperor
197	950	Septimius Severus sacks Lugdunum and disposes of last rival	243	996	Timesitheus defeats Shapur I of Persia
205	978	Birth of Plotinus	244	997	Assassination of Gordian III; Philip the Arabian becomes Emperor
211	964	Death of Septimius Severus: Caracalla and Geta become co-Emperors	245	998	Birth of Diocletian
212	965	Assassination of Geta; Citizenship granted to all free men of Empire; Birth of Aurelian	248	1001	Celebration in honor of completion of thousandth year of Roman history
217	970	Assassination of Caracalla	249	1002	Philip the Arabian dies in battle; Decius becomes Emperor
218	971	Elagabalus becomes Emperor	250	1003	Decius institutes persecution of Christians
222	975	Assassination of Elagabalus; Alexander Severus becomes Emperor	251	1004	Decius dies in battle against Goths; Gallus becomes Emperor; death of Origen
225	978	Death of Tertullian	253	1006	Gallus dies in battle; Valerian and Gallienus become co-Emperors
226	979	Sassanid (Neo-Persian) Empire established			

OUR DATE	A.U.C.	
259	1012	Valerian captured by Shapur I of Persia
260	1013	Western provinces break away and become independent
267	1020	Goths sack Athens; Odenathus of Palmyra, after driving back Persians, is assassinated
268	1021	Assassination of Gallienus; Claudius II becomes Emperor; Zenobia, widow of Odenathus, seizes eastern provinces: Rome at nadir.
270	1023	Claudius defeats Goths, dies natural death; Aurelian becomes Emperor; Death of Plotinus
271	1024	Aurelian begins construction of fortified wall around Rome; abandons province of Dacia
272	1025	Death of

OUR DATE	A.U.C.	
		Shapur I of Persia
273	1026	Aurelian destroys Palmyra and retakes the East
274	1027	Aurelian takes western provinces and rules over united Empire once more
275	1028	Assassination of Aurelian
276	1029	First Tacitus, then Probus, become Emperors
280	1033	Birth of Constantine I
281	1034	Assassination of Probus; Carus becomes Emperor and dispenses with Senatorial confirmation
283	1036	Assassination of Carus; Diocletian becomes Emperor
285	1038	Anthony founds monasticism
286	1039	Diocletian accepts Maximian as co-Emperor; Divides Empire into East and West; Maxim-

OUR DATE	A.U.C.		OUR DATE	A.U.C.	
		ian establishes capital at Milan	311	1064	Death of Galerius
293	1046	Galerius and Constantius Chlorus accepted as Caesars	312	1065	Constantine I wins battle of Milvian Bridge and shifts favor to Christianity
297	1050	Constantius Chlorus reconquers Britain	313	1066	Edict of Milan establishes religious toleration in the Empire; Death of Diocletian
301	1054	Diocletian attempts, unsuccessfully, to control wages and prices	321	1074	Birth of Valentinian I
303	1056	Diocletian initiates persecution of Christians; Armenia becomes officially Christian	324	1077	Death of Licinius; Constantine I sole Emperor
			325	1078	Council of Nicaea
305	1058	Abdication of Diocletian; Galerius becomes Emperor	330	1083	Establishment of Constantinople as Eastern capital
			331	1084	Birth of Julian
306	1059	Death of Constantius Chlorus. Constantine I proclaimed Emperor	337	1090	Death of Constantine I; his three sons become co-Emperors
309	1062	Birth of Shapur II of Persia	340	1093	Birth of Ambrose and Jerome; Death of Constantine II
310	1063	Death of Maximian; Licinius made co-Emperor	345	1098	Birth of John Chrysostom
			346	1099	Birth of Theodosius I

OUR DATE	A.U.C.		OUR DATE	A.U.C.	
350	1103	Death of Constans			westward and attack Goths
351	1104	Constantius II establishes himself as sole Emperor	375	1128	Death of Valentinian I; Gratian and Valentinian II become Western co-Emperors
354	1107	Birth of Augustine			
355	1108	Julian becomes Caesar; begins Gallic campaign	376	1129	Visigoths cross Danube in flight from Huns
359	1112	Shapur II takes Amida; Birth of Stilicho	378	1131	Roman legions smashed and destroyed by Gothic cavalry at the battle of Adrianople; death of Valens; Theodosius becomes co-Emperor
361	1114	Death of Constantius II; Julian becomes Emperor and attempts to reestablish paganism			
363	1116	Failure of Julian's invasion of Persia; Death of Julian; Jovian becomes Emperor; Final victory of Christianity	379	1132	Death of Shapur II
			382	1135	Gratian gives up title of "Pontifex Maximus"; Removes pagan altar of victory from Roman Senate
364	1117	Death of Jovian; Valentinian and Valens become co-Emperors	383	1136	Assassination of Gratian
370	1123	Birth of Alaric the Visigoth	390	1143	Ambrose forces Theodosius to do penance for sack of Thessalonica; Birth of Gaiseric the
374	1127	Ambrose becomes bishop of Milan; Huns sweep			

OUR DATE	A.U.C.		OUR DATE	A.U.C.	
		Vandal; Birth of Leo (later Pope Leo I)			Constantinople
392	1145	Assassination of Valentinian II	400	1153	Alaric invades northern Italy
394	1147	Empire unified with Theodosius sole Emperor; Theodosius puts an end to the Olympian games; finally makes Roman Empire officially Catholic	402	1155	Stilicho defeats Alaric at the battle of Pollentia
			404	1157	Western capital shifted from Milan to Ravenna; John Chrysostom exiled
395	1148	Death of Theodosius; Arcadius becomes Eastern Emperor and Honorius becomes Western Emperor; Augustine becomes bishop of Hippo	406	1159	Birth of Attila the Hun; Germans cross Rhine — permanently
			407	1160	Romans abandon province of Britain
396	1149	Alaric the Visigoth invades Greece; sacks Eleusis and destroys the Temple of Ceres; Birth of Aetius	408	1161	Execution of Stilicho; Alaric again invades Italy; Death of Arcadius; Theodosius II becomes Eastern Emperor
			409	1162	Suevi, Alani, and Vandals settle in Spain
397	1150	Death of Ambrose	410	1163	Sack of Rome by Alaric; Death of Alaric
398	1151	John Chrysostom becomes patriarch of	415	1168	Visigoths defeat other German tribes in Spain
			418	1171	Theodoric I

becomes East-
ern Emperor;
Emperor;
Ricimer the
Sueve real
power in
West; Makes
Majorian the
Western Em-
peror

460   1213 West Roman
expedition
against Gai-
seric in Car-
thage fails
completely

461   1214 Death of Ma-
jorian; Death
of Pope Leo I

466   1219 Death of
Theodoric II
the Visigoth;
Euric suc-
ceeds to the
Visigothic
throne; Birth
of Clovis

468   1221 East Roman
expedition
against Gai-
seric in Car-
thage fails
completely

472   1225 Death of Ricimer

473   1226 Julius Nepos
made Western
Emperor by
Leo I

474   1227 Death of Leo
I; Zeno be-
comes Eastern
Emperor;

Theodoric I
becomes king
of Ostrogoths

475   1228 Forced abdi-
cation of
Julius Nepos.
Romulus Au-
gustulus be-
comes Roman
Emperor

476   1229 Abdication of
Romulus Au-
gustulus; Odo-
acer rules in
Italy; "Fall of
the Roman
Empire"

477   1230 Death of Gai-
seric

480   1233 Assassination
of Julius
Nepos

481   1234 Clovis be-
comes king of
Franks

484   1237 Death of
Euric; Alaric
II becomes
king of Visi-
goths

486   1239 Clovis con-
quers king-
dom of Sois-
son, wiping
out last vestige
of Roman rule
in the West

488   1241 Theodoric I
and the Ostro-
goths invade
Italy

491   1244 Death of

OUR DATE	A.U.C.		OUR DATE	A.U.C.	
		Zeno; Anastasius becomes Eastern Emperor	493	1246	Theodoric I takes Ravenna; kills Odoacer

INDEX